KARPOV · KASPAROV

KARPOV - KASPAROV

1990

by

Don Maddox
Ron Henley
Michael Rohde
Leonid Shamkovich
Michael Valvo

with contributions by
Roman Dzinzichashvili and Semion Palatnik

 Published in the United States by David McKay Company, Inc., a subsidiary of Random House, Inc., New York. Distributed by Random House, Inc., New York, and Random House of Canada Limited, Toronto.

Library of Congress Cataloging-in-Publication Data

Karpov-Kasparov, 1990 / by Don Maddox . . . [et al.] ; with contributions by Roman Dzinzichashvili and Semion Palatnik. — 1st ed.

p. cm.

ISBN 0-812-91923-8

1. Chess—Tournaments, 1990. 2. Kasparov, G. K. (Garry Kimovich) 3. Karpov, Anatloy. I. Maddox, Don.

GV1455.K2614 1991

794.1'57—dc20 90-50677

Designed by M 'N O Production Services, Inc.

Manufactured in the United States of America

98765432 24689753 23456789

First Edition

ACKNOWLEDGMENTS

A world chess championship is a unique event in the world of sports. This book is intended to share that experience with you and to teach you how to think about top-level chess games. To show you all sides of this spectacular event, we have assembled a special team of grandmasters and analysts, each with a unique perspective. The result is an in-depth analysis of every aspect of the championship: how a professional chess player thinks and feels, what it means to make million-dollar decisions over the board, how an opening is chosen, how mistakes are made, and how brilliant moves are conceived.

International Grandmaster Ron Henley, one of Karpov's seconds, offers an insider's view of a world champion's training camp, from the candidates' qualifiers through the confrontation with Kasparov. Ron also presents detailed analysis of Karpov's qualifying games and a comprehensive look at Karpov's adjournment analysis at critical points in the match.

Grandmasters Michael Rohde and Leonid Shamkovich join forces to bring you as close to analytic truth as is humanly possible. Rohde, one of America's youngest grandmasters and a player known for his aggressive and probing style, served as a live commentator during the New York leg of the match. Shamkovich, a world-famous tactician and the author of a renowned book on chess sacrifices, provided live commentary via computer and modem during the match to viewers on the *USA Today* Sports Center.

For the first time, a computer took part in the esoteric debate that is championship chess. IBM's Deep Thought, with its 720,000 moves per second search capability, followed the match live over the *USA Today* Sports Center. International Master Mike Valvo and I were able to query Deep Thought at critical points during and after the games. You will find references to Deep Thought's analysis throughout the book. Valvo, one of the world's foremost authorities on computer chess, examines Deep Thought's emergence as a force in world championship chess in Chapter 5. In a real sense, Deep Thought and its creators—Feng-hsiung Hsu, Thomas Anantharaman, and Murray Campbell—must also be listed as contributors to this book.

I offer special thanks to grandmasters Roman Dzindzichashvili (USA) and Semion Palatnik (USSR) and to International Master Bjarke Kristensen (Denmark) for their contributions to the analysis of the match. Eric Schiller's contributions, both as pressroom consultant and as a generous sounding board for my more outrageous theories, were invaluable.

The following people contributed directly to the successful completion of this project: FIDE Master David Gertler, National Master Alan Kantor, Jason Luchan, Dawn Maddox, John Maddox, Darren Rose, National Master Yuri Zaderman, and the onsite bulletin staff: Adam Black, FIDE Master Al Chow, FIDE Master Billy Colias, International Grandmaster Nick de Firmian, International Grandmaster Max Dlugy, National Master Eric Schiller, and International Master Elliott Winslow. Thanks also go to Linda Henley for patiently enduring extended separation from Ron both during and after the match while we went over and over the games.

Finally, the entire American chess community owes a dept of gratitude to match sponsor Ted Field and Interscope for bringing a world championship to New York. This book was made possible through the direct support of Mr. Field's World Professional Chess Promotions Inc., including Bob Burkett, Rick Hobish, and Stephanie Jagerson.

In this brave new world of electronic information processing, I would like to acknowledge ChessBase International, NICBase, and Chess Laboratories for their contributions to producing this book. I used ChessBase to build, sort, and print the game files that form the foundation of this volume. Chess Laboratories's chessplaying computer program, Zarkov, was essential to producing the necessary diagrams accurately and efficiently, and NICBase contributed relevant games from its data files.

CONTENTS

KARPOV · KASPAROV

1

THE PLAYERS

by
Don Maddox

The world chess championship is accustomed to marathon confrontations. In 1834, French superstar Louis de la Bourdonnais played a match with British Champion Alexander McDonnell that spanned eighty-five games between June and October. The British player lost the series +27 =13 −45. Between 1954 and 1959, Mikhail Botvinnik met Vasily Smyslov sixty-nine times in three matches for the title, winning from the third match to continue his reign as world champion though trailing in the series by one game (+17 =34 −18). Finally, in more recent times, Anatoly Karpov crossed swords with Soviet defector Viktor Korchnoi seventy-four times in three matches, including the 1974 candidates' match won by Karpov before assuming Bobby Fischer's title by default in 1975. Final tally for Karpov: +15 =50 −9.

But the titanic struggle between Garry Kasparov and Anatoly Karpov is unprecedented in chess history for several reasons.

First, two players of their caliber are rarely in the lists at the same time. Perhaps the closest comparison to this contemporary rivalry was the heated and extended negotiation for a rematch between Alexander Alekhine and José Raúl Capablanca. The two never met in a rematch after Alekhine upset Capablanca +6 =25 −3 in 1927.

Second, never in chess history have two players struggled so long to prove so little. After 120 championship games in four matches, the two Soviet giants came to New York in 1990 with only one slim point between them in the final count, Kasparov leading +17 =87 −16. Only a last-minute comeback in Seville, Spain, in 1987, where Kasparov had lost the penultimate game of the match to fall behind by a point entering the final round, allowed the young world champion to retain his title with a draw: +4 =16 −4.

In September 1984, challenger Garry Kasparov sat down across from Anatoly Karpov for the first time, having blown through the candidates' cycle like a hurricane: +4 =4 −1, Belyavsky; +4 =6 −1, Korchnoi; and +4 =9 −0, Smyslov. World Champion Karpov was unimpressed, reeling off wins in games 3, 6, 7, and 9 before Kasparov was forced to face reality: Karpov simply could not be blasted off the face of the earth. The match would go the first player to win six games, and Karpov had already won four.

Kasparov's old teacher Botvinnik advised him to keep his wits about him: "If you cannot win, draw." Botvinnik later confessed that he had little hope that Garry could exercise the iron will required to fight such a thankless rear-guard defense.

Miraculously, the young challenger stalled his savvy opponent for seventeen straight draws. After a fifth loss and four more draws, he finally won game 32. Then came another string of fourteen gut-wrenching draws, and now Garry seemed to break through, winning games 47 and 48 brilliantly.

On February 15, 1985, President Florencio Campomanes of the International Chess Federation (FIDE) stopped the match and scheduled a new match for September 1985.

Amid the controversy and recrimination that resulted, only one thing was clear: Garry Kasparov was a genuine threat to the throne.

In September, Kasparov took the world championship by a score of +5 =16 −3 (Match 2). But FIDE's match rules provided that Karpov would retain his title in the event of a draw and be given a rematch within six months if he were to lose. Kasparov, the youngest world champion in chess history, might also have the shortest reign.

On July 28, 1986, Kasparov began his mandatory defense (Match 3), ultimately winning by a single game and retaining his title. The following year in Seville, the world champion again retained his title by drawing their fourth match.

One thing that sets both players apart from the rest of us is the self-assuredness born of a talent that is measured in absolute terms. In chess, you don't have to worry about whether you're better than other players; you *know*. You get used to being superior in a way that few of us ever experience. This makes you freer and more confident, but it also can create the impression that the rest of the world is dealing

Table 1 Kasparov–Karpov Matches

	Kasparov Wins	Kasparov Losses	Draws	Winner
Match I, 1984–85	3	5	40	Undecided*
Match II, 1985	5	3	16	Kasparov
Match III, 1986	5	4	15	Kasparov
Match IV, 1987	4	4	16	Drawn**
Match V, 1990	4	3	17	Kasparov

* In a controversial decision, the World Chess Federation president Florencio Campomanes halted the match without decision, citing concerns for the players' health.

** As champion, Kasparov retained the title.

Table 2 The Road to Kasparov–Karpov 1990

Kasparov's Record from 1988 to 1990

Event	Wins	Losses	Draws	Place
Amsterdam 1988	6	0	6	1
Belfort 1988	9	1	5	1
USSR Championship 1988	6	0	11	1–2
Koln 1988 (Match with Vlastimil Hort)	2	0	1	1
Reykjavik 1988	6	1	10	1
Thessaloniki 1988 (Board 1)	7	0	3	NA
Barcelona 1989	7	1	8	1–2
Skelleftea 1989	4	0	11	1–2
Tilburg 1989	10	0	4	1
Belgrade 1989	8	0	3	1
Linares 1990	6	1	4	1
Svendborg 1990 (Match with Curt Hansen)	1	0	1	1
Murcia 1990 (Match with Lev Psakhis)	4	0	2	1
New York 1990 (Match with Deep Thought)	2	0	0	1

with a spoiled child who is used to having his own way. In quite opposite ways, both of these great players struggle with this aspect of their personalities.

Table 3 Karpov's Record from 1988 to 1990

Event	Wins	Losses	Draws	Place
Wijk aan Zee 1988	6	1	6	1
Euwe Memorial 1988	2	1	3	2–3
Brussels 1988	7	1	8	1
Amsterdam 1988	3	2	7	2
Belfort 1988	7	1	7	2
USSR Championship 1988	6	0	11	1–2
Tilburg 1988	7	0	7	2
Thessaloniki (Board 2)	6	0	4	NA
Seattle 1989 (Candidates' Quarter-Final with Johann Hjartarson)	2	0	3	1
Linares 1989	5	1	4	2
Marostica 1989 (Match with Ulf Andersson)	1	0	3	1
Rotterdam 1989	7	3	5	2
Skelleftea 1989	4	0	11	1–2
London 1989 (Candidates' Semifinal with Artur Yusupov)	2	1	5	1
Kuala Lumpur 1990 (Candidates' Final with Jan Timman)	4	0	5	1
Biel 1990	5	0	9	1
Cambridge 1990 (Match with Deep Thought)	1	0	0	1
Haninge 1990	5	1	5	2–3

GARRY KASPAROV

On meeting Garry Kasparov, I was struck immediately by the force and honesty of his character. Whether you agree with him or not, you know what he thinks. He has the bearing of a leader, not a diplomat, which may account for his occasional insensitivity to the reaction of strangers.

Darkly handsome and charismatic, conspicuous in the Western press for his outspoken criticism of the Communist system, Kasparov, at twenty-seven, is a man with a passion for ideas and for action. His every gesture, every nuance of voice, urges you to join him in changing the particular corner of the universe under consideration. When he talks about politics, in chess or the real world, he fervently espouses democratic ideals that some of his fellow grandmasters doubt he understands. After losing a vote recently in the Grandmasters Association (GMA), an organization he founded in reaction to what he views as failures in FIDE, the governing international body of chess, he resigned as president in a pique. That elicited quiet smiles from players who had been saying, "Garry's definition of democracy is: everybody votes for me."

But Garry is one of those remarkable people who know they are right, doomed to be viewed by others as saints or devils. Reared on the psychic battlefield of the chessboard, Kasparov neither gives nor expects quarter.

"When you beat your opponent in a chess game," he wrote for *The European* during the match, "you destroy his ego, for a time you make him lose confidence in himself as a person."

What sets Kasparov apart from most other men is his energy. Kasparov seems to explode with energy like a Claymore mine, set to spray shrapnel in all directions when it's triggered. A businessman, a politician, a writer, an organizer, Garry Kasparov pours his attention into more projects than most people can find time to think about. Some observers say that Kasparov's biggest weakness as a chess player is this fragmentation. It is hard enough, they argue, to play chess at world championship level without dabbling in a half-dozen other fields—and Garry never "dabbles" in anything!

In 1986 Kasparov, at twenty-two, became the youngest world champion in history by defeating Karpov for the first time, 5 wins to 3. Earlier this year he became the highest rated player in chess history, surpassing Bobby Fischer's old mark of 2785 and settling in at 2800.

The first Karpov–Kasparov match, in 1985, had been aborted after forty-eight games by Florencio Campomanes, the president of FIDE, while Kasparov was trailing 3 wins to 5 after having been behind 5 to 0. Kasparov (and others) have consistently criticized Campomanes's unprecedented decision as a transparent attempt to save his friend, a tired and failing Karpov. The two players have been bitter enemies both at and off the board ever since, and Kasparov has dedicated himself to separating professional chess from the auspices of FIDE, which he sees as a corrupt and ineffectual amateur organization.

His one remaining goal in chess, he says, is to prove he can beat Karpov decisively.

Interview with Garry Kasparov, April 1990

DON MADDOX: You have worked long and hard to bring the world championship to New York City. Why is it so important to you that this match be held in the United States?

GARRY KASPAROV: Chess is already a popular sport in Europe, where I organized a series of large tournaments called the World Cup. Unfortunately, all the events we've held up to now could more accurately be called the European Cup.

I've always felt badly about this situation, and I thought we should start something in America. Since [Bobby] Fischer left the chess stage, nothing big has happened in America. I conceived a plan to develop chess in this country, and I've spent a reasonable amount of time here playing exhibitions, giving interviews, and making appearances. But the main target was to organize a big event, and the biggest chess event of all is the world championship match.

I believe this match will open a new era in American chess because even Fischer played most of his important tournaments outside the country. He was an American, but he was forced to earn his living outside his native country. In spite of his success and achievements, the impetus he gave to chess in America disappeared quickly.

Now, I suspect things are much better because two foreigners are playing here and the prize fund is enormous. American sponsors have increased the prize fund from three million Swiss francs to three million dollars. This has in turn forced the French sponsors to increase their contribution.

DM: Garry, your political activism outside as well as inside chess is startling for an American audience. I've heard reports of a new political party called the New Radical Socialist party . . .

GK: No. It's called very simply the Democratic party. In my country there is still no political life as you understand it here in the West, but I decided to join a group of well-known parliamentary deputies and politicians who had already made the decision to create a new, anti-Communist party. I had the same idea independently, and we agreed to unite our efforts. Now we have this organization—not an all-Union party, just a Russian party. I think it will be successful. We have the support of many important and influential people.

DM: What is your official position in the party?

GK: I am deputy chairman of the party, responsible for foreign affairs. Among other things, I promote the party abroad.

DM: In America it's unusual for a sportsman to speak out like this early in his career. We have a number of political figures who began in athletics and gradually built a base in local politics before moving up. But it's rare to hear a sports celebrity speak up as loudly and critically as you have everywhere. Why did you decide to speak out?

GK: My position is very simple. I had a choice—to leave the country, or to live in it and speak loudly. You cannot live there as a citizen and keep silent. If I keep silent, who will speak? Who will encourage people to join the democratic forces? I couldn't just leave the country—I didn't want to emigrate.

DM: You've said that one of the problems with Gorbachev's reforms is that they are taken seriously only by people in the West who want to believe them. Is there some danger that the same thing will happen with your words? That they will be heard by people in the West who want to believe them, but not by people in your own country?

GK: Life is dangerous if you insist on living at the top or on the edge. But I saw something really dangerous [ethnic and nationalistic violence] in Baku last January. Compared with that tragedy, these other fears are not very serious.

Personally, I would have preferred to wait until after the world championship match to start my political activity, but when I saw what happened in Baku, I couldn't wait. If I were to wait, at the end of the world championship match I might return to find a country completely destroyed, perhaps in the middle of a civil war.

DM: Is that where you think what's happening is leading to an explosion?

GK: Yes. The country is disappearing. It's completely disintegrated.

DM: In your first autobiography, *Child of Change*, you clearly identify yourself at least with the forces that drove the government to perestroika, and you identify Anatoly Karpov with a kind of "old guard." But now you seem to believe Gorbachev is moving too slowly toward change.

GK: In the beginning, yes. Gorbachev started his reforms, but he had another goal—to save the system and rebuild it. I made one mistake in my first autobiography: I failed to make the distinction between the system and the society. Karpov represents the system, and since the system has changed, Karpov has changed, too. But he is still on one side, and I'm on another.

DM: How do you handle the conflicting demands on your time? You are here promoting the world championship, you pursue political agendas inside and outside chess, and you have to prepare to play chess. Are you worried about the conflicts between these roles?

GK: Yes, but as I told you, I have no choice. I have to find enough time to prepare for a world championship match, and I hope I do. But if I feel the moment is right to do something, I have to do it. To become involved in politics, for instance, I can't escape.

I believe it's a crucial moment right now in the country, and the result of this perestroika, this change in my country, will be very important for the entire world. It will affect you as well. It is extremely important how the largest country in the world will look in a year or two—and I feel I have the ability to help make sure it turns out okay.

DM: Your results suggest you are a much stronger player than when you drew with Karpov three years ago, and most people think he is playing more weakly. What do you think of his chances in October?

GK: I do believe I will win the match. I play better now than I did three years ago, definitely—I know that. And I think Karpov plays worse than three years ago. But that's not the most important thing in the match because you can play much better overall than your opponent and still play this particular match worse than he does.

And there are so many psychological factors between us because we have played four matches, 120 games, and we have spent something like 600 hours opposite each other. Under the circumstances, you cannot predict the result.

DM: You have said that, in the final game of your previous match, when you came back from a point down to retain your title, you could tell from Karpov's eyes that he was broken.

GK: Absolutely. Absolutely.

DM: Do you think that carries over?

GK: Yes, but I will be able to make a better prediction right before the match, when I know my condition and I can feel Karpov's. Now I have no idea. I haven't started real preparation yet. I've done some work, but it's not real preparation. I start that four days from now, in Spain.

ANATOLY KARPOV

Anatoly Karpov's world championship tenure represented ten years of quiet dominance sandwiched between two of the most controversial events in chess annals. In 1975, at the age of twenty-four, he was awarded the title by default when World Champion Bobby Fischer refused to defend it; ten years later, he lost the title to Kasparov after the FIDE president's intervention had stopped the previous match.

Though Karpov has proven to be one of the game's most enduring and dominant players, his career has been haunted by controversy. It has been said that his position as world champion gave him virtually unlimited power over the chess careers of other Soviet players and that he wielded this power ruthlessly for his own ends. First Viktor Korchnoi and then Garry Kasparov accused him of complicity in government "dirty tricks" to prevent them from winning the title.

My impressions of Karpov are far removed from those areas of controversy. I met him in New York City a few weeks before his fifth encounter with Kasparov. He seemed shy and distant at first, and although eventually he talked openly and frankly, he was more careful with his words than Kasparov had been, and never quite shed a certain caution. Garry's striking and immediate openness with strangers was unusual compared with Anatoly's slight, temporary reticence. In any case, before our conversation was over, I felt I had learned a great deal about Karpov.

Slight, fair-haired, almost childlike, Karpov combined a refreshing demeanor with a surprising toughness, a quality that, early in his career, lured many opponents to underestimate him. But no one underestimates Karpov today.

The key to Karpov's character seems to be economy. He is a chess player first, last, and foremost. There is none of Kasparov's frenetic grasping at causes and targets. Karpov wants to be world champion; he gives the impression that he knows exactly what he has to do to reach that goal and that he will not waste an ounce of energy on the way.

He reminded me of a desert lizard, conserving energy by sitting absolutely still, its throat pumping quietly for air until prey ventures into reach. Then, with an incredible burst of energy, the hunt ends as quickly as it began, prey devoured, throat pumping, at rest again. This impression was heightened by Karpov's eyes, his most striking physical feature—lucid and clear almost to the point of making you uncomfortable. They seemed inhuman, almost reptilian. I felt I was in the presence of an alien creature, one for whom chess is the only universe.

If Kasparov's energy explodes, Karpov's is set like a fixed charge carefully measured and placed by a demolition expert: Garry will destroy anything or anyone in his way; Anatoly chooses his targets with great care.

Interview with Anatoly Karpov, September 1990

DON MADDOX: What is the difference between the match's single venue in Spain and this one being scheduled in both the United States and France? How does that affect your preparations and expectations?

ANATOLY KARPOV: I have to admit the difference between playing the match in one place and in two places is most important. We had a relatively unsuccessful experience splitting the third match between London and Lenigrad. That's why I have some doubts about this year, because the distance is even greater. On the other hand, I believe the organizers in New York and Lyon are very serious, and they will do their job properly. Of course, even if they do their jobs perfectly, we have a lot of problems.

DM: What's the biggest problem with the move—is it the need to acclimate yourself?

AK: Yes, jet lag is a problem. But also, we have a lot of literature to move. And even just to get used to a new bed and a new pillow might be a problem.

DM: Are you satisfied with the time you've had to acclimate yourself?

AK: This is always a dilemma. Maybe you need more time to get used to a new time zone and a new place, but at the same time you get bored if you stay too long away from your home. This is my character anyway; maybe other people feel differently.

DM: So one reason you waited longer to come is that you find it harder to establish a routine away from home?

AK: Yes, you have to consider that our stay will be as long as three months including an acclimatization period. So this is the absolute limit to be out of your country and away from your home.

DM: I talked to Kasparov in April. One of the things he said was that in the time since Seville, your play seemed to have gotten weaker while his has gotten stronger, that your results are less even than they were before. What do you think of that characterization?

AK: I don't agree completely because this year was quite good for me. I played well in Biel, and I played well against Timman. Of course, we made mistakes. The match [their 1990 candidates' match in Kuala Lumpur] gave a very strange impression because of a few big mistakes Timman and I made, so most journalists decided the quality of the match was low. But we didn't make many small mistakes, just big mistakes as the result of tension. Even in a world championship match, you have big mistakes. But in general the quality was quite high. I was satisfied with my play against Timman. Then in Sweden I played not badly, and if I hadn't lost a game on time against Seirawan, I would have won that tournament as well. So I don't agree with Kasparov's judgment of my play.

Concerning Kasparov's play, we have two sides: one side is the points he scored in tournaments, the other is the quality of his games. I think he played much stronger in 1987 or 1988 than in 1989, for instance. If you look through the games, I would say that mostly the wind was in his favor, he was lucky.

DM: How have the changes in the Soviet Union over the last two or three years affected the way you prepared for a match and the way you look at travel?

AK: For me, it hasn't changed very much because I've never mixed chess and politics. Of course, now we have a different financial situation. We need to find sponsors, and we pay our own way because the old system of financing chess and other sports has changed. So it has its positive side and its negative side, like most things do. But it has become easier in recent years to travel with your family. Now I have full freedom to travel with my wife; before, it was an exceptional case. Kasparov has been traveling with his mother since 1982. This was maybe a unique case, his being allowed to travel with a parent.

I also have much more freedom choosing seconds. I couldn't imagine seven years ago having such an international team as now. It would have been impossible because of the position of Soviet officials, but now we're free, so I can invite Ron Henley to be my second.

DM: That's interesting, because one of the things Kasparov does consistently is to equate the way you play chess with a kind of political conservatism, as if these two things were the same thing. How do you feel about that? He seems to have had a certain amount of success in making this equation.

AK: I just don't care what he says—this is rubbish. When he speaks about politics he is very inexperienced, of course. But he knows how to impress people. Most of what he says flies in the face of the facts—mostly stupid accusations he cannot prove. But you can't change him. I respect him as a chess player, but I have no respect for him as a politician or, as he calls himself, a "democrat." We know how he acted as president of the GMA. His ego is just to get as much power as possible, just to have people around as servants, not as friends. Just, "If I say this, it should be done."

DM: Is it especially important to you to beat Kasparov?

AK: No, I just play chess at the maximum level I'm capable of at the moment. It doesn't matter whether I'm playing Kasparov, Timman, or Spassky. I just play chess and try to play my best.

If we look at my previous encounters with Kasparov, he was very lucky to save the match in Seville—several times, not only in the last game, which I need not have lost. But I did lose, and then the score was equal. After that, he beat me twice in Holland—but one game was ridiculous, and the other I lost on time with three pieces more, a completely winning game. In Sweden he had an advantage, but miscalculated and ended up with a draw in a completely winning position. We played together in tournaments in Holland, in the Soviet championship, two tournaments in Sweden and France. In France he came in first, but I beat him in our personal game. In the Soviet championship and in Sweden, we shared first place. So I don't see that he was especially superior. It's even worse for him if he thinks I wasn't playing at my best level.

DM: How do you protect yourself psychologically from moments like your collapse in the final game in Seville?

AK: I just like to play immediately in another tournament. I followed Seville with Wijk aan Zee and won that tournament brilliantly. I just put that match and that failure behind me. It's not easy, but I just look forward, not back. It's the best way—just forget about what happened.

DM: Henley is impressed with your practical approach to chess, the fact that you refuse to waste energy but spend your time only on the most useful and productive ideas. How do you discipline yourself to do that? How many years did it take you to get to the point of your chess career where you said, "I've only got so many brain cells, and I'm not going to fill them up with nonsense"?

AK: That comes with experience, and, of course, I've played and won the most number of tournaments. That's why I have the level of experience to overcome problems.

DM: Is there anything that particularly worries you about this match?

AK: No, I don't see any problems besides my own, and whether I'm in good form and good shape or not. But you never know until the final game. You have no test as in other sports; you can't train like a runner. I never play training games because I don't feel them and I don't like them. You play at home and nobody is watching. I don't know how to play when it doesn't matter whether I win or lose. They can't tell me whether I'm in good shape or not, they don't show me anything.

DM: When you played the supercomputer Deep Thought earlier this year in an exhibition at Harvard, did you have the same kind of trouble that you have with training games? [Karpov, in sharp contrast to Kasparov's earlier crushing wins over Deep Thought, barely squeaked out a win.]

AK: No, it was different—but it wasn't easy, because I didn't take it very seriously like Kasparov did. He looked at many games, I saw maybe just one. So I didn't know its level, I didn't know its style, and I wasn't ready for possible mistakes. It was also difficult because I flew in from Moscow just for that game and I was playing between 3 A.M. and 5 A.M. Moscow time. In the previous thirty hours, I'd had less than five hours' sleep.

Interview with Garry Kasparov, September 1990

DM: I interviewed Karpov last week, and he said Kasparov "just wants to have people around as servants, not as friends. His ego is just to get as much power as possible."

GK: It's hard to answer this question—you should ask my friends. But I can say it's not true. I believe I have more friends than Mr. Karpov has. If power were my goal, I have better ways to exercise it than spreading my support to so many organizations outside chess. Power is easiest to attain in the arena where you have the most talent. I'm definitely not interested in power.

DM: Other people have also complained that your definition of democracy is "everybody votes for me." Do you think your resigning from the GMA may have been a mistake, giving ammunition to people who want to see your attempt to lead professional players as a personal ego trip?

GK: Well, there were two positions on the floor in Murcia [Spain]—one clearly identified with Bessel Kok, and the other with me. It's easy to see how players came to feel they were voting for personalities instead of issues.

I had good technical reasons for resigning from the GMA, but the truth is that I was fed up with what was happening. I thought the board had made a big mistake, and I wanted to wait until after the match to sort things out. Bessel Kok has said that I'm welcome back on the board, that I can serve as president anytime I want. My resignation has always been listed as "temporary" in official GMA documents. I just wanted to postpone this fight until I have a clear mind. I will reassess the situation later. I don't know if I will go back, but I will consider it.

The fact is that I am the first world champion to work for the interests of other professional players, and I'm not even sure at this moment that I represent a professional sport. If even the world championship loses money, how can we claim to be a professional sport? The only thing I am sure of is that I will use my capabilities to help chess in the best way possible.

I've thought about the possibility that my resignation might be misunderstood. But if you understand the background of the vote, you realize it basically pitted Americans and Soviets against West Europeans. What this shows me is that Europeans are satisfied with conditions as they are—change scares them a little bit. Under the new system, their old capital—their names—might not be as good. Talented young players might be able to take their places too easily. So Americans and Soviets basically voted for the immediate professionalization of chess; the West Europeans were against it.

DM: When we talked last, you expressed concern over changes in the Soviet Union and their impact on your ability to focus on the world championship. How has the situation altered since April, and have those alterations affected your match preparation?

GK: These changes deeply affected my match preparation. There were so many distractions. I lost valuable time. I lost thirty to forty days of preparation time, perhaps one third of my normal schedule. Although I feel better now and I had a great time in Martha's Vineyard [preparing for the match], a great time, it was not enough. I'm still behind. Still, I think my chess strength is more than enough to beat Karpov.

DM: Karpov thinks your play has deteriorated a bit since 1987–88, and he feels his chances in the match are very good. Is he wrong, or is the climb in your rating over the past two years a genuine reflection of increased power over the board? How do you estimate your chances in this match?

GK: Karpov plays worse than he did in 1987–88. I'm not better—my best year was 1988–89, when I played some fantastic chess. My match in Spain with Psakhis was very strong. I've lost energy, but I'm more experienced now. I think my chess strength is more than enough to beat Karpov. If my normal level of energy on a scale of one to ten is ten, then Karpov's is five, at least half as much. Because of my nonchess activities, we come to the board almost even, but I will mobilize all of my psychological resources—I can do it.

DM: Karpov said the biggest impact on him by internal Soviet changes has been the freedom to travel with his wife and to select foreigners for his training team. How have these changes affected you and the way you train?

GK: I suspect that these changes haven't affected Karpov very much, except that in the old days players who served on his team were rewarded with permission to travel to international tournaments. These terms never appealed much to foreigners.

As for me, I lost my native town (Baku) and my primary training base [when ethnic unrest forced him to leave in January]. That's a major loss and disruption—now there are no Armenians in my city. They have all been forced out.

I suspect the real reason that Karpov did most of his training in the U.S.S.R. is that it's too expensive to be here. His team is still furnished by the Soviet Sports Committee. Mine is privately financed, paid for out of my own pocket. I value my freedom more than money.

2

A SURVEY OF PREVIOUS KASPAROV–KARPOV MATCHES

by International Grandmaster
Leonid Shamkovich

Queen's Gambit Declined: 1 d4 d5 2 c4 e6

By far the most frequent opening in the first four world championship encounters between Kasparov and Karpov has been the Queen's Gambit Declined (QGD). In Match 1 it appeared eighteen times, with a 3-1 edge for Karpov almost exclusively with the white pieces. In Match 2, there were eight Queen's Gambits. Karpov won Games 4 and 22; the rest were drawn. Of five QGDs in Match 3, Kasparov won Games 8 and 22 with white; three were draws. Finally, there were four draws with this opening in Match 4, Kasparov playing white three times.

In all, the two rivals have contested thirty-five QGD games, with Karpov leading 5–3. Of all opening variations, only the QGD has appeared in all four matches leading up to 1990. In spite of Kasparov's negative score with this opening, he won two brilliant games with it (Match 3, Games 8 and 22), playing with white.

Nimzo-Indian Defense: 1 d4 Nf6 2 c4 e6 3 Nc3 Bb4

Kasparov has been particularly successful against Karpov's Nimzo-Indian, winning four of eight games (six were played in Match 2, two in Match 3). Karpov seems to have given up defending with the Nimzo-Indian against Kasparov.

Queen's Indian Defense: 1 d4 Nf6 2 c4 e6 3 Nf3 b6

In eleven appearances, the Queen's Indian has produced three decisive results. In Match 1, Kasparov won Game 32 with white, Karpov won Game 6 with black, and there were six draws. Karpov picked up another point with black in Game 18 of Match 3.

Grünfeld Defense: 1 d4 Nf6 2 c4 g6 3 Nc3 d5

After his relatively unsuccessful use of the QGD in Matches 1 and 2, Kasparov shifted to the Grünfeld Defense in Match 2, an opening he had never before played with black. In spite of a disastrous failure in Match 3 (0–3), the world champion stuck with the Grünfeld in Match 4 (1–2). Notwithstanding his bad results against Karpov, Kasparov has been successful with this opening against a long list of top-flight opposition, including Robert Hübner and Yasser Seirawan.

King's Indian Defense: 1 d4 Nf6 2 c4 g6 3 Nc3 Bg7 4 e4 d6

Kasparov held a draw with black in Game 17 of Match 4. Aside from the failure of his main alternatives, the QGD and the Grünfeld, there was no reason for him to repeat this opening in Match 5.

English Opening: 1 c4

In the first three matches, both players opened with 1 c4 as white, producing a total of six draws. In Match 4, Kasparov used the English five times as white, winning two, losing two, and drawing one.

King's Pawn Openings: 1 e4

In sixty games with white in the first three matches, Kasparov played 1 e4 only ten times, scoring +3 =6 −1. Karpov defended the Ruy Lopez (1 e4 e5 2 Nf3 Nc6 3 Bb5) six times (+2 =3 −1 for Kasparov) and the Petroff (1 e4 e5 2 Nf3 Nf6) four times (+1 =3 −0 for Kasparov). In Game 14 of Match 4, Karpov eschewed his favorite Ruy Lopez for the Caro-Kann, a quick draw.

There was certainly nothing in the record to indicate that Kasparov would resort exclusively to 1 e4 in the 1990 World Championship match.

Sicilian Defense: 1 e4 c5

This is Kasparov's favorite answer to 1 e4. Co-author of a famous book on the Sicilian (*Sicilian . . . e6 and . . . d6 Systems*, with Alexander Nikitin), Kasparov is the world's foremost expert on this opening. His chief successes have occurred in the sharp Scheveningen Variation, in which only Grandmaster Andrei Sokolov has managed to beat him.

Kasparov played the Sicilian fourteen times against Karpov in Matches 1 and 2, losing one game in Match 1 and winning two in the rematch. His expertise with this opening seems to have discouraged Karpov from playing 1 e4.

THE THREE BEST GAMES FROM MATCHES 1–4 ANNOTATED BY GM LEONID SHAMKOVICH

Match 2, Game 4 (1985)
Queen's Gambit Declined

White: Anatoly Karpov *Black: Garry Kasparov*

1 d4	d5
2 c4	e6
3 Nc3	Be7
4 Nf3	Nf6
5 Bg5	h6
6 Bxf6	

This exchange, in contrast to the usual 6 Bh4, is a contemporary idea. Today's grandmasters are very flexible in their attitude toward the concept of the bishop-pair as an advantage. Kasparov is especially well known for his willingness to play this exchange in a variety of settings. Here he plays against himself, as it were.

6 ...	Bxf6
7 e3	0-0
8 Qc2	Na6!?

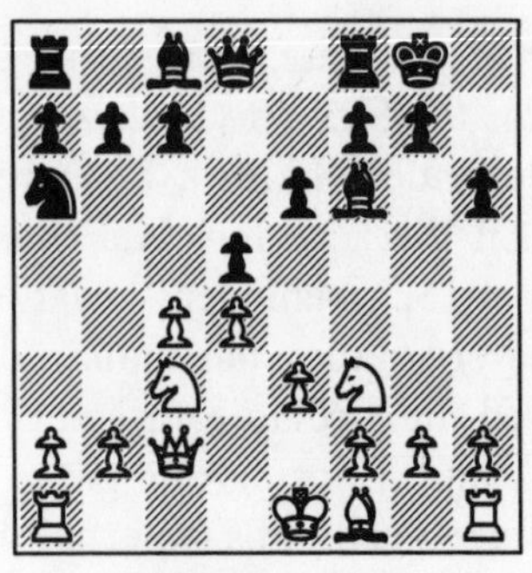

After 8 ... Na6

Kasparov tries a new and interesting idea. Dubious is 8 . . . c5?!, since 9 dxc5 Qa5 10 cxd5 exd5 11 0-0-0 Be6 12 Nxd5 (Kasparov–Timman, USSR vs. World 1984) gives White considerable advantage. After 9 . . . dxc4 10 Bxc4 Qa5 11 0-0 Bxc3 12 Qxc3 Qxc3 13 bxc3, Karpov defeated Kasparov with white in Game 27 of Match 1. It is interesting to see both super-Ks willing to defend these Queen's Gambit systems with either white or black.

9 Rd1!

A strong and logical reply. An attractive alternative is 9 c5 with the idea 9 . . . b6 10 c6!, with an advantage for White. But Black can also consider 9 . . . Nb4!? 10 Qa4 Nc6 11 b4 e5 12 b5 exd4.

9 . . .	**c5**
10 dxc5	**Qa5**
11 cxd5	**Nxc5**

This is the point of Kasparov's novelty on move 8, and it's typical of his style: he has excellent compensation for the pawn after 12 dxe6 Bxe6. Karpov is not tempted by this gift.

12 Qd2! Rd8

An interesting try is 12 . . . Bxc3 13 Qxc3 Qxc3+ 14 bxc3 exd5 15 Rxd5 b6, with some compensation for the pawn (weak pawns on c2 and a2). But such an endgame gambit is just too risky against Karpov's superb defensive technique.

13 Nd4 exd5

The isolated center pawn at d5 blockaded by the knight is a common situation, providing White with a significant advantage. The question is always just how stable the knight's position really is.

14 Be2 Qb6
15 0-0

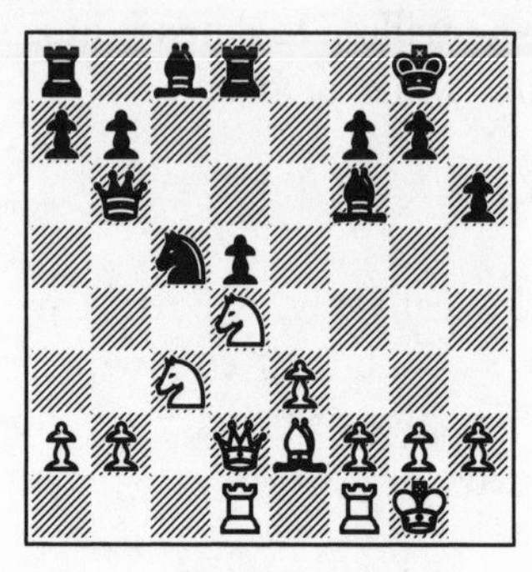

After 15 0-0

15 . . . Ne4

More logical is 15 . . . Ne6 to lure the powerful knight away from d4. Both Kasparov and Karpov analyzed that move. Kasparov rejected it in view of 16 Nf3! d4 17 Ne4, concluding that the black knight is forced to retreat to c7. According to Kasparov in *Informant 40* (Game 538), White has a slight edge after 17 . . . dxe3 18 Nxf6+ gxf6 19 Qxe3.

But neither player mentioned the interesting 17 . . . Bg5!?. The game might continue 18 Nexg5 (18 Nfxg5? hxg5 19 exd4 Nxd4 is good for Black) 18 . . . dxe3! 19 Qxe3 (unplayable is 19 Qc2 exf2+ 20 Rxf2 Rxd1+ or 20 . . . hxg5) 19 . . . Rxd1 (another intermezzo) 20 Rxd1 Qxe3 21 fxe3 hxg5 22 Ne5 (best—not 22 Bc4 Kf8, equalizing immediately) 22 . . . Kf8 23 Rf1 f6 24 Ng6+ Kf7 25 Bh5 Nf8! 26 Rcl Nxg6 27 Rc7+ Kf8 28 Bxg6 Be6, equalizing.

Of course, choosing such a sharp variation over the board is not easy without advance preparation, even for the world champion. And Black may be able to hold the game with calmer methods.

16 Qc2	Nxc3
17 Qxc3	Be6

More interesting is 17 . . . Bf5, avoiding exchange of the bishop. Kasparov noted that during the game he was dissatisfied with 18 Qd2 Be4 19 Bg4!—justifiably so, in my opinion. But after 19 . . . Rd6 or 19 . . . a5, he added, "Black is out of danger." He may be right, but I would hate to defend such a position against Karpov after the strong 20 Rc1!.

18 Qc2	Rac8
19 Qb1	Rc7
20 Rd2	Rdc8?

This serious positional blunder permits White to keep control of the light squares on the weak Black kingside and to create two hanging center pawns in the Black camp. Later, Kasparov suggested 20 . . . Bxd4! 21 Rxd4 Rcc8 22 Bd3 Qc7 with an even game, the open c-file providing adequate compensation for the passive bishop at e6.

21 Nxe6!	fxe6
22 Bg4!	

White's superiority is now obvious. Karpov finished the game superbly, while Kasparov faltered.

22 . . .	Rc4
23 h3	Qc6

24 Qd3	Kh8
25 Rfd1	a5
26 b3	Rc3
27 Qe2	Rf8
28 Bh5	Bd8
29 Bg6	b5
30 Bd3	b4
31 Qg4	Qe8
32 e4!	

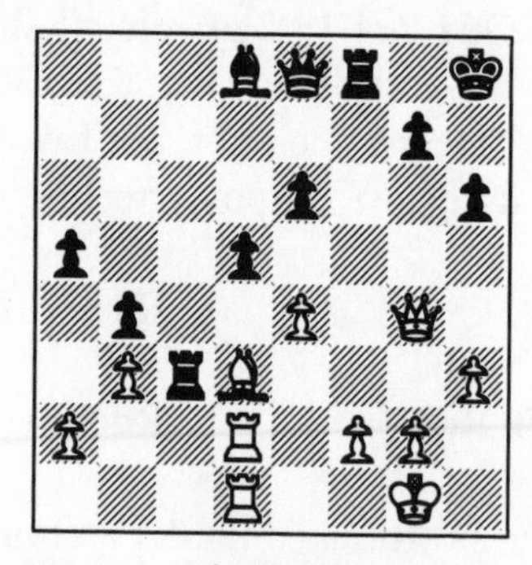

After 32 e4

32 ..	Bg5

Kasparov suggested 32 . . . Bb6, but White maintains a clear plus after 33 Re2 Qf7 34 Kh1!.

33 Rc2	Rxc2?

Garry commits one more—apparently fatal—inaccuracy. Correct is 33 . . . Qc8! with some chances to survive. Kasparov concluded his analysis with 34 exd5 (34 Qe2 Qc5!) 34 . . . exd5 (34 . . . Rxc2? 35 Qe4! wins) 35 Qxc8 Rfxc8 36 Re2 Rc1 37 Rxc1 Rxc1 + 38 Kh2 Rc8 39 Bg6, with only a slight advantage for White. It is difficult to see how he can make progress.

34 Bxc2	Qc6
35 Qe2	Qc5
36 Rf1	Qc3
37 exd5	exd5
38 Bb1!	

White's general plan is to create threats along the b1-h7 diagonal. The text move subtly extends the long diagonal.

38 ...	Qd2
39 Qe5	Rd8?

According to Kasparov, this mistake is the last straw. He later recommended 39 . . . Bf6 40 Qf5 Kg8 41 Bc2! Rd8 42 Rd1 Qg5 43 Re1, but Black's game is still unpleasant.

40 Qf5	Kg8
41 Qe6+	

Karpov sealed this move. "Karpov conducted his strategical plan after 21 . . . fxe6 very strongly and logically," wrote Kasparov.

The game concluded:

41 . . . Kh8 42 Qg6 Kg8 43 Qe6+ Kh8 44 Bf5! Qc3 45 Qg6 Kg8 46 Be6+ Kh8 47 Bf5 Kg8 48 g3 Kf8 49 Kg2 Qf6 50 Qh7 Qf7 51 h4 Bd2 52 Rd1 Bc3 53 Rd3 Rd6 54 Rf3! Ke7 55 Qh8! d4 56 Qc8 Rf6 57 Qc5+ Ke8 58 Rf4 Qb7+ 59 Re4+ Kf7 60 Qc4+ Kf8 61 Bh7! Rf7 62 Qe6 Qd7 63 Qe5 1-0

Match 3, Game 4 (1987)
Nimzo-Indian Defense

White: Garry Kasparov *Black: Anatoly Karpov*

1 d4	Nf6
2 c4	e6
3 Nc3	Bb4
4 Nf3	

The Nimzo-Indian has not been very successful for Karpov against Kasparov, though he played the defense regularly with great success before his four matches with Garry. Before and since his encounters with Karpov, Kasparov has tried many approaches to the Nimzo-Indian—4 Qc2, 4 e3, 4 a3, and recently 4 f3. But against the former world champion he has resorted almost exclusively to 4 Nf3 followed by g3.

4 ...	c5
5 g3	cxd4

In previous matches, Karpov tried other moves. Here he proves that the exchange is quite playable.

6 Nxd4	0-0
7 Bg2	d5
8 Qb3	

Kasparov's general plan is to obtain the advantage of the bishop-pair. Commenting on the game later, he pointed out the interesting alternative 8 0-0!? dxc4 9 Qa4 (Romanishin–Ribli, Reggio Emilia 1985–86), in the spirit of a gambit.

8 ...	Bxc3+
9 bxc3	

Interesting is 9 Qxc3!? e5 10 Nb3 (Ubilava–Novikov, Tbilisi 1988, and Piket–Belyavsky, Amsterdam 1989). The text creates a potentially weak pawn on c3.

9 . . . Nc6!

Both players had deeply analyzed this new line in their opening preparations, so it held no surprises for either. The text move is best, threatening 10 . . . Na5, while 10 Nxc6 bxc6 favors Black. The reason Black avoids the "normal" 9 . . . dxc4 is not 10 Qxc4 e5! 11 Nb5 a6 12 Nc7 Ra7!, with an acceptable position, but the gambit idea 10 Qa3!.

10 cxd5 Na5!
11 Qc2 Nxd5

After 11 ... Nxd5

12 Qd3

This may be slightly inaccurate. Kasparov himself demonstrated the best continuation for Black after the game: 12 Ba3! Re8 13 Qd3 (not 13 c4? Nf4!) 13 . . . Bd7 (13 . . . Qc7 14 Nb5 Qc6 15 Nd6, with a definite advantage for White) 14 c4 Nb6 15 Rc1! (15 c5 Nbc4 is unclear) 15 . . . Rc8 16 c5 Nd5 17 Nb5, with a small plus for White. Unfortunately, there has been no serious test of this system since the match because of the increased popularity of 4 f3 and 4 Qc2.

12 . . . Bd7?!

Strangely, Karpov passes up the natural 12 . . . Qc7! preventing c4; Black is OK after 13 Nb5 Qc6 14 Ba3. More interesting is Kasparov's 14 0-0 Bd7 15 a4 a6 16 e4 axb5 17 exd5 Qc4, which he says "proves risky, but how else can White play for a win?" Still, White is slightly better after 18 Qxc4 Nxc4 (or 18 . . . bxc4 19 Ba3 Rfd8 20 Rad1) 19 dxe6 Bxe6 20 Bxb7 Rxa4 21 Rb1.

13 c4!

This is even stronger than transposition to the previous variation after 13 Ba3 Re8 14 c4, etc.

13 . . . Ne7!

White is better after 13 . . . Nb4 14 Qc3 or 13 . . . Nb6 14 c5 Nbc4 15 0-0! (Kasparov). The text is more flexible, increasing control over the c6-square and attacking the c4-pawn, the object of Black's counterplay. Kasparov later gave 14 Ba3 Re8 15 0-0 Nec6! 16 f4 Nxd4 17 Qxd4 Bc6 18 Qc3 Bxg2 19 Kxg2 Qc7 20 Bb2 f6, with an edge for Black. It is curious that Kasparov avoided playing the obvious Ba3 even though he approved it in his analysis immediately following the game.

14 0–0

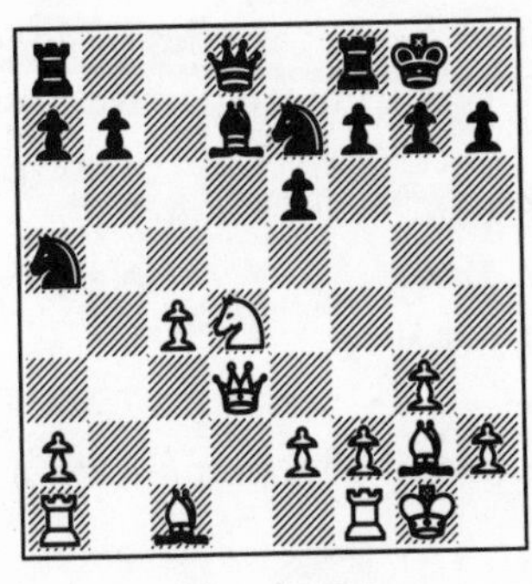

After 14 0-0

14 . . . Rc8?

Who would guess that this natural move would turn out to be perhaps the decisive mistake? Karpov is overlooking a witty tactical point.

Kasparov suggested 14 . . . Bc6!? 15 Nxc6 Nexc6, noting: "It was psychologically not easy to allow the opponent the two bishops." Still, the game is basically even in this line: 16 Bb2 Qxd3 17 exd3 Rad8 18 Rfd1 Nd4 19 Kf1 Rd7 20 Bc3 Nac6.

Instead of 15 Nxc6, Kasparov recommended 15 Ba3! (at last!) 15 . . . Bxg2 16 Kxg2, with a defensible position. He is absolutely right, but Black must play precisely: 16 . . . a6! (not 16 . . . Rc8 or 16 . . . Re8, when 17 Nb5! gives White a definite advantage; no better is 16 . . . Qc7 17 Nb5 Qc6+ 18 Qf3!) 17 Qc3 Nac6 (17 . . . b6? 18 Bb2!) 18 Rfd1 Qc7 19 Bb2 e5!.

15 Nb3!

This strong maneuver compels Black to exchange White's weak c-pawn for the b-pawn.

15 . . . Nxc4
16 Bxb7

Now Kasparov begins a series of exquisite maneuvers to drive Black's pieces to more passive positions.

16 . . .	**Rc7**
17 Ba6!	**Ne5**
18 Qe3!	

White must avoid the simplification resulting from 18 Qd6 Bc8!.

18 . . .	**Nc4**
19 Qe4	**Nd6?**

After this retreat, White's advantage is manifest. Kasparov thought Black could still hold on after 19 . . . Qa8! 20 Qxa8 Rxa8 21 Bg5! Nd5 22 Rfc1 Ncb6 23 Bd2, but I am not so sure he can after 23 . . . Bc8 24 Bd3 Bd7 25 e4 Rxc1+ 26 Rxc1 Ne7 27 Rc7.

20 Qd3!

White has realized his plan, leaving Karpov no chance for consolidation and escape.

20 . . .	**Rc6**
21 Ba3	**Bc8**
22 Bxc8	**Ndxc8**
23 Rfd1!	

The queen trade is good for White here because Black's pieces are poorly coordinated.

Kasparov is normally just as quick as Karpov to transpose to an endgame, but after a completely different middlegame. Kasparov's approach is to exploit every possible tactical and

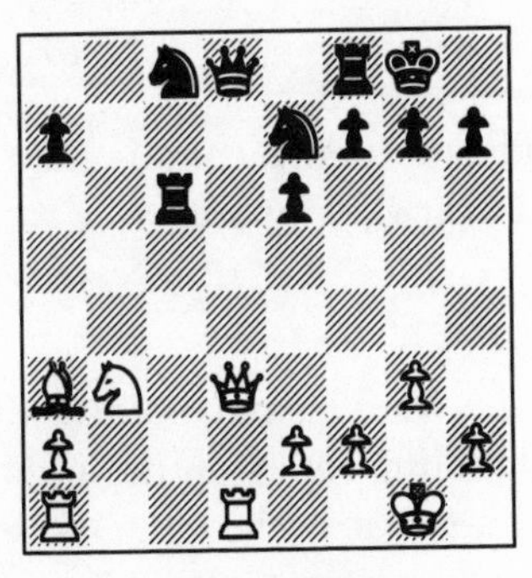

After 23 Rfd1

combinative resource in the middlegame, while Karpov is willing to move more quietly through the middlegame, playing leisurely and risk-free chess without surrendering tactical vigilance.

23 ...	Qxd3
24 Rxd3	Re8
25 Rad1	

His control of the d-file and activity for his pieces give White a decisive advantage. Karpov, of course, offers stubborn resistance.

25 ...	f6
26 Nd4	Rb6
27 Bc5	Ra6

After 27 . . . Rb2, Kasparov suggested 28 Nxe6 Rxe2 29 Nc7 Rf8 30 Ra3!, with an advantage for White.

28 Nb5!	Rc6

The alternative 28 . . . Rxa2 fails to 29 Nc7 Rf8 30 Nxe6 Re8 31 Nc7 Rf8 32 Re3 Kf7 33 Rd7.

29 Bxe7!	Nxe7

Black avoids the petite combination 29 . . . Rxe7? 30 Rd8+ Kf7 31 Rxc8!, winning.

30 Rd7!

Kasparov wins the a7-pawn because of the threat 31 Nd6 followed by doubling rooks on the seventh rank and pushing his passed a-pawn. "The game is decided despite Karpov's desperate resistance," wrote Kasparov.

30 . . .	Ng6
31 Rxa7	Nf8
32 a4	Rb8
33 e3	h5
34 Kg2	e5
35 Rd3!	Kh7
36 Rc3	Rbc8
37 Rxc6	Rxc6
38 Nc7	Ne6
39 Nd5!	

The crucial centralization.

39 . . .	Kh6
40 a5	e4
41 a6!	1-0

Faced with 41 . . . Rd6 (41 . . . Nc5 42 Rc7!) 42 Ne7 Rd1 43 Ra8 Kh7 44 a7 Ra1 45 Nc6 Ng5 46 Re8, Black resigned.

Kasparov has been quoted as saying that this was one of his very best efforts against Karpov. In addition, this game seems to have ended the sharp debate between these Soviet superstars over the Nimzo-Indian Defense. Karpov abandoned the opening in their last match. The bottom line: +4 −0 =3 in favor of Kasparov.

Match 3, Game 22 (1986)
Queen's Gambit Declined

White: Garry Kasparov ***Black: Anatoly Karpov***

1 d4	**Nf6**
2 c4	**e6**
3 Nf3	**d5**
4 Nc3	**Be7**
5 Bg5	**h6**
6 Bxf6	

This exchange, known as the Petrosian Variation, has been examined many times from both sides by both players. Kasparov's play after Bxf6 in similar positions in the Catalan and Tarrasch as well as in this variation has shaken conventional wisdom about the advantage of two bishops.

6 . . .	**Bxf6**
7 e3	**0-0**
8 Rc1	**c6**
9 Bd3	**Nd7**
10 0-0	**dxc4**

This is the traditional prelude to a break with . . . c5 or . . . e5. The alternative is 10 . . . b6?!, but this is questionable after 11 e4 dxe4 12 Nxe4 Be7 13 Bb1 Bb7 14 Qd3, with strong threats against the black kingside. No better is 11 . . . dxc4 12 Bxc4 e5 13 d5, with a solid advantage for White.

Also 10 . . . Qe7 and 10 . . . Be7 have been tried here, but without much success for Black. In either case, White keeps a plus by combining his spatial advantage with an e4 break.

11 Bxc4

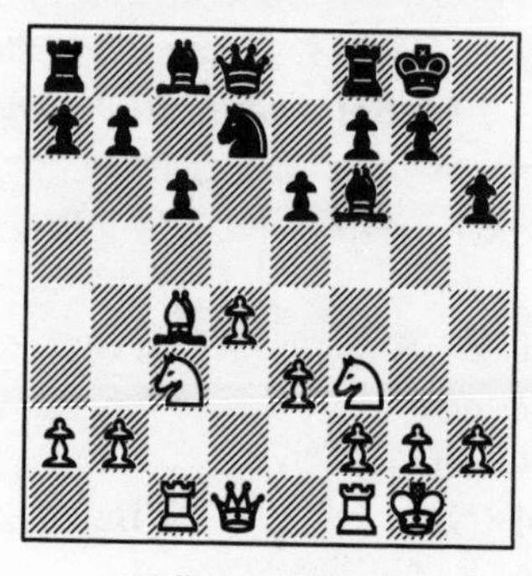

After 11 Bxc4

11 . . .	**e5!?**

In Match 3, Game 12, Black equalized with 11 . . . c5 12 Qe2 a6 13 Rfd1 cxd4 14 Nxd4 Qe7 15 Ne4 Be5 16 Nf3 Bb8, but Kasparov improved with 16 Qh5 in Kasparov–Olafsson, Dubai 1986. Still dubious is 11 . . . b6?! because of 12 e4! Bb7 13 e5 Be7 14 Qe2 b5 15 Bd3 c5 16 Nxb5 cxd4 17 Be4! (Karpov–Spassky, Lucerne 1985).

12 h3!

One of Kasparov's small but venomous innovations, preventing . . . Bg4.

12 . . .	**exd4**
13 exd4	**Nb6**
14 Bb3	**Bf5**
15 Re1	**a5?**

This attempt to drive the bishop from its strong position at b3 weakens b6, a square that later plays a critical role.

16 a3

Now the bishop loses its pawn support, but the black knight is in the same boat.

16 . . . Re8!

Karpov sometimes repeats Kasparov's opening ideas with the same color. Against Belyavsky in the 1986 European Cup, he met 16 . . . Qd7 with 17 Ne5! Bxe5 18 Rxe5 Rfe8 19 Qe2, with a clear edge for White.

17 Rxe8 + Qxe8
18 Qd2!

The white queen steers for the active f4-square.

18 . . . Nd7?

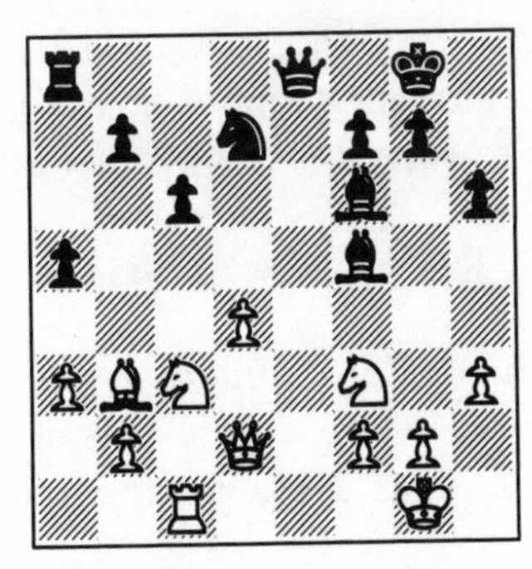

After 18 ... Nd7

More sensible is 18 . . . Qb8, with an eye on f4.

19 Qf4! Bg6

Why not 19 . . . Be6, getting rid of the annoying bishop at b3? Kasparov suggests 20 Bxe6 Qxe6 21 Qc7 Qb3 22 Ne4! Qxb2 23 Re1 Nf8 24 Nxf6 + gxf6 25 Qf4, with a clear lead for White. But Black seems to hold after 25 . . . Ng6 26 Qxf6 Qb3 27 Ne5 Re8 28 Re3 Qe6, or 26 Qxh6 Qxa3 with an unclear game.

20 h4 Qd8
21 Na4!

A very farsighted and effective concept, hindering Black's queenside coordination and starting an attack.

21 . . . h5

Black stops h5 but at the cost of another critical weakness on g5. Commentators criticized this move, but further analysis uncovered nothing better; e.g., 21 . . . Bh5 22 g4 Bg6 23 h5 Bh7 24 Ne5!, and White wins; or 21 . . . Qb8 22 Qg4 Nf8 23 h5 Bh7 24 Nb6! is also very strong (24 . . . Ra6 25 Nd7 Nxd7 [25 . . . Qd8 26 Nde5!] 26 Qxd7 Qf8 27 Re1 Ra8 28 Qxb7, and Black cannot save c6); and 21 . . . Nf8 22 Re1 also fails to solve Black's problems.

22 Re1 b5

The only chance for counterplay, but the pawn at c6 is dangerously weak. More resistance is offered by 22 . . . Qb8 23 Qe3 Qd6 24 Nc3 Nf8, but the game is still good for White.

23 Nc3 Qb8
24 Qe3

An interesting alternative is 24 Ne5 Bxe5 25 dxe5 Nc5 26 Ba2 b4, with tremendous complications that resolve in White's favor.

24 . . . b4

25 Ne4	bxa3
26 Nxf6+	Nxf6
27 bxa3	Nd5!

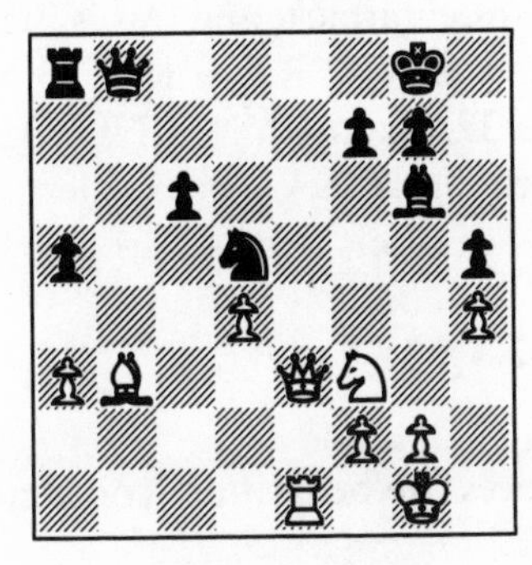

After 27 ... Nd5

As usual, Karpov perseveres in a difficult position. On 27 . . . Ng4, Kasparov suggested 28 Qc3 Qd6 29 g3, threatening Ne5.

28 Bxd5	cxd5
29 Ne5	

Finally Black has removed White's pesky bishop, but Kasparov now demonstrates the knight's domination of Black's bishop.

29 . . .	Qd8!
30 Qf3!?	

Kasparov later preferred 30 Qf4!.

30 . . .	Ra6

Karpov hopes to create counterplay by moving the rook to f6 or g6. Kasparov suggested 30 . . . Rc8.

31 Rc1	**Kh7!?**

Black should try 31 . . . Qxh4. The h4-pawn is an important part of White's attack, and this is Black's only chance to grab it: 31 . . . Qxh4 32 Rc8 + Kh7 33 Nxf7 Bxf7 34 Qxf7 Rf6 holds; or 32 Qxd5 Kh7 33 Nf3 Qg4!, and White still has an edge, though Black has excellent drawing resources. Still, Karpov's cautious text is also playable.

32 Qh3!

White's pieces are beautifully coordinated.

32 . . .	**Rb6**
33 Rc8	**Qd6**
34 Qg3	**a4?**

A serious, perhaps fatal, mistake, the idea of which is clearly to establish an outpost at b3. Kasparov's postmortem analysis uncovered Black's best chance to escape: 34 . . . Rb1 + 35 Kh2 Qa6!, with the idea . . . Qf1. Kasparov then claimed that 36 Re8! Qf1 37 Qf3 wins; e.g., 37 . . . a4 38 Nxf7! Bxf7 39 Qxf7 Qg1 + 40 Kg3 Rb3 + 41 f3, when Black can't play . . . Qe1 +. My own analysis uncovered 37 . . . f6 38 Rh8 + ! Kxh8 39 Nxg6 + Kg8 40 Qxd5 + Kh7 41 Ne7!, and White wins. Kasparov himself suggested 36 . . . Qb5!, dislodging the rook from e8, as an improvement since 37 Ra8 "deprives Black of counterplay." But I think 37 . . . Qf1 38 Qf3 Rd1! gives Black real chances to survive.

Usually these study-like puzzles have little practical value, but in a few moves we will see the rare exception.

35 Ra8!

This is a triumph of tactical play. Black cannot defend a4: 35 . . . Ra6 36 Nxf7! Bxf7 37 Qd3+ wins; and 35 . . . Rb3 36 Rh8+! Kxh8 37 Nxf7+ also fails.

35 . . .	**Qe6!**

Karpov is not easy to crush—he doesn't miss a single tactical point.

36 Rxa4	**Qf5**
37 Ra7!	**Rb1+**
38 Kh2	**Rc1**
39 Rb7	**Rc2**
40 f3	**Rd2**
41 Nd7!!	

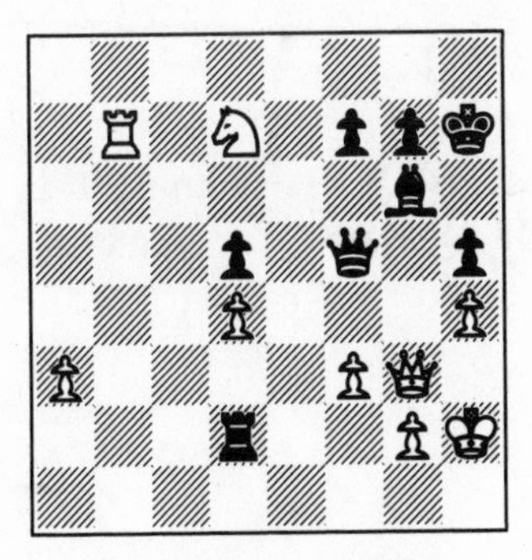

After 41 Nd7

This is perhaps the most remarkable sealed move in championship history. Everyone expected the straightforward 41 Rb4? f6 42 Nxg6 Qxg6 43 Qxg6+, when Black has chances to survive. A draw was universally expected.

Upon resumption, Black immediately accepted the offered pawn.

41 . . .	**Rxd4**
42 Nf8 +	**Kh6**
43 Rb4!!	

The final point of Kasparov's combination: 43 . . . Rxb4 44 axb4 d4 45 b5 d3 46 b6 d2 47 b7 d1Q 48 b8Q Qc1 49 Nxg6 Qxg6 50 Qh8 + Qh7 51 Qgxg7 mate. White also wins after 43 . . . Rd1 44 Rb8 Bh7 45 Qg5 +.

43 . . .	**Rc4**
44 Rxc4	**dxc4**
45 Qd6	

Black cannot stop Qe3 +—a study-like conclusion, incorporating a neat fortress formed by White's knight.

45 . . .	**c3**
46 Qd4	**1-0**

White threatens Qe3 +, winning after either 46 . . . Bh7 47 Qxc3 g5 48 Qe3, or 47 . . . Bg8 48 Qe3 +.

GARRY KASPAROV, INTERREGNUM

by International Grandmaster
Leonid Shamkovich

Garry Kasparov, the defending 13th world champion, is notable even among world champions—an absolutely integrated and complete chess player, strong both positionally and tactically, and with a combinative bias and a unique skill for gambit play in a variety of opening settings.

Kasparov is a significant opening innovator, regularly creating new ideas in a range of different schemes. Like Bobby Fischer, he is famous for researching known opening positions for new and surprising interpretations.

Although Kasparov has apparently not yet attained Fischer's level of technical expertise in realizing an advantage in the middlegame and ending, he seems to outstrip him in the dynamic interpretation of the game as a whole, especially in his ability to give up material in exchange for piece activity.

Kasparov and Karpov have met four times previously:

Match 1, Moscow 1984–85: +3 =40 −5, stopped without decision (Karpov leading).

Match 2, Moscow 1985: +5 =16 −3, Kasparov became the youngest world champion in history.

Match 3, London–Leningrad 1986: +5 =15 −4, Kasparov retained his title.

Match 4, Seville 1987: +4 =16 −4, Kasparov retained his title by drawing the match.

Kasparov's incredible will power is demonstrated by the fact that he has won three of the four final games in the matches, excluding only the draw in Match 2 that guaranteed him the title.

Perhaps the most fertile period in his career was that between Seville and the start of the 1990 match, during which he took the tournament circuit by storm, achieving a record 2800 FIDE rating and displacing Fischer as the highest-rated chess player in history. The list of Kasparov's successes in this period is overwhelming:

Amsterdam 1988: 1. Kasparov 9; 2. Karpov 6.5, a full 2.5 points back!

Belfort World Cup 1988: 1. Kasparov 11.5; 2. Karpov 10.5, including his only tournament victory over Kasparov.

U.S.S.R. Championship 1988: 1–2. Kasparov–Karpov 11.5.

Reykjavik 1988: 1. Kasparov 11 (lost to Andrei Sokolov); 2. Alexander Belyavsky 10.5.

Thessaloniki Olympiad: 8.5/10 on first board for the U.S.S.R.

Barcelona World Cup 1989: 1. Kasparov 11; 2. Ljubomir Ljubojevic 11.

Skelleftea 1989 World Cup: 1–2. Kasparov–Karpov 9.5.

Tilburg 1989: 1. Kasparov 12/14!; 2. Viktor Korchnoi 8.5.

Belgrade 1989: 1. Kasparov 9.5/11; 2–3. Jan Timman–Jan Ehlvest 6.5. Here Kasparov passed Bobby Fischer's record 2785 FIDE rating.

Linares 1989: 1. Kasparov 8; 2. Boris Gelfand 7.5.

During this period, Kasparov also played three training matches with grandmasters Vlastimil Hort (2.5-.5), Kurt Hansen (1.5-.5), and Lev Psakhis (5-1!). This added to a string of match victories over grandmasters Robert Hübner, Jan Timman, Tony Miles, and Ulf Anderssen, and demonstrated his dominance over the contemporary field, with the exception of Karpov.

The world champion lost only four games between 1988 and 1990 (Karpov lost 10): against Karpov (Belfort 1988); Sokolov (Reykjavik 1988); Artur Yusupov (Barcelona 1989); and Boris Gulko (Linares 1990).

Following are, in my opinion, Kasparov's finest match and tournament victories in this period.

U.S.S.R. Championship 1988
English Opening

White: Garry Kasparov ***Black: Vasily Ivanchuk***

1 c4 Nf6 2 Nc3 e5 3 Nf3 Nc6 4 g3 Bb4 5 Bg2 0-0 6 0-0 e4 7 Ng5 Bxc3 8 bxc3 Re8 9 f3 exf3 10 Nxf3 d5 11 d4!

Always dangerous in the opening, Kasparov comes up with a new plan. Previously played was 11 cxd5 Qxd5 12 Nd4 Qh5! with a complicated and unclear position.

11 . . .	**Ne4**
12 Qc2!	

In the same tournament against Dzandzgava, Vaiser played 12 cxd5 Nxc3 13 Qd2 Nxd5 14 e4 Nf6 15 e5 Ne4 16 Qe3 f5 17 Bb2 Ne7 18 g4 Nd5 19 Qb3 c6 20 gxf5 Bxf5 21 Rae1, with an unclear position.

12 . . . dxc4
13 Rb1!!

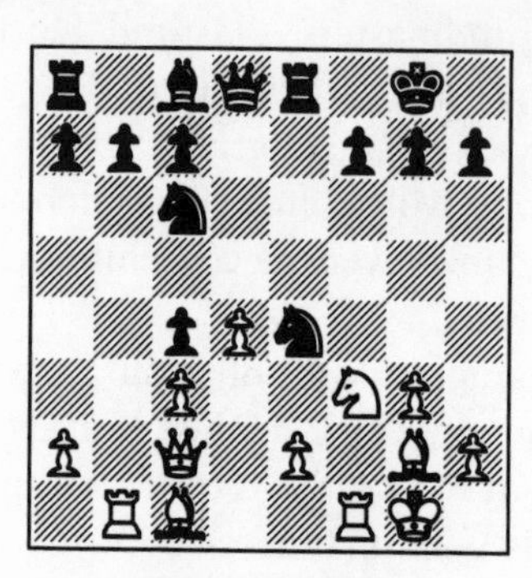

After 13 Rb1

13 . . . f5 14 g4 Qe7? 15 gxf5 Nd6 16 Ng5 Qxe2 17 Bd5 + Kh8 18 Qxe2 Rxe2 19 Bf4 Nd8 20 Bxd6 cxd6 21 Rbe1!

White uses the back-rank threat to remove Black's only active piece.

21 . . . Rxe1 22 Rxe1 Bd7 23 Re7 Bc6 24 f6! 1-0

Black's back is broken. If 24 . . . Bxd5 25 Re8 + Bg8 26 f7 Nxf7 27 Nxf7 mate.

Tilburg 1989
King's Indian Defense

White: Jeroen Piket *Black: Garry Kasparov*

1 d4 Nf6 2 Nf3 g6 3 c4 Bg7 4 Nc3 0-0 5 e4 d6 6 Be2 e5 7

0-0 Nc6 8 d5 Ne7 9 Ne1 Nd7 10 Be3 f5 11 f3 f4 12 Bf2 g5 13 b4 Nf6 14 c5 Ng6 15 cxd6 cxd6 16 Rc1 Rf7 17 a4 Bf8

Once again Kasparov comes up with a new plan deep in the opening. Older alternatives are 17 . . . h5 and 17 . . . b6.

18 a5	**Bd7!**
19 Nb5?!	

Better is 19 Kh1 Rg7.

19 . . .	**g4!**

Kasparov goes for the throat.

20 Nc7?!	**g3!**

In this tremendously complicated position, Kasparov counts on breaking through to White's king, using the exchange as bait to buy the necessary time.

21 Nxa8?	**Nh5!**

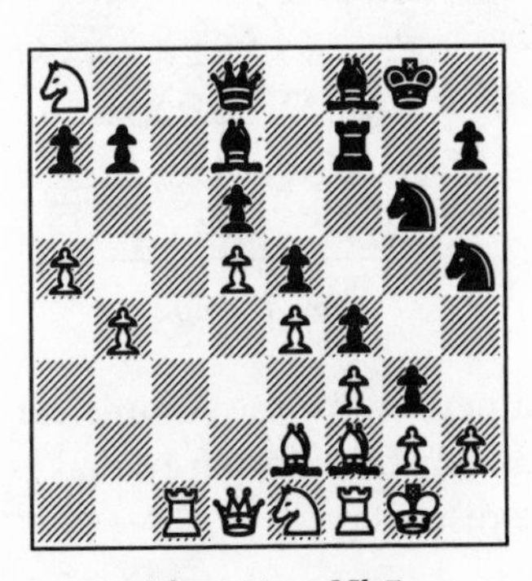

After 21 ... Nh5

22 Kh1

Forced. If 22 Bxa7 Qh4 23 h3 Bxh3 24 gxh3 Qxh3 25 Rf2 gxf2+ 26 Kxf2 Nh4 27 Bf1 Qh2+ 28 Ng2 Rg7 and Black wins. Notice how the g7-square vacated by the bishop comes into play.

22 . . . gxf2 23 Rxf2 Ng3+! 24 Kg1 Qxa8 25 Bc4 a6! 26 Qd3 Qa7! 27 b5 axb5 28 Bxb5 Nh1! 0-1

Linares 1990
Nimzo-Indian Defense

White: Garry Kasparov *Black: Boris Spassky*

1 d4 Nf6 2 c4 e6 3 Nc3 Bb4 4 Qc2 d5 5 cxd5 exd5 6 Bg5 h6 7 Bh4 c5 8 dxc5 Nc6 9 e3 g5 10 Bg3 Ne4 11 Nf3 Qf6 12 Bb5!

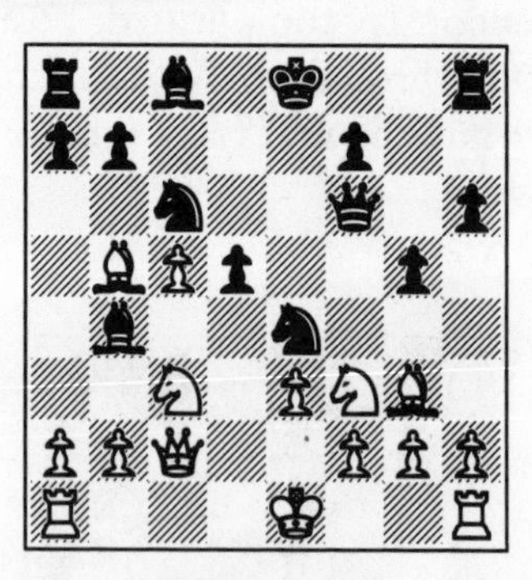

After 12 Bb5

A precise (and new) response An unclear position results from the previous 12 Rc1. Kasparov makes his living from this kind of little discovery.

12 . . .	Nxc3
13 Bxc6+	bxc6?

White has only a small edge after 13 . . . Qxc6 14 bxc3 Bxc5 15 0-0.

14 a3!	g4!
15 Be5!	

Black can stir up trouble after 15 Nd4 Nb5+.

15 . . .	Ne4+
16 axb4	Qf5
17 Bxh8	gxf3
18 Rg1!	Qg4?

Spassky finally cracks under the pressure. He still has some chances after 18 . . . fxg2!.

19 Qd1!

Pinning the f-pawn. White is in good shape here.

19 . . . Ng5 20 Qd4! Ne4 21 Qe5+ Be6 22 Qf4 Qg6 23 Qxf3 f6 24 Qf4 Kf7 25 f3 Ng5 26 Kd2 Qf5 27 h4 Qxf4 28 exf4 Nh7 29 g4 1-0

White has a dominating position after Black takes the bishop. He will have three pawns for the piece, the black knight is worthless, and the black king will be trapped on the back rank for some time.

Linares 1990
Sicilian Defense

White: Vasily Ivanchuk *Black: Garry Kasparov*

1 e4 c5 2 Nf3 d6 3 d4 cxd4 4 Nxd4 Nf6 5 Nc3 a6 6 Bg5 e6 7 f4 Qb6 8 Qd2 Qxb2 9 Rb1 Qa3 10 f5 Nc6 11 fxe6 fxe6

12 Nxc6 bxc6 13 Be2 Be7 14 0-0 0-0 15 Rb3 Qc5+ 16 Be3 Qe5 17 Bf4 Qc5+ 18 Kh1 Ng4 19 h3 e5 20 Na4 Qa7 21 Bc4+ Kh8 22 hxg4 exf4 23 Nb6 d5!

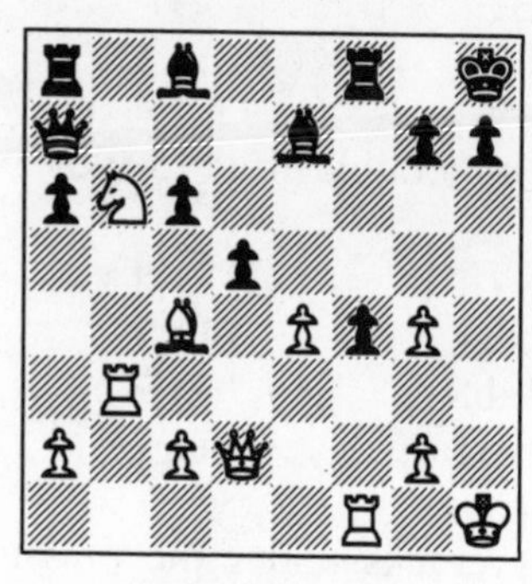

After 23 ... d5

No matter how deep in the opening you survive, you are still in danger of stumbling over a Kasparov land mine. Previously played was 23 . . . Rb8.

24 exd5 cxd5 25 Bxd5 Rb8 26 Nxc8 Rbxc8 27 Rh3! Qb6 28 Re1 Bg5 29 Re6 Qd8!

Kasparov finds the only move. White is much better after 29 . . . Qb1+? 30 Kh2 Qxc2 31 Qxc2 Rxc2 32 Be4.

30 c4?!

Ivanchuk stumbles a bit. White maintains equality after 30 Rd6 Qxd6 31 Rxh7+ Kxh7 32 Be4+ Qg6 33 Qd3; or 30 Qd3 Bh4 31 Be4 Qxd3 32 Bxd3 g5 33 Re7 Rfe8 34 Rxh7+ Kg8 35 R3xh4 gxh4 36 Rxh4.

30 . . . Rb8! 31 Qd3 Bh4 32 Be4 Qg5! 33 Bxh7 Rfd8 34 Qc2 f3 35 Rxf3 Rd2 36 Qe4 Rd1+ 37 Kh2 Re1?

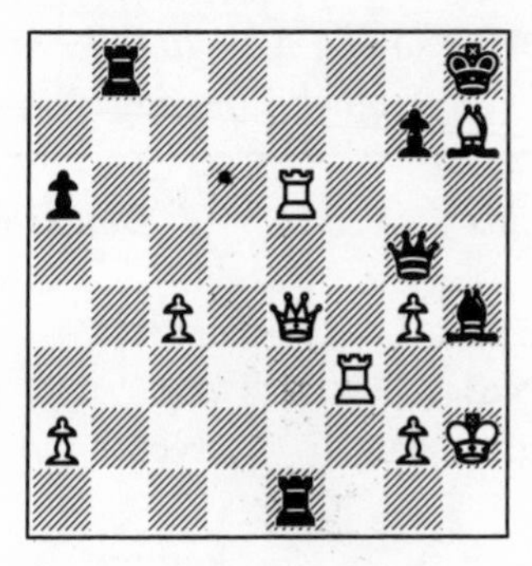

After 37 ... Re1

Correct is 37 . . . Qc1! 38 Re8 + Rxe8 39 Qxe8 + Kxh7.

38 Qf5	**Rxe6**
39 Qxe6	**Kxh7**
40 Qe4 +	**g6**

This is forced. If 40 . . . Kg8? 41 Rf5 and White is winning.

41 Rh3?

White's final mistake. He holds after 41 Rf7 + Kh6 42 Qd4 Rg8 43 g3 Qd8 44 Rd7 Qb8 45 Qd2 + Bg5 46 Qg2 Bh4.

41 . . .	**Kg7**
42 Qd4 +	**Kg8**
43 Qe4	**Qf6!**
0-1	

Kasparov finishes brilliantly: 44 Rf3 Qd6 + 45 Kh3 Kg7!! 46 c5 Rh8, winning.

Murcia (La Mangua) 1990
English Opening

White: Lev Psakhis *Black: Garry Kasparov*

1 c4	g6
2 Nc3	Bg7
3 g3	Nc6

The alternative is 3 . . . c5. Now the game transposes to an older line of the English opening.

4 Bg2	d6
5 Nf3	

Another try is 5 e3 e5 6 Nge2.

5 . . .	e5
6 d3	f5

The game now takes on the characteristics of the Closed Sicilian. This game is an excellent example of the contemporary tendency to transpose from one opening setup to another.

7 0-0	Nf6
8 Rb1	h6!

Black prepares a kingside pawn storm while preventing thrusts such as Bg5 or Ng5.

9 b4

Whose attack is more dangerous? White's on the queenside or Black's on the kingside?

9 . . .	0-0
10 b5	Ne7
11 a4	Be6

Black takes control of the critical d5-square. White may now be regretting that he avoided the safer, more flexible 5 e3 and 6 Nge2 so as to meet Black's attack with f4. It's still not too late.

12 Ba3?

Unclear is 12 Ne1!? Rb8 13 f4.

12 . . .	Rc8
13 Nd2	b6
14 e3	g5!
15 d4?	

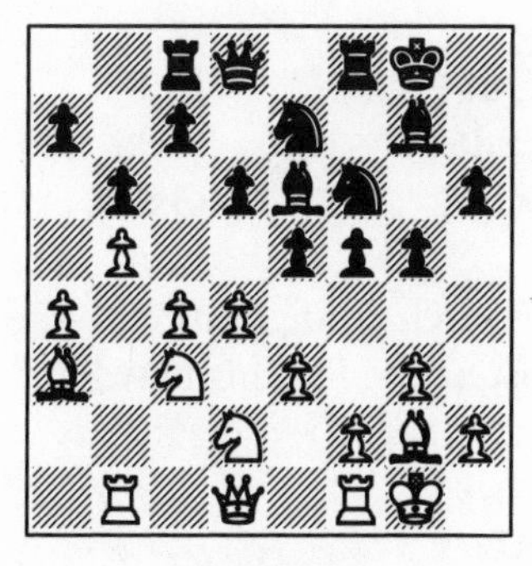

After 15 d4

Simultaneously creating weak pawns at d4 and c4, but 15 f4 is dubious because of the weak e3-pawn. Better is 15 Qe2 Qd7 16 Rbe1, preventing . . . f4.

15 . . .	exd4
16 exd4	f4!

Black creates more scope for his pieces, especially the bishop at e6 and the knight at e7. The hole at e4 is unimportant.

17 Re1	**Bg4**
18 Nf3?!	

Maybe 18 Bf3!?.

18 . . .	**Qd7**
19 c5	

This counterattack comes too late.

19 . . .	**Rce8**
20 Rc1	**Nf5**

Black's pressure intensifies with every move.

21 Qd3	**Kh8**
22 cxd6	**cxd6**
23 Rxe8	**Qxe8!**

An idea from Dutch configurations—the queen transfers to a powerful post at h5. Psakhis may have considered only 23 . . . Rxe8.

24 Rf1

Black gets a strong attack after 24 h3 fxg3! 25 hxg4 (25 fxg3 Qh5!) 25 . . . gxf2+ 26 Kxf2 Nxg4+ 27 Kg1 Qh5.

24 . . .	**Qh5!**

Black's kingside threats are very strong.

25 Ne4

Strong for Black is 25 Ne2 Re8.

25 . . .	**Nxe4**
26 Qxe4	**Bh3!**
27 Ne5!?	

White makes one last attempt to complicate. Otherwise, the threat 27 . . . Bxg2 28 Kxg2 g4 and 29 . . . f3+ is crushing.

27 . . .	**Bxg2**

Not 27 . . . dxe5? 28 Bxf8 Bxf8 29 Qxe5+ when White is better.

28 Kxg2	**g4**
29 Bxd6!?	**Rf6!**

The final point of Black's attack. A mistake would be 29 . . . Nxd6? 30 Ng6+ Kg8 31 Qe6+ Nf7 32 Ne7+ Kh8? (32 . . . Kh7!? 33 Qe4+ draw) 33 Ng6+ Kh7 34 Nxf4, and Black's position is no longer crushing.

30 Bb8	**Qh3+**
0-1	

White resigned in view of 31 Kg1 f3 32 Nxf3 gxf3 33 Qxf3 Nh4!. This game is a brilliant example of Kasparov's remarkable skill in conducting a kingside attack.

It's clear that Karpov is Kasparov's only real opposition in the chess world today, and the quality of that opposition is equally clear in the score of their games against one another (60.5–59.5 in 120 match games). Against other grandmasters, Kasparov's record speaks for itself—he has dominated them much more convincingly than Karpov. This single fact led many observers coming into Match 5 to predict a convincing and easy win for the world champion.

But Karpov has learned his lessons well, taking great pains to neutralize Kasparov's creativity with unparalleled defensive skill, brilliant endgame technique, and thorough opening preparation. Faced with Kasparov's enormous will power, outstanding tactical skill, flexibility and erudition in the opening, and the tremendous pressure he brings to bear on an opponent, many players simply fold. Karpov's stubbornness in face of this whirlwind is half the match, but Kasparov's unpredictable genius is the fire that illuminates the whole show.

4

INSIDE THE KARPOV WORLD CHAMPIONSHIP TEAM

by International Grandmaster
Ron Henley

I first met Karpov in 1988 at the World Active Chess Championships in Mazatlan, Mexico, when I asked him to autograph a copy of his book, *Chess at the Top*. We discussed the possibility of my working on his team in the upcoming quarterfinal match with Johann Hjartarson in Seattle, Washington, in February 1989. Karpov later gave me a couple of opening assignments and some games to research, and we agreed to meet in Seattle.

The way I see it, a second does whatever is required to see to it that the player he is working for is able to perform at his peak. This is not an easy role for many people. It demands that you should subordinate your own ego to another player's success.

Anatoly and I are quite often asked why he chose an American to be his second for this world championship run. In an interview with a Dutch journalist in Malaysia before the match with Jan Timman, he summed it up nicely, saying that in a second one looks for certain personality traits and that nationality is relatively unimportant. What *is* important is trust and the ability to contribute. Such a relationship transcends geographical or political boundaries. I have tremendous respect for Karpov, which has increased as I have observed his behavior and how he has treated other people.

When I arrived at Karpov's hotel, I had very little to show him. But Mike Valvo and I had analyzed in great detail one of the games Karpov had given me, and we had come up with some tremendous ideas and variations.

Karpov coolly took in everything I showed him and admitted that his team hadn't really considered the approach I presented. I was impressed by how practical Karpov is. Once it becomes apparent that a variation is not important, he quits looking at it. He's very disciplined in this respect. Many top players, even very strong players, get sidetracked and continue to analyze far past the point where it is practical. This discipline is probably a critical factor in his accumulation of the vast chess knowledge he brings to the board.

Hjartarson, though relatively unknown, had recently beaten Korchnoi by an impressive margin. Karpov's main concern, however, was that this match was for only six games, and in such a short match you are in serious trouble if you fall one game behind early on.

The match started rather well, as Karpov drew the first game with black. He told me later that drawing with black in the first round of a match gives you greater leverage in the final game, in which you have white. For a short match, Anatoly feels it's an advantage to play black in the first game—an interesting and useful insight into match play.

The second game was an English Opening in which Hjartarson played a slightly inferior setup for Black. Karpov introduced a novelty on the twelfth move and attained a slight positional advantage. On the twentieth move he sacrificed an exchange, and in a queenless ending, played a beautiful endgame in which his minor pieces dominated Hjartarson's position.

The key to any match at this level is success with the black pieces. In the Hjartarson match, the Ruy Lopez in particular stood Karpov in good stead. In Game 3, he won a very nice game with black. It is still not clear what Hjartarson's mistake was.

In Game 4, Karpov achieved the advantage of two bishops against Hjartarson's bishop and knight, but Karpov's isolated d-pawn created enough disadvantages to balance the position. Although Seirawan and I thought that Hjartarson might have had a slight edge at some point, Karpov felt he was never worse—in fact he had recently won a similar ending against Swedish GM Ulf Anderssen at Rotterdam.

In the final game, Hjartarson, requiring a win to stay alive, tested Karpov's Ruy Lopez again. Hjartarson developed a very nice initiative, but Karpov played sharply, sacrificing his queen for a rook, a minor piece, and a pawn to maintain the balance. In the final drawn position Karpov actually stood slightly better.

With the match firmly under our belts, we all went to Karpov's apartment for dinner. I proposed a toast to Igor Zaitsev, for it was his variation in the Ruy Lopez that had scored 1.5 points for us with black: that defense had been the key to Karpov's success in this match. Igor, quietly embarrassed, pointed out that we should give Misha Podgaets credit, since Igor and Anatoly had wanted to play the Caro-Kann, but Podgaets had recommended the Ruy Lopez.

During the Hjartarson match, Soviet GM Artur Yusupov was edging out Canadian GM Kenneth Spraggett in an intense and hard-fought match that was eventually decided by a fifteen-minute playoff game.

Karpov's match with Yusupov was scheduled for October 1989 in London. Meanwhile, Dutch GM Jan Timman would be meeting British GM Jonathan Speelman.

The Yusupov match was an extremely difficult one for Karpov, for he ran into a number of unexpected problems. Though Yusupov is a solid player and extremely well prepared theoretically, Karpov was considered a prohibitive favorite. In fact, bookmakers in London stopped taking bets three days before the match.

In spite of the public's faith in Karpov's chances, the team was concerned. Yusupov is always prepared, and we were afraid Kasparov might help him block our road to a rematch.

In addition, match conditions were relatively poor. The floors of Sadlers Wells Theatre, where the match was being played, creaked when people walked around, and the site was far from where we were staying. To make matters worse, the organizers had put up all four teams—Karpov's Yusupov's, Speelman's, and Timman's—in the same row of apartment buildings. It was uncomfortable even to go grocery shopping because we often ran into people from the other teams. Everyone felt claustrophobic.

The match turned out to be much more difficult for Anatoly than anyone expected. We consistently had problems with white in the opening and were unable to obtain any advantage against Yusupov with the Queen's Gambit. In a couple of games, Karpov actually stood worse with white.

Game 1 began as a Queen's Indian. Karpov, as black, improved on a beautiful game he had played as white against GM Lajos Portisch. Karpov's 16 . . . b4 was an improvement and led to a balanced play and a 44-move draw.

In the second game, Karpov consumed a great deal of time on a Classical Nimzo-Indian with 4 Qc2. His position at times teetered on the brink of disaster, and he had to show amazing resourcefulness to hold off Yusupov.

In these first two games, Anatoly had already been in time trouble twice. Later in the match, when I urged him to do something about his time trouble, he said it was necessary to play his way out of it. It was clear that he was not in his best form.

In Game 3, Yusupov employed the Sämisch Variation

against Karpov's Nimzo-Indian. In this very sharp and double-edged variation, White accepts doubled pawns in hopes of securing the two bishops and mounting a serious kingside initiative. Kasparov has tried this approach with some success. Karpov, however, though well prepared, once again spent over an hour on the first fifteen or twenty moves, much of it trying to remember previous analysis.

Yusupov sacrificed the exchange for an attack. Karpov took the material, fended off the attack, and reached a virtually won position. But then in time trouble, he overlooked a chance to win a piece.

After the time control, Karpov had a rook for a minor piece and two pawns, but it was far from clear who stood better because of White's potentially dangerous passed pawns on the kingside. However, Karpov continued to press for the win. After making the first time control in a traumatic scramble, both players, especially Yusupov, quickly ran short of time again in the very complicated second session.

Television monitors in the press room allowed you to watch the faces of the players as well as the board position. The ending of this game was one of the few times during these matches that I saw Karpov working so intensely. On the monitor, I could see his lips silently moving as he calculated variations. It was like watching the internal workings of a clock—only this was a human calculating machine humming at maximum efficiency under maximum load.

Ultimately Yusupov left a piece hanging on move 59 after throwing away his winning chances on move 57. The game was adjourned after move 60, and Yusupov resigned after seeing Anatoly's sealed move.

After this tough loss, Yusupov used his timeout. Anatoly was now one game ahead in an eight-game match, but uncharacteristically, had been in time trouble four times in three games.

After the timeout, Karpov had white in Game 4. We were still unable to demonstrate any appreciable advantage against the Lasker Defense. After sixteen moves Karpov stood slightly worse and was forced to play extremely accurately to maintain the balance. He outplayed Yusupov in the major piece ending and was close to obtaining an advantage when Yusupov sacrificed a rook to force a perpetual check.

A narrow escape, but the fact that Karpov had stumbled repeatedly into severe time trouble was a recipe for impending disaster. I urged him to do something about this, but to no avail. I hoped that with the arrival of his wife, Natalie, Anatoly would relax and return to form.

Yusupov took his final timeout before Game 5, hoping to capitalize on having the white pieces. With four games remaining, he would have only two more chances with white.

During the two-day timeout, Karpov showed Natalie around London. He seemed happy that she was there, but I was puzzled and worried at his lack of interest in preparing for Game 6.

Two days later his plan became clear when he said to me, "Well, now I think it's time for us to take a timeout."

The idea was to take advantage of the pressure Yusupov was under and to keep his team cooped up for a couple more days in their chessic sweat-box. Unfortunately, this psychological gambit didn't work.

Candidates' Match (5), London 1989
Torre Attack

White: Artur Yusupov ***Black: Anatoly Karpov***

1 d4 Nf6 2 Nf3 e6 3 Bg5 c5 4 e3 b6?

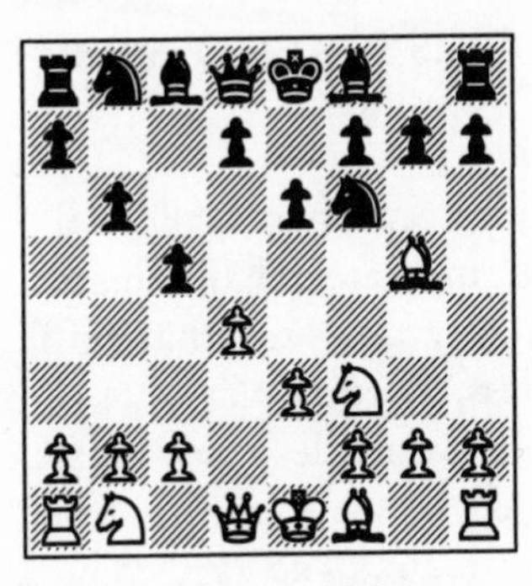

After 4 ... b6

5 d5 exd5 6 Nc3 Be7 7 Nxd5 Bb7 8 Bxf6 Bxf6 9 c3 0-0 10 Bc4 a6 11 0-0 b5 12 Bb3 d6 13 Qd2 Nd7 14 Rfd1 Bxd5 15 Bxd5 Rb8 16 Qc2 Nb6 17 Rd2 g6 18 Rad1 Qc7 19 Qe4 Kg7 20 h4 Qe7 21 Qf4 Be5 22 Nxe5 dxe5 23 Qg3 Rbd8 24 h5 Rd7 25 b3 Rfd8 26 e4

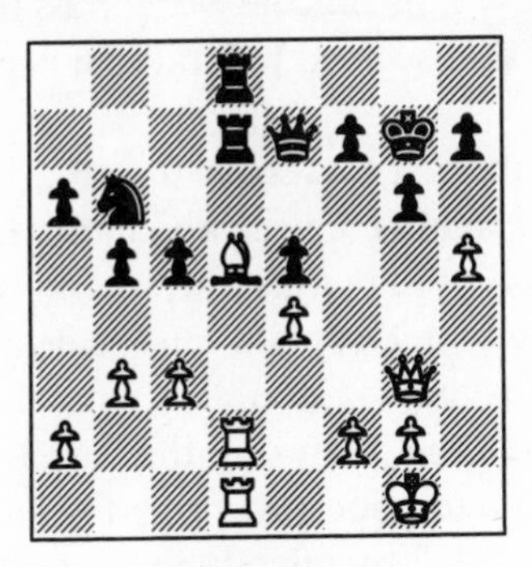

After 26 e4

26 . . . g5 27 Qe3 h6 28 c4 Rc7 29 Rd3 Nd7 30 Bxf7 Kxf7 31 Qd2 Ke8 32 Qa5 bxc4 33 bxc4 Rcc8??

This is a time pressure mistake. After the game, Karpov recommended 33 . . . Rc6! 34 Qa4 Qe6, when Black plans . . . Ke7 and . . . Rc7.

34 Qa4 Rc7 35 Qxa6 Rb8 36 Qg6+ Kf8 37 Rf3+ 1-0

Karpov's blunder on move 4 allowed 5 d5. British GM Tony Miles told me later that American GM Lubomir Kavalek had recently analyzed that position as better for white. Nevertheless, Karpov was able to outplay Yusupov positionally. Yusupov made a few mistakes and was left with a bishop on d5 versus Karpov's strongly posted knight. Karpov pressed with 26 . . . g5 27 Qe3 h6 28 c4 Rc7 29 Rd3 Nd7, virtually forcing Yusupov to sacrifice a piece with 30 Bxf7+.

Theoretically, Black should still have been able to draw the game, and Karpov could have drawn after the sacrifice in two or three ways. Once again, however, time pressure reared its ugly head, and he made a mistake. His position fell apart very quickly. This time he was forced to pay a price for the sluggishness that seemed to land him perpetually in time trouble.

The team continued to search for an advantage against Lasker's Defense in the Queen's Gambit Declined. I suggested the method of play that Karpov followed in Game 6. We aimed to combine Bg5 with queenside pressure, but we had to permit Yusupov to double a pair of pawns. Karpov and I spent some time analyzing the variation, and we decided that White had good prospects for an advantage.

Yusupov responded by introducing a wonderful novelty, 17 . . . Rac8, an extremely deep move which Karpov later said was "the best move of the match." I have to agree with him.

I watched the game from the balcony of the theater, and I was quite happy because Karpov played the first fifteen moves very quickly. He was in no danger of time trouble, and he was in a position we were familiar with.

Candidates' Match (6), London 1989
Queen's Gambit Declined

White: Anatoly Karpov *Black: Artur Yusupov*

1 d4 Nf6 2 c4 e6 3 Nf3 d5 4 Nc3 Be7 5 Bg5 0–0 6 e3 h6 7 Bh4 Ne4 8 Bxe7 Qxe7 9 cxd5 Nxc3 10 bxc3 exd5 11 Qb3 Rd8 12 c4 dxc4 13 Bxc4 Nc6 14 Qc3 Bg4 15 0–0 Bxf3 16 gxf3 Qf6 17 Be2 Rac8!

After 17 ... Rac8

Most annotators would consider the game equal at this point. The main problem for White is that . . . Rac8 defends Black's queenside and prepares to maneuver the knight to e7, followed by a pawn break at c5. Black also has various ways to bring his pieces to bear on White's kingside.

Karpov and I concluded independently that Black's prospects were actually better. I was devastated; if Karpov lost this game, he would be down one, and I felt I could have cost him the match.

Karpov later said that . . . Rac8 had probably been prepared by Yusupov's team in advance. It was quite normal for moves as deep as this one to be overlooked in match preparation by one or both teams.

Fortunately for us, Karpov escaped the noose again. Despite tremendous winning chances, Yusupov erred in a rook ending and allowed Karpov to escape with a draw.

18 Rab1 b6 19 Rfc1 Ne7 20 Kh1 Rd5 21 Qc2 Qh4 22 f4 Qxf2 23 Bg4

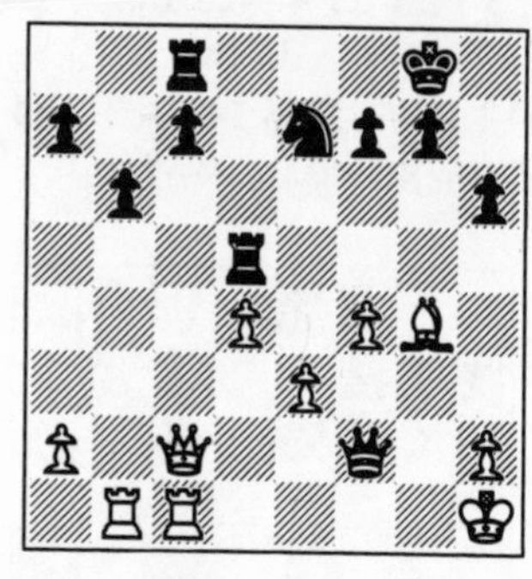

After 23 Bg4

By sacrificing his f-pawn and posting his bishop at g4, Karpov has reached an ending with some drawing chances—brilliant resourcefulness in a bad position.

23 . . . Qxc2 24 Rxc2 f5 25 Bf3 Rd7 26 Rbc1 Nd5 27 Bxd5+ Rxd5 28 Rxc7 Rxc7 29 Rxc7 Ra5 30 d5 Kf8 31 d6 Ke8 32 Rxg7 Rxa2 32 Kg1 a5 34 Re7+ Kd8 35 e4 fxe4 36 Rb7 e3 37 Kf1 a4?

After 37 ... a4

Anatoly has managed to play himself back into trouble, but now Yusupov errs, allowing Karpov to save the game with some study-like resources.

38 Rxb6 a3 39 Ra6 Rf2+ 40 Ke1 a2 41 f5 Kd7 42 f6 Ke6 43 Ra8 Kxd6 44 f7 Rxf7 45 Rxa2 Ke5 46 Ra6 Draw

After the close call in Game 6, we realized that there was a distinct possibility of a playoff, a two-game mini-match. The Timman–Speelman match had also come down to the final game, Timman losing a promising position in Game 7.

In Game 7 of our match, Yusupov again unleashed the Torre Attack. Before the game began I had to return to New York on business. I received word that Karpov had defended well this time, and actually stood better at several points before losing a pawn in time pressure and settling for a draw on move 61.

Game 8 of both matches was played on the same day. Timman defeated Speelman with black after obtaining an advantage in the opening, thus ensuring his spot as a qualifier. Karpov finally solved the Queen's Gambit Declined, Lasker Defense, and played his best game of the match. Perhaps Yusupov had gone to the well once too often. He varied from the *Encyclopedia of Chess Openings* (ECO) recommendation by playing 17 . . . Nd5. Karpov simply built up a tremendous kingside attack and later converted his advantage into a winning rook ending. Yusupov resigned on move 53.

Candidates' Match (8), London 1989
Queen's Gambit Declined

White: Anatoly Karpov ***Black: Artur Yusupov***
Annotated by GM Semion Palatnik

1 d4	Nf6
2 c4	e6
3 Nf3	d5
4 Nc3	Be7
5 Bg5	0-0
6 e3	h6
7 Bh4	Ne4

Neither player is a stranger to Lasker's Defense to the Queen's Gambit.

8 Bxe7	Qxe7
9 Rc1	c6
10 Bd3	Nxc3
11 Rxc3	

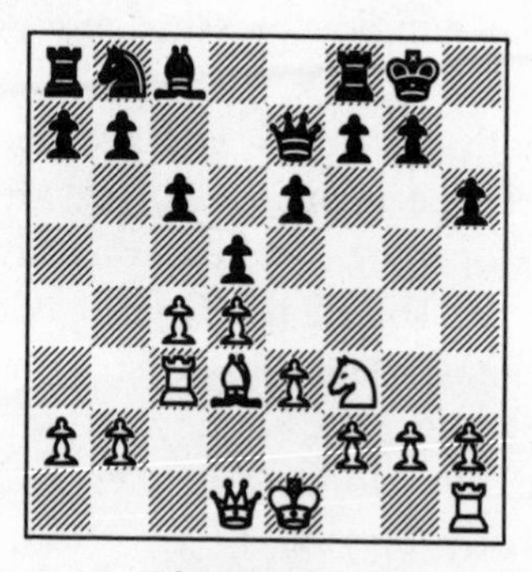

After 11 Rxc3

In spite of the apparent simplification, Black still has problems with his development—look at the bishop at c8!

11 . . .	dxc4
12 Bxc4	Nd7
13 0–0	e5
14 Bb3	

A useful prophylactic move, anticipating . . . Nb6.

14 . . . exd4

Black has other possibilities; e.g., 14 . . . e4; or 14 . . . Re8 15 d5 cxd5 16 Qxd5 Nf6 17 Qc5 Ne4 18 Qxe7 Rxe7 19 Rc2 Ng5 20 Nxg5 hxg5 21 Rd1 Bf5 22 Rc3 Kf8, with equality (Nikolic–Yusupov, Belgrade 1989).

15 exd4 Nf6!?

An alternative is 15 . . . Nb6.

16 Re1

Gaining a tempo on the queen.

16 . . . Qd6
17 Ne5

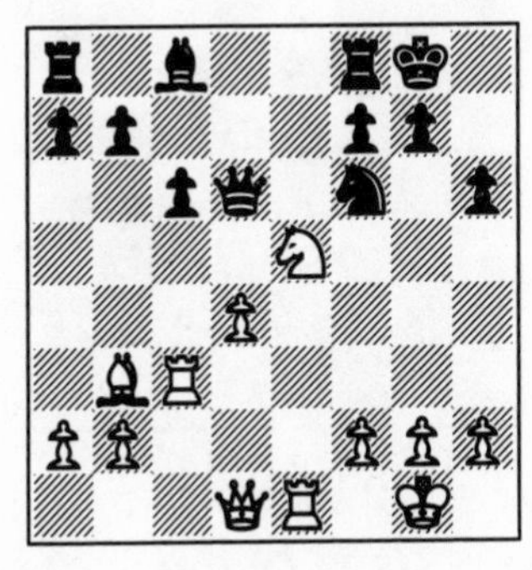

After 17 Ne5

Hinting at an f7-weakness.

17 . . . Nd5

White has better prospects after 17 . . . Be6 18 Bxe6 fxe6 19 Rg3.

With the match firmly under our belts, we all went to Karpov's apartment for dinner.

18 Rg3 Bf5

The sixth rank is blocked after 18 . . . Be6 19 Qd2 Bf5 20 Bxd5 cxd5 (20 . . . Qxd5? 21 Qxh6) 21 Qf4 Be4 22 f3 Bh7 23 Qg4 g5 24 f4, and White has the advantage.

19 Qh5 Bh7
20 Qg4 g5

It is usually risky to open the king with pawn moves, but Black has no choice.

21 h4 f6

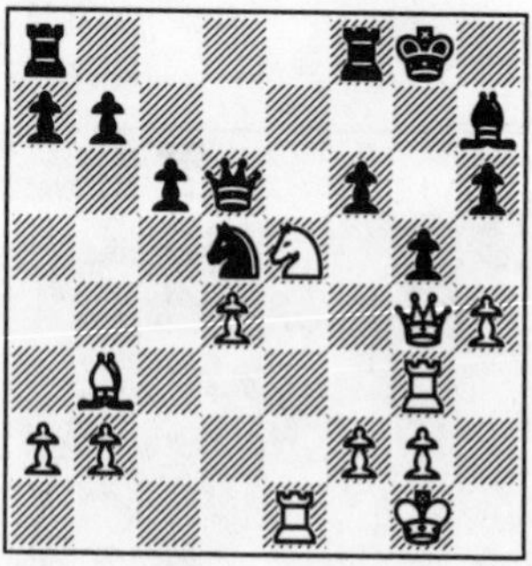

After 21 ... f6

Alternatives: 21 . . . f5 22 Qh5 g4 23 Nxg4! wins; 21 . . . Nf6 22 Qf4!? (22 Qf3 is also good for White) 22 . . . Nh5 23 Qf3 Nxg3 24 Nxf7 Qc7 (or 24 . . . Qxd4 25 Re7!, with a better position) 25 Qf6 Rxf7 26 Re7!, winning.

22 hxg5

Another choice is 22 Qh5!?: 22 . . . fxe5 23 hxg5 Kg7! (23 . . . Kh8 24 g6!; or 23 . . . Bg6 24 Qxh6 with an attack) 24 Bxd5 cxd5 25 Rxe5, again with an attack; or 22 . . . Kg7 23 Bxd5 cxd5 (23 . . . fxe5 is unclear) 24 Ng4 f5 25 Nxh6 Qxh6 26 Rxg5 + Bg6 27 Re7 +, with a winning position for White.

22 . . .	**hxg5**

White answers 22 . . . fxg5 with 23 f4.

23 f4!?

White has the initiative after 23 Qh5 Rae8 24 Ree3, and he has a strong position after 23 Rh3 Qe7!? (23 . . . fxe5?24 Rxh7 Kxh7 25 Bc2 + Kg7 26 Qxg5 + Kf7 27 dxe5 Rae8 28 Qh5 +, winning) 24 Ree3!. Another try is 23 Nf3!? Kh8 (23 . . . Rae8 24 Rxe8 Rxe8 25 Nxg5 Re1 + 26 Kh2, and the game is over) 24 Re6, and now:

(A) 24 . . . Qd7 25 Nxg5! fxg5 (25 . . . Rg8 26 Rxf6! Qxg4 27 Rxg4 Nxf6 28 Nf7 mate) 26 Qxg5 Rg8 27 Qe5 + Rg7 28 Rh6! Rf8 (28 . . . Re8 29 Rxg7; or 28 . . . Rg8 29 Rxh7 + !; or 28 . . . Qe7 29 Rxg7 Qxg7 30 Bc2, winning) 29 Rhg3 Kg8 30 Bc2! Bxc2 31 Rh8 + Kf7 32 Rf3 +, winning (White also wins after 30 . . . Rff7 31 Bxh7 + Rxh7 32 Qb8 + Rf8 33 Rxh7);

(B) 24 . . . Qc7! 25 Bxd5 cxd5 26 Nxg5 Rg8 27 Qf4;

(C) 24 . . . Qf4 25 Qh5.

23 . . .	**Rae8**
24 fxg5	**fxe5**

White has a won endgame after 24 . . . Bf5 25 gxf6 + ! (25 Qxf5 fxe5) 25 . . . Bxg4 26 Rxg4 + Kh8 (26 . . . Kh7 27

Bc2+ Kh6 28 Rg6+ Kh7 29 f7, and White wins) 27 Nf7+ Rxf7 28 Rxe8+ Rf8 29 f7 Nf6 30 Rxf8+ Qxf8 31 Rg8+ Nxg8 32 fxg8Q+ Qxg8 33 Bxg8.

25 g6	**Bxg6**
26 dxe5	

Unclear is 26 Rxe5!? Kh7 27 Qh5+ Kg7 (27 . . . Bxh5? 28 Rxh5+ Qh6 29 Bc2+ Kh8 30 Rxh6 mate) 28 Rxg6+ Qxg6 29 Rg5 Re1+ 30 Kh2 Re6.

26 . . .	**Qe6**
27 Bxd5	**cxd5**
28 Qxg6+	**Qxg6**
29 Rxg6+	**Kh7**
30 Rd6	

After 30 Rd6

The voltage in the position drops as White transitions to a simple technical win.

30 . . .	**Rc8**
31 Re3	**Rc2**

32 Rd7+ Kg6
33 Rxb7

Black is hopeless.

33 . . . Re8 34 a3 d4 35 Rd3 Rxe5 36 Rxd4 Rg5 37 Rd6+ Kh5 38 Rh7+ Kg4 39 Rd4+ Kf5 40 Rd5+ Kg6 41 Rg7+ Kxg7 42 Rxg5+ Kf6 43 Rb5 a6 44 Rb6+ Ke7 45 Kh2 Kd7 46 Kh3 Kc7 47 Rb3 Kd6 48 g4 Ke5 49 Kh4 Kf6 50 Rb6+ Kg7 51 Kh5 a5 52 Rb7+ Kg8 53 a4 1-0

When I came home from work that day and phoned the theater, I got the good news on a recording: Anatoly had played his best game of the match to advance to the finals. Yusupov never had a chance in that game. Some people felt it was a sad finale for him: He had put up a much greater fight than anyone had expected, losing in the end by just one game.

Pilkington Glass, an English firm, considered sponsoring the final match; in fact, it had been announced that the entire series would be played in London. But since both players had been dissatisfied with the London arrangements, neither of them endorsed this proposal.

Finally, Malaysia hosted the match, and did a wonderful job.

The match was scheduled for March, which we felt was to our advantage, one of them being Malaysia's warm climate. Karpov had asked me to come to Moscow for the month of February to work with Zaitsev and Podgaets, and the new schedule and site dovetailed nicely.

We were housed outside Moscow on an isolated army base with four primitive barracks and a cafeteria. Our team consisted of Zaitsev, IM Alexei Kuzmin (not to be confused with the older GM Gennadi Kuzmin), Podgaets, GM Oleg Romanishin, who stayed a few weeks before leaving for a tournament, and me. Occasionally, other masters and grandmasters would visit, and from time to time we received various dignitaries who were visiting the camp.

Every morning we woke to the rat-a-tat of gunfire. The other three barracks were occupied by young men between eighteen and twenty-five years old, who hit the range every morning. It was humbling to watch some of these boys score as high as 25 out of 25 shots.

We generally gathered for breakfast at about 9 A.M. We spent most of the day studying chess, primarily because the cold weather restricted most other activities. We did get outdoors to shoot skeet. I had no talent for it, but Anatoly was quite good.

The only diversion aside from skeet, cards, and occasional trips to the gym to play tennis was a Russian pocket billiards table. You have to use much greater force in Russian pocket billiards than in the American version of the game. The balls are very heavy, and the pockets are extremely narrow. None of the other players on the team could hold a cue to Karpov in pocket billiards.

We were in high spirits en route to Malaysia. Romanishin brought the most recent game bulletins from Russian tournaments, and we had just received the bulletins from the Bulgarian Zonal tournament, which had hosted some very strong Eastern European players, so we set out with plenty of material to study on the plane. Karpov, having just finished a series of political meetings, was exhausted and slept most of the trip.

In general, our preparation for Timman was much more thorough and professional than previously. I felt we could eliminate our time-pressure problem, which was often due to uncertainty or difficulty remembering openings. If Karpov were better prepared theoretically, his practical chances would be greatly improved.

In the first round, Karpov donned familiar Spanish gloves, once again answering 1 e4 with the Ruy Lopez. Timman varied from theory on move 18, and Karpov was quick to pounce on the opportunity to equalize. Four moves later, the Dutch grandmaster offered a questionable pawn sacrifice, and Karpov—in his usual boa constrictor style—squeezed out a win to kick off the match.

Following this demoralizing start, Timman came out in full battle regalia for Game 2, but after an initial demonstration seemed content to withdraw into a damage control formation, accepting a draw with the black pieces before shooting to even the match with White in Game 3.

In Game 3, Timman held a hungry Karpov at bay in a position that most observers expected him to lose.

Game 4 turned out to be an epic seesaw battle. Karpov let a beautiful position deteriorate to what many considered Timman's best chance to score a point. But Timman repeatedly held back the critical . . . h5 or . . . b5 pawn break, and the game reached a complicated adjournment during which our team came closer to the truth. In the end, that's all that mattered.

Candidates' Match (4), Kuala Lumpur 1990
King's Indian Defense

White: Anatoly Karpov ***Black: Jan Timman***

1 d4 Nf6 2 c4 g6 3 Nf3 Bg7 4 g3 c6 5 Bg2 d5 6 cxd5 cxd5 7 Nc3 0-0 8 Ne5 e6 9 0-0 Nfd7 10 f4 Nc6 11 Be3 f6 12 Nd3 Nb6 13 b3 Qe7 14 a4 Bd7 15 Bc1 Rfd8 16 e3 Be8 17 Ba3 Qf7 18 Rc1 Bf8 19 Bxf8 Qxf8 20 g4 Qe7 21 Qd2 Rac8 22 Ne2 Rc7 23 Rc5 Nc8 24 f5!

After 24 f5

"Crisis time," said Dutch GM Gert Ligterink. "Very pleasant, without risk for Karpov," added Soviet GM Oleg Romanishin.

24 . . . g5

On 24 . . . gxf5, White has 25 Ndf4 Nd6 26 Nxe6!

25 Ng3 e5
26 Qc1?

Better is simply 26 Bxd5 + Kh8 27 Rfcl exd4 28 e4.

26 . . . b6
27 Rc2 e4
28 Nf2 Nd6
29 Qd2 Rdc8
30 Rfc1 a5

Preferable is 30 . . . Na5! (Ligterink).

31 Bf1 Nb4 32 Rc3 Qd7 33 Nd1 Rc6 34 Rxc6 Rxc6 35 Rxc6 Qxc6 36 Nc3 Kf8 37 Kf2 Ke7 38 Ke1 Kf8 39 Kd1 Qc8 40 Ke1 Kg7

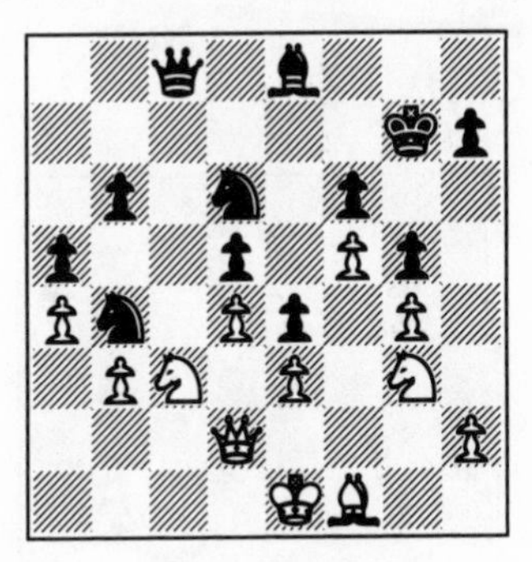

After 40 ... Kg7

Black has the possibilities of . . . h5 and . . . b5; White has an utterly static position. In fact, Timman should play 40 . . . h5! right away.

41 Na2!

According to Hans Ree, the position is now actually better for White: 41 . . . Nxa2 42 Qxa2 Qc3+ 43 Kf2 b5 44 axb5 Bxb5?! (44 . . . Nxb5 is unclear) 45 Nh5+ Kf8 46 Bxb5 Nxb5 47 b4! The consensus was that Timman has missed his best chance for a meaningful edge.

41 . . . Nxa2 42 Qxa2 Qc7 43 Kf2 Kf8 44 Qb2 Ke7 45 Be2 Kd8 46 Ke1 Kc8

Romanishin liked 46 . . . b5!.

47 Kd2	**Kb7**
48 Qc1	**Qe7**
49 Ke1	

Of course not 49 Qa3? Nxf5.

49 . . .	**Bd7**

50 Kf2	Ne8
51 Qh1!?	

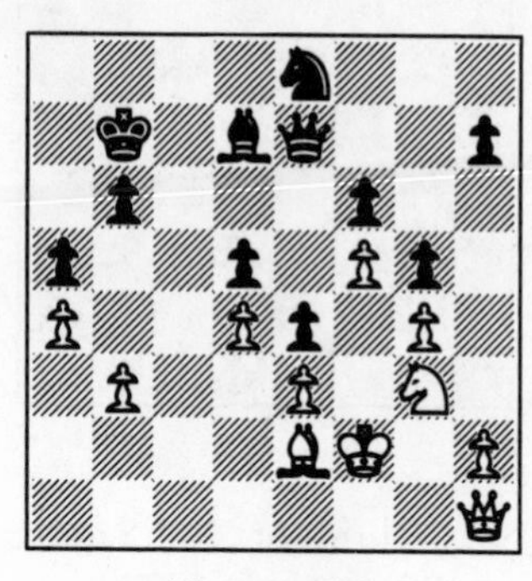

After 51 Qh1

Simpler is 51 Qc3 to maintain the position. Karpov elects to seek active play even at the cost of his queenside pawns. Timman accepts the challenge.

51 ...	Qb4
52 h4	Qxb3

Too slow are 52 . . . gxh4 53 Qxh4 Qxb3 54 Qxh7 Qxa4 55 g5 fxg5 56 Qe7 Qc6 57 Nh5 a4 58 f6, and 52 . . . h6 53 hxg5 hxg5 54 Qh7 Kc8 55 Qf7 Qxb3 56 Nxe4 Bxa4? 57 Ba6+ Kd8 58 Nxf6.

53 hxg5	fxg5
54 Qxh7	Qxa4
55 Qe7	Qc6
56 Qxg5	

Black must be better here.

56 ...	a4
57 Qe7	Qd6!

58 Qxd6	**Nxd6**
59 Bd1!	**Bb5?**

A terrible blunder just before time control. After 59 . . . b5!, Romanishin and Ligterink thought Karpov was lost. Later Karpov said he thought he could hold the position after 59 . . . b5 and agreed that 59 . . . Bb5 was a mistake.

60 Ne2	**a3**
61 Nc1!	

After 61 Nc1

Timman sealed his move after twenty-two minutes' thought. The position is unclear with chances for both sides and two days to analyze.

None of the seconds attended Game 5—which naturally turned out to be one of the most exciting of the match—since we were all too busy with the extremely complicated adjourned position of Game 4. Many observers thought Timman stood better at adjournment; the Karpov camp was silent.

61 . . .	**Kc7**
62 Kg3	**Nc4**
63 Be2	**Be8**
64 Kf4!	

Karpov used fifteen minutes to make his choice here. Interesting is 64 g5 Nxe3 65 Kf4 Nc2 (if 65 . . . Ng2+ 66 Ke5 Nh4 67 g6! Bxg6 68 fxg6 Nxg6+ 69 Kf5, with a White advantage) 66 Ke5 Nb4 67 Kf6 Kd6 68 g6 Nc6 69 Bb5 e3 70 g7 Ne7 71 Bxe8!! e2 72 Nxe2 a2 73 Nc3! Ng8+ 74 Kf7 Nh6+ 75 Kf8 a1Q 76 Nb5 mate (Podgaets).

We discovered that Black could draw after 64 g5 Kd6! 65 Bxc4 (otherwise Black has counterplay after 65 Kf4 Nb2!) 65 . . . dxc4 66 Na2 Ba4 67 Nc3 Bb3 68 Nb5+ Ke7 69 Nxa3 c3 70 Kf4 b5! 71 Kxe4 b4 72 Kd3! bxa3 73 Kxc3 Bd5, draw (Karpov team). The text gives Black more problems.

64 . . . Nb2?!

Because Timman didn't see the coming 72 Bg8!, he thought his counterplay here would be enough to draw. Better is 64 . . . b5!? 65 Na2 Nb2 (But not 65 . . . Kd6? 66 g5 Nb2 67 g6 b4 68 Kg5! [68 Nxb4? Nd3!] b3 69 Nc1 Ba4 70 g7 a2 71 g8Q a1Q 72 Qb8+! Kd7 73 f6!, and now 73 . . . Qxc1 allows 74 Bg4+ Kc6 75 Qc8+ with a winning position for White). Our analysis leaned toward 66 f6 Nd3+ 67 Kf5 b4 68 Bd1, with some promise for White.

65 Kg5

In retrospect, maybe 65 Na2!? is a better try: e.g., 65 . . . Kd6 66 Kg5 Ke7 (66 . . . Nc4 67 Bxc4 dxc4 68 Kf6 supporting the pawns from g7) 67 Kh6 Kf6 68 Nb4!, with a good shot at winning. At the time, we gave 65 Kg5 an exclamation point. Later, Hungarian GM Gyula Sax turned up a hidden resource at move 73 we had missed, but it was too late to help Timman.

65 . . . Nd3

The attempt to repeat the position with 65 . . . Nc4 66 Kf4 fails to 66 Kf6! Nxe3 67 Ke7, with a White advantage.

66 Nb3!

The knight is a better "stopper" at a1 than at a2.

66 . . .	**a2**
67 Na1	**b5**
68 Bd1	**b4**

Worse is 68 . . . Kd6 69 Bb3 Nc1 70 Kh6! b4 71 f6 Ke6 72 Kg7 Nxb3 73 Nxb3 Ba4 74 Nc5+! Kd6 75 f7 a1Q 76 f8Q+ and mates.

69 Bb3	**Nc1**
70 Bxd5	**Kd6**
71 Bc4	**Bb5!**

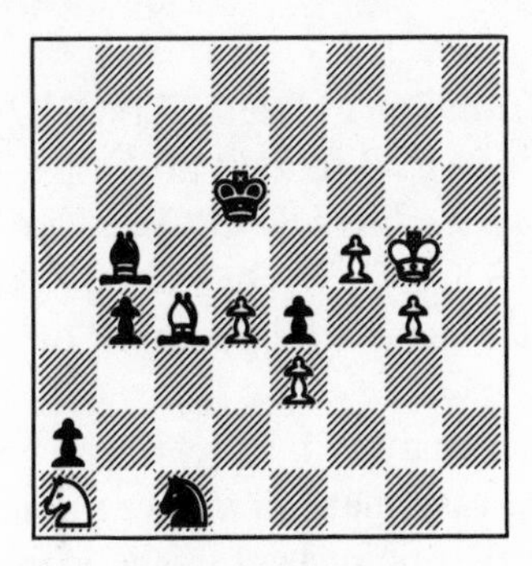

After 71 ... Bb5

If 71 . . . Ba4 72 f6 b3 73 Kh6!! (73 Kg6?? Be8+ wins—for Black!) 73 . . . b2 74 f7 bxa1Q 75 f8Q+ Kd7 76 Qf5+ Kc7 77 Qa5+ wins. Or 71 . . . b3 72 Bxb3 Nxb3 73 Nxb3 Kd5 74 Na1 Kc4 75 Kf6 Kc3 76 Ke7 Kb2 77 Kxe8 Kxa1 78 f6 Kb2 79 f7 a1Q 80 f8Q Qa4+ 81 Kf7 Qb3+ 82 d5!! (a postmortem improvement over Zaitsev's original 82 Kf6) 82

. . . Qxe3 83 Qb4 + Kc2 84 g5 Qf3 + 85 Kg7 e3 86 Qc4 + Kb2 87 Qb5 + Kc1 88 d6 e2 89 Qc5 + Kb2 90 Qb6 + Kc1 91 d7 e1Q 92 d8Q Qec3 + 93 Qdf6, and White wins. Computers have demonstrated forced wins for queen and g-pawn against queen.

72 Bg8!!	**Ke7**
73 Kh6	**Kf8?**

This was the point at which Sax discovered a hidden resource for Black: 73 . . . b3!! 74 Bxb3 Nxb3 75 Nxb3 Bc4! 76 Na1 Kf6!. In spite of his two-pawn edge, White is unable to make progress; he is playing without his knight, and the black bishop controls the key diagonal.

74 Be6	**Bd7**
75 g5	**b3**
76 g6	**1-0**

Mate results from 76 . . . Bxe6 77 fxe6 b2 (77 . . . Kg8 78 e7) 78 g7 + Ke7 79 g8Q bxa1Q 80 Qf7 + Kd6 81 Qd7 +. After 78 . . . Kg8 79 e7 Kf7 80 g8Q + ! Kxe7! (80 . . . Kxg8 81 e8Q mate) 81 Qg5 + !, White picks off the b2-pawn with check or plays d5 + and a queen check on the h8–a1 diagonal.

Some fantastic analysis by the Karpov team combined with his ability to assimilate a massive number of variations had given him a two-point lead in the match.

While we were wrestling with the adjourned position of Game 4, Karpov and Timman conspired to play perhaps the most exciting game of the match in Game 5. Anatoly missed another golden opportunity, and Timman must have felt shaky indeed after losing the adjourned position of Game 4 the next day. He took a timeout before Game 6 to try to recover from that unexpected setback.

Candidates' Match (5), Kuala Lumpur 1990
Ruy Lopez

White: Jan Timman *Black: Anatoly Karpov*

1 e4 e5 2 Nf3 Nc6 3 Bb5 a6 4 Ba4 Nf6 5 0-0 Be7 6 Re1 b5 7 Bb3 d6 8 c3 0-0 9 h3 Bb7 10 d4 Re8 11 Nbd2 Bf8 12 a4 h6 13 Bc2 exd4 14 cxd4 Nb4 15 Bb1 bxa4 16 Rxa4 a5 17 Ra3 Ra6 18 Rae3

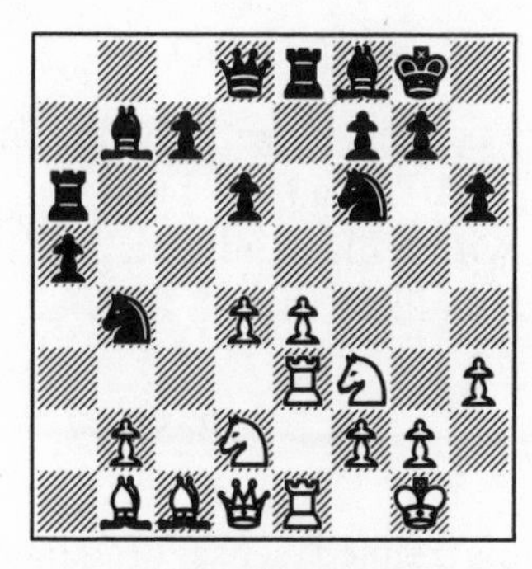

After 18 Rae3

Timman deviates from 18 Nh4?!. The irony is that it was Karpov who explained why Nh4 doesn't work in *New In Chess*, #7 (Hjartarson–Karpov, Seattle 1989), a journal of which Timman is the editor.

18 . . .	a4!
19 Nh4	c5!
20 dxc5	

Good for Black is 20 d5? Nfxd5! 21 exd5 Rxe3 22 fxe3 Qxh4.

20 . . .	dxc5
21 Nf5!	

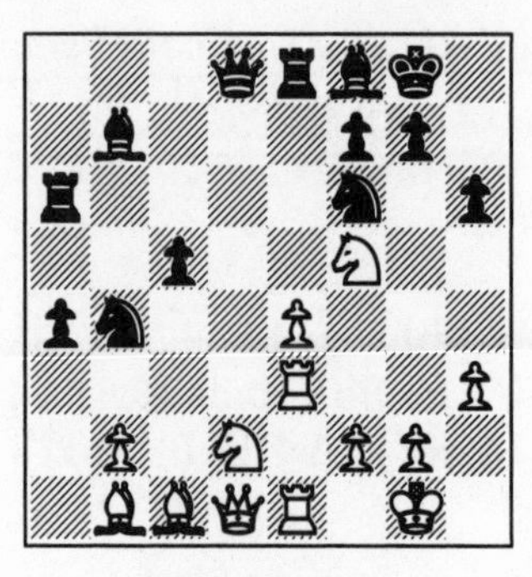

After 21 Nf5

Timman is very dangerous with the initiative. Premature here is 21 e5 Nfd5 22 Re4 a3! 23 bxa3 Nc3 24 Qg4 Nxb1 and 25 . . . Bxe4, with a Black advantage. The text begins a promising kingside buildup.

21 . . .	Bc8!?

Karpov, with his refined sense of danger, decides the knight has to be eliminated.

22 e5	Nd5
23 Rg3	Nf4
24 Qf3	Bxf5!
25 Bxf5	Ne6
26 Bb1!	Nd4
27 Qg4	Nbc2!!

It would all be over if White had time to play Nc4, unleashing the bishop-pair. Karpov finds a resource to keep the delicate balance, turning the game into a tactical melee.

28 Qe4	f5
29 Qd3	Nxe1

30 Qxa6	**Rxe5**
31 Re3?!	

This mistake gives Karpov chances to win. Fantastic is 31 Qxh6 (with the idea Ba2 mate) 31 . . . Qd5! 32 Qh4? Qxg2+!! 33 Rxg2 Nef3+ 34 Nxf3 Nxf3+ 35 Kh1 Re1+ 36 Rg1 Rxg1 mate (Alexander Roshal). White's best is 31 Ba2+! Kh8 32 Bc4 f4 33 Rg4 f3, with a small Black edge.

31 . . .	**Qg5**
32 Kf1!!	

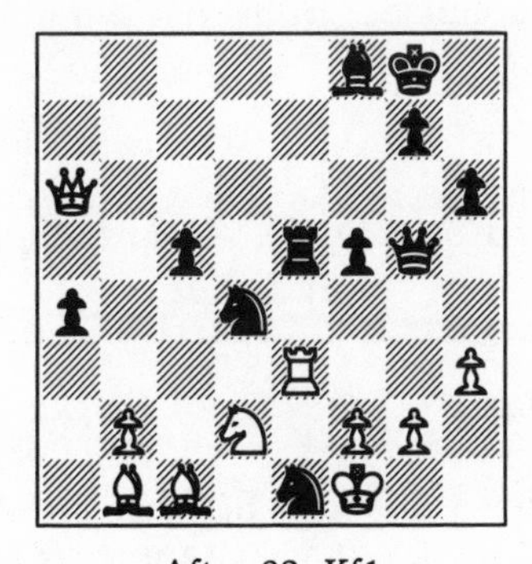

After 32 Kf1

Timman finds the only chance: 32 Qf1 Ne2+ 33 Rxe2 Rxe2, etc.

32 . . .	**Rxe3**
33 fxe3	**Qxe3**
34 Qc4+	**Kh7?**

A natural attempt to avoid Ba2 and Qg8 mate, but Karpov overlooks 34 . . . Kh8!! 35 Ba2 Qd3+! and either 36 Qxd3 Nxd3 with a Black advantage, or 36 Kxe1 Nc2+ 37 Kf2 (37 Kd1 Ne3+) 37 . . . Qe3+ 38 Kf1 Qe1 mate.

35 Ba2	**Nd3?**

Karpov misses 35 . . . Qd3 + !, when White has to play 36 Kf2! Qxc4 37 Bxc4 Nec2 38 Nf3, with excellent chances for Black.

36 Qg8 +	**Kg6**
37 Qf7 +	**Kh7**
38 Qg8 +	**Draw**

Karpov now took his first timeout. We were pretty confident. Anatoly seemed a cinch to sew up his challenger's berth in the next four or five games unless Timman managed to pull several rabbits out of his hat simultaneously. But in Game 7, hopping with tactical possibilities, Timman let his position slide.

Candidates' Match (7), Kuala Lumpur 1990
Ruy Lopez

White: Jan Timman ***Black: Anatoly Karpov***

1 e4 e5 2 Nf3 Nc6 3 Bb5 a6 4 Ba4 Nf6 5 0–0 Be7 6 Re1 b5 7 Bb3 d6 8 c3 0–0 9 h3 Bb7 10 d4 Re8 11 Nbd2 Bf8 12 a4 Qd7 13 axb5 axb5 14 Rxa8 Bxa8 15 d5 Ne7 16 Nf1 h6 17 Ng3 c6 18 dxc6 Bxc6 19 Nh2 d5 20 Nh5 Nxe4 21 Ng4

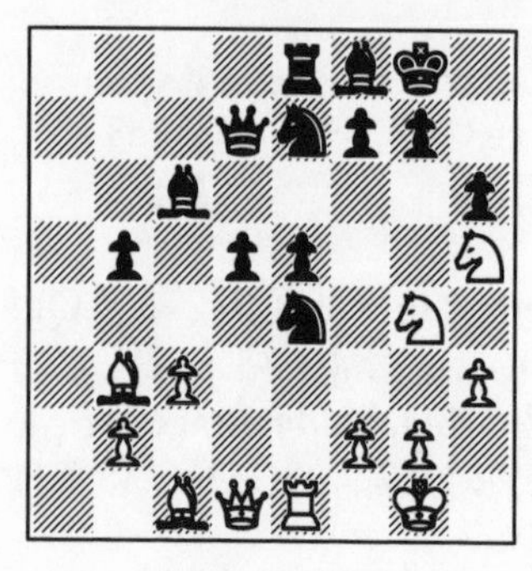

After 21 Ng4

Timman sacrifices a pawn to stir up complications. The threat is 22 Rxe4! and 23 Nf6+.

21 . . .	Qf5!
22 f3?	

Ree and Ligterink suggested 22 Rxe4!. The attack seems extremely dangerous: e.g., 22 . . . dxe4! 23 Ng3! Qc8! 24 Nxe5 Rd8 25 Qh5 Bd5 26 Bxd5 Rxd5 27 Qxf7+ Kh7 28 Bf4 Rd6 29 Ng4 Rg6 30 Bxh6!. With Karpov's next finesse the tide begins to turn.

22 . . .	Nxc3!
23 bxc3	Qxh5
24 Rxe5	Qh4!

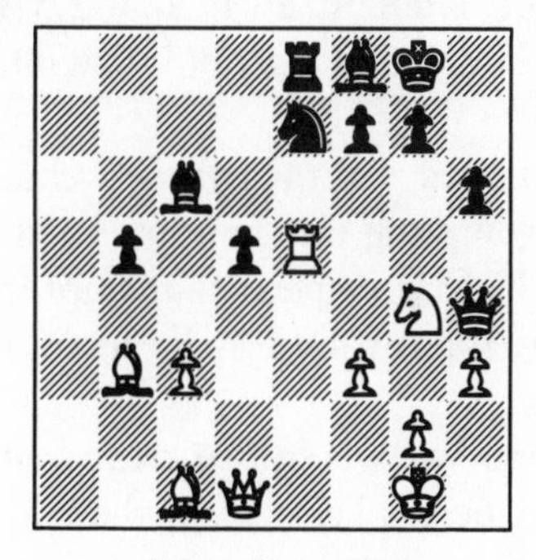

After 24 ... Qh4

25 Be3	Ng6

Karpov returns the pawn to clear the way to d8 and maintain the balance.

26 Bf2	Qd8
27 Rxe8	Qxe8
28 Bxd5	h5

Romanishin felt this was drawish, suggesting that Karpov might have tried for more considering the shortage on Timman's clock, but Karpov had the calendar on his side.

29 Ne3 Nf4 30 Bxc6 Qxc6 31 Bg3 Ne6 32 Nd5 Qc4 33 Qd2 Qb3 34 Kh2 Qb1 35 Qe1 Qxe1 36 Bxe1 Bd6+ 37 Bg3 Bc5 38 Be1 Kf8 39 g4 hxg4 40 fxg4 Ke8 41 Kg2 Kd7 42 Bg3 Kc6 43 Nb4+ Bxb4 Draw

In Game 8, Timman essentially committed suicide: He had reasonable compensation for a pawn but misplayed a blitzkrieg attack. Karpov blew him out in the center and crashed through on the kingside.

Karpov had now extended his lead to 5.5–2.5 and was in a position to put Timman away 6.5–2.5 in this best-of-twelve match. He did not disappoint, winning a 56-move thriller.

Karpov had missed several winning chances in the five drawn games, prompting one famous American grandmaster to remark, "He hasn't been that impressive. You can't afford to let those opportunities slip away in world championship play."

In Kuala Lumpur we weren't so critical of Karpov's play. If he had indeed been playing less than his best chess to establish this commanding lead, perhaps that grandmaster's observation was high flattery. At any rate, Karpov seemed relaxed and was playing very smoothly.

Game 9 was a fabulous struggle. After Karpov mishandled an interesting opening, Timman obtained a dangerous central pawn mass, then missed some real chances with . . . e5. Karpov found some fantastic resources, and then, just when everyone thought he had managed a draw, it became apparent that he was playing for a win.

Candidates' Match (9), Kuala Lumpur 1990
Ruy Lopez

White: Jan Timman *Black: Anatoly Karpov*

1 e4 e5 2 Nf3 Nc6 3 Bb5 a6 4 Ba4 Nf6 5 0–0 Be7 6 Re1 b5 7 Bb3 d6 8 c3 0–0 9 h3 Bb7 10 d4 Re8 11 Nbd2 Bf8 12 a4 h6 13 Bc2 exd4 14 cxd4 Nb4 15 Bb1 c5 16 d5 Nd7 17 Ra3 f5 18 Rae3

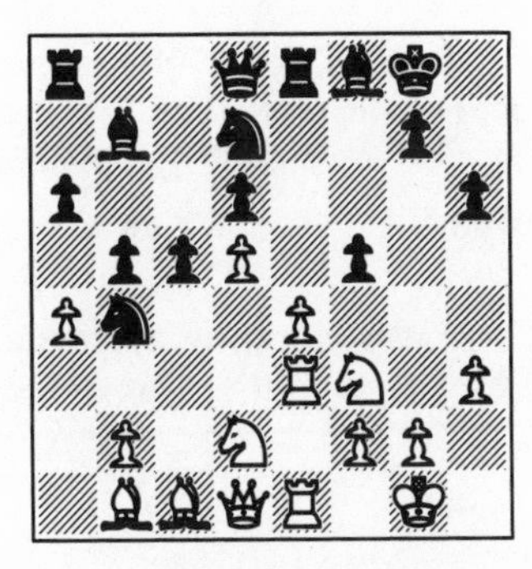

After 18 Rae3

First seen in de Firmian–A. Ivanov (Chicago 1988).

18 . . . f4!?

In *Informant 48*, Ivanov gives "?!" and recommends 18 . . . Nf6.

19 R3e2

Ivanov played 19 Ra3—this is a novelty.

19 . . . Ne5!?

An interesting strategic fight is shaping up.

20 Nf1 Nxf3+ 21 gxf3 Qh4 22 Nh2 Re5 23 Qd2 Qxh3 24 Qxf4 bxa4 25 Qg4 Qxg4+ 26 Nxg4!? Ree8 27 f4 a5 28 f3 Ba6 29 Rg2 Kf7 30 Rd1 Bc4

Now after 31 e5!?, Black can try 31 . . . Bb3 32 Rdd2 Nxd5 33 Be4 Nxf4, or 31 . . . a3 32 e6+ Ke7 33 bxa3 Nxd5 34 Be4 Nc3 (Garcia), in either case with an unclear position.

31 Ne3	**Bb3**
32 Re1	**c4**
33 e5	**dxe5**
34 Bg6+	**Kg8**

Gufeld and Torre were looking at the game continuation through 37 . . . Kh8, concluding it was unclear.

35 Ng4

Black might consider here 35 . . . Red8!?, or 35 . . . Bc5+ to free f8 for the king.

35 . . .	**Nd3**

Anatoly was down to two minutes on the clock.

36 Nxh6+	**gxh6**

Not 36 . . . Kh8? 37 Nf7+ Kg8 38 Rh2, with the idea Rh8 mate.

37 Bxd3+	**Kh8**
38 Bg6	**Red8**
39 Bd2?!	**Bb4**

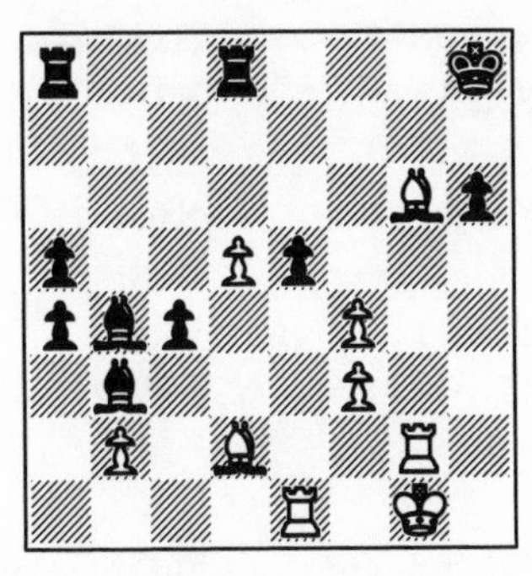

After 39 ... Bb4

With his flag hanging, Karpov thought for twenty seconds—an eternity for the audience!

40 Bc3	Bxc3
41 bxc3	a3
42 fxe5	Rxd5
43 e6	Rd1
44 Rxd1	Bxd1
45 e7	Ba4!
46 Bf7	Rb8!

Now 47 e8Q + ? Bxe8 48 Bxe8 Rb1 + loses quickly. Good for White is 47 Bxc4 Rb1 + 48 Kh2 Rb2, but an immediate 47 . . . Rb2 gives Black the advantage.

47 Re2	Rb1 +
48 Kf2	Rb2
49 Bxc4	Kg7

To draw, White must get his king to h1 and win Black's h-pawn.

50	Ke1	Rxe2+
51	Kxe2	h5!?
52	Bb3	Bd7
53	Ke3	Kf6
54	Kf4	Bc6!
55	c4	Kxe7
56	c5	Be8
	0-1	

Tremendous fighting chess and a great result for Karpov.

After the match, Karpov and I sat down for about an hour to discuss the world championship match and our problems during Karpov–Timman. We were especially concerned about our analysis of the fourth game. Though Karpov was satisfied with the outcome, he wasn't satisfied with the quality and efficiency of our analysis. Despite our seventy man-hours of analysis, we had missed the drawing move that Sax found a few days later. Worse, it was only four hours before the second play session that Podgaets and I discovered winning chances for Anatoly after 64 g5. Since that try occurred a mere four moves after the adjourned position and was identified only a few hours before play, it was impractical for Karpov to test the line. Sax's discovery of a drawing resource in the line actually played makes this lapse all the more critical.

We felt that the percentage of adjournments would certainly be higher in the world championship match. In the last twenty-four game match, eight games were adjourned. In Kuala Lumpur, we'd had only one adjournment, although it turned out to be a significant one.

5

DEEP THOUGHT AND THE KS

by Don Maddox
and International Master Mike Valvo

In years to come, Kasparov–Karpov 1990 is likely to be seen as a watershed in the history of chess, dividing chess as a purely human endeavor from chess as electronic information management.

Until recently, chessplaying computer programs have been the butts of intellectual jokes. Serious players dismissed them as weak, vaguely irritating intruders into the world of tournament chess.

Meanwhile, thousands of people were being introduced to chess by programs such as Chessmaster 2100 and by dedicated chessplaying machines such as those in the Fidelity line. Not until the arrival on the scene of Deep Thought did anyone consider these electronic monsters legitimate denizens of the upper levels of professional chess.

This year, for the first time, a chessplaying computer had some say in the analytical component of the match. In Game 1, Deep Thought, with its 720,000-move-per-second search capability, actually discovered a way for Karpov to win a pawn, and in the marathon win of Game 16, some observers feared that Deep Thought's analysis may have influenced the outcome, a rumor that proved groundless. In Game 20, a commercial computer discovered a mate-in-six missed by the world champion in his annihilation of the challenger.

Fidelity even provided Karpov with an $11,000 prototype as an electronic "coach in the corner," and the challenger's team actually used the machine to check variations and to test their own analysis.

A quick look at the adjournment analysis provided by Ron Henley in this book might suggest that the use of world-class computers differs only in degree from that of seconds and overnight team analysis. After all, the onus still falls on the player to absorb and select from an enormous volume of chess data, whether presented by the team or the computer.

But as computers become stronger, the idea of deciding the outcome of an adjourned game by means of human analysis becomes absurd. Machines will soon be strong enough to work out any adjourned position to an objective conclusion, erasing even the current level of human skill—and error—from the equation. When that happens, computers will change the face of tournament chess; adjournments will become obsolete.

Already computers are having other, more subtle influences on chess. Both the champion's and the challenger's teams could follow the games live in their training camps via computer: the *USA Today* Sports Center in New York, and the Minitel in France.

More important, both camps used computers as training aids, sorting through thousands of games using ChessBase, a games data base capable of storing, sorting, and retrieving more than 100,000 games and organizing them into digestible reports.

Kasparov is a child of the computer information age in chess. He carries, wherever he plays, a portable machine equipped with ChessBase and a hard drive, enabling him to isolate the games of an opponent in seconds and to prepare instantly for an unanticipated adversary.

A visit to Kasparov's rooms during the New York leg of

the match revealed reams of carefully stored and sorted computer readouts and several computers, indicating an organized and efficient use of ChessBase to prepare and research openings. Garry is an experienced ChessBase user, and most of his seconds were at home on the computer and with the program. Kasparov's team has become sophisticated enough in the use of ChessBase to have contributed a number of professional-level utilities to its developers' electronic toolbox.

It is not inconceivable that Kasparov's involvement with chess databases has helped him become the best-prepared tournament player in history and to break Bobby Fischer's long-standing record with a 2800 rating.

Karpov, on the other hand, has little to do with computers, and none of his team except Henley came to New York with any experience with ChessBase or the computer. The computers used by Karpov in Malaysia, New York, and France were all borrowed and rounded up by Henley, at first almost as an afterthought.

Karpov is the product of a generation preceding the information revolution, and he still prefers preparing the "old-fashioned way." He relies on heavy, focused analysis by trusted seconds, counting on his great experience and the depth of his knowledge in his chosen repertoire to hold him in good stead against all comers. Kasparov's frenetic preparation and determination to learn all he can about an upcoming opponent is alien to Karpov, who treats all prey the same.

The two players use computers differently. In Kasparov's camp they were used for research and retrieval, and for gathering, collating, and comparing analysis. Kasparov came to America with a massive database for this purpose and showed an enormous appetite for new games while he was here, requesting access even to games from local tournaments.

Karpov and his aides brought significantly less data with them and demonstrated a much smaller appetite for games. They used ChessBase primarily to gather and collate analysis they had done themselves, apparently satisfied with far less in the way of research and barely aware of the gap between the two camps in terms of the number of games available for study in electronic format.

Perhaps the clearest indication of the difference is that Kasparov regularly reviews material himself on screen, while Karpov seems to depend on hard copy printouts to review the results of his team's work, rarely touching the machine himself.

After visiting both camps early during the New York leg, I believed that the difference in the two players' ratings could be attributed to their different approaches to computers and information retrieval. I went so far as to predict that the outcome of the match itself might be determined by the computer, thinking that ChessBase as a "multiplier" to make every hour's study more productive, might widen the study gap already created by the players' different attitudes toward preparation.

Having lived through the match with the players, my understanding has shifted somewhat. Kasparov's fanatic dedication to personal preparation coupled with modern computer technology gives him an enormous edge in the tournament environment, where his natural superiority is magnified by his ability to focus on an individual opponent's weaknesses. Head to head with a player of Karpov's limited range but enormous depth, the advantages of computer preparation are to a large extent nullified; reviewing a thousand games might reveal a weakness in an opponent, but it can't create one.

The point is that Kasparov plus a computer is more dangerous to a random opponent than Karpov is without one.

The personal attention Kasparov is able to give each and every opponent is beyond Karpov's (computerless) reach at this point, and the result is a higher kill ratio on the tournament floor, exaggerating the difference between these two great players in that arena.

Kasparov believes that every game and every opponent, down to the lowest board in a clock simultaneous exhibition, is worth preparing for. Karpov believes in conserving his energy for the game. As Valvo observed, the Karpov camp's attitude toward computers is a reflection of Karpov's own attitude. He probably wouldn't use the information even if it were available.

In that sense, Karpov is a dinosaur—living and dangerous, but a throwback to a previous era, surrounded by strong young players such as Kasparov, to whom this new technology is as natural as the grass. Once Karpov is gone, it is not likely that another world champion will ever emerge without access to the power residing in a personal computer and without an appetite for the information it creates.

Chess-playing computers began to appear in strong tournaments in the period following the Kasparov–Karpov match in Seville in 1987. Although they were achieving respectable results in human tournaments, winning various state championships, skeptics continued to doubt that computers could seriously challenge strong human players. "Computers play well," they would say, "but not well enough to challenge tournament players." Then "tournament players" rapidly changed to "masters" and, by 1988, to "grandmasters."

The Software Toolworks Open Chess Championship at Long Beach, California, in 1988 changed everything. Deep Thought, the creation of several graduate students at Carnegie-Mellon (Hsu, Anantharaman, Browne, Campbell, Jansen, and Nowatzyk), emerged from the smoke tied for first with GM Anthony Miles. The program beat GM Bent Larsen along the way and achieved a USCF performance rating of 2745! Against the other titled players in that event, Deep Thought defeated IMs Vince McCambridge, Alex Fishbein, and Jeremy Silman, losing only to GM Walter Browne. The win against Larsen was the first by a computer against a strong grandmaster in a serious competition.

American Open, Long Beach, Cal.
November 1988, Round 3
English Opening

White: Bent Larsen ***Black: Deep Thought***

1 c4 e5 2 g3 Nf6 3 Bg2 c6 4 Nf3 e4 5 Nd4 d5 6 cxd5 Qxd5 7 Nc2 Qh5 8 h4 Bf5 9 Ne3 Bc5 10 Qb3 b6 11 Qa4 0–0 12 Nc3 b5 13 Qc2 Bxe3 14 dxe3 Re8 15 a4 b4 16 Nb1 Nbd7 17 Nd2 Re6 18 b3 Rd8 19 Bb2 Bg6 20 Nc4 Nd5 21 0–0–0 N7f6 22 Bh3 Bf5 23 Bxf5 Qxf5 24 f3 h5 25 Bd4 Rd7 26 Kb2 Rc7 27 g4 hxg4 28 Rhg1 c5 29 fxg4 Nxg4 30 Bxg7 Rg6 31 Qd2 Rd7 32 Rxg4 Rxg4 33 Ne5 Nxe3 34 Qxd7 Nxd1+ 35 Qxd1 Rg3 36 Qd6 Kxg7 37 Nd7 Re3 38 Qh2 Kh7 39 Nf8+ Kh8 40 h5 Qd5 41 Ng6+ fxg6 42 hxg6+ Kg7 43 Qh7+ Kf6 0-1

One year later, at the 1989 American Open, Deep Thought played an exhibition playoff game against 1988 co-winner Anthony Miles.

Now the chess world began taking Deep Thought and computers in general very seriously. Grandmasters became curious about how strong Deep Thought really was. Though no one was very impressed by the quality of the victory over

Larsen, the machine had garnered in a full point against a strong grandmaster.

Professional players had been fearing the advent of computers for years. Was that time here already? GM Ken Spraggett added fuel to the fire by making Deep Thought one of his seconds in his candidates' match against Yusupov. The program's main task during their match was to critically examine Yusupov's previous games and openings. Successful or not, psychologically this technique can be powerfully intimidating.

Meanwhile, chess organizations tried to prevent computers from playing in human tournaments. FIDE refused to rate computers or to permit them to play in FIDE-sanctioned events. American tournament organizers began maintaining "no computer" lists: If you didn't want to play against computers, you signed the list and the tournament director wouldn't pair you against them. Since many computers were by then of master strength or better, they began to influence the final standings. Though they generally are not eligible for money prizes, professionals were strongly against their participation anyway. Today many tournaments are advertised as "non-computer" events. Computers have to organize their own events, it seems, and invite humans to play!

There are several very strong computer programs, but Deep Thought is clearly the strongest and best-known. I first came across its principle author, Feng-hsiung Hsu, while directing the ACM North American Computer Championships in Dallas in 1986. He was operating an earlier version of Deep Thought called Chiptest.

Twice during the tournament I was called over to a Chiptest game when the computer attempted to castle while in check, an illegal move. Though I was unsure what to do about this—given the circumstances a computer will generally do what it did before—I decided to apply the human rule: if you make an illegal move, you must take it back and make a legal move. At my request, Hsu retracted the illegal previous move. Chiptest thought a bit, then claimed its previous try had been illegal and made a legal move! I was flabbergasted. If Chiptest had insisted on repeating its previous illegal move, I would have been forced to forfeit it. This machine, which had difficulty making legal moves four years ago, is today intimidating ranking chess players!

The Software Toolworks result made Deep Thought the darling of many post-game barroom speculations. Everybody wanted to try their skills against it.

In the summer of 1989, chess columnist Robert Byrne of *The New York Times* began research for an article on Deep Thought. Feng-hsiung had recently begun working at IBM's Thomas J. Watson Research Center in Yorktown Heights, New York, which gave Byrne access to the machine as well as to its designers. After playing a series of speed games with Deep Thought, drawing two and losing one, he became entranced with the machine's capabilities, and a two-game match over the *USA Today* Sports Center was proposed.

Byrne, though one of America's best grandmasters, was unfamiliar with computer play and devised his own strategy against Deep Thought. It completely backfired. He conceded space in the first game and allowed the machine whatever setup it desired. The two factors that bring out the best in computer play are more space and tactical opportunities. The machine had no difficulties in handling such a challenge, and Byrne made some errors that the machine eventually capitalized on.

A couple of weeks later, the second game was played and both sides then agreed to two more games. The four-game match, though interrupted by challenges by Kasparov and Karpov (see below) eventually ended in a 2–2 tie. Game 3 is presented here.

USA Today *Match (3), February 1990*
English Opening

White: Deep Thought *Black: Robert Byrne*

1 c4 g6 2 Nc3 Bg7 3 g3 e5 4 Bg2 Nc6 5 d3 f5 6 e3 Nf6 7 Nge2 0–0 8 f4 d6 9 Qb3 Kh8 10 0–0 Ne7 11 c5 c6 12 cxd6 Qxd6 13 fxe5 Qxe5 14 Nf4 g5 15 Nh3 h6 16 Bd2 b6 17 Qa3 a5 18 Na4 Rb8 19 Nf2 Ba6 20 Bc3 Qe6 21 Bxa5 Bxd3 22 Nxd3 bxa5 23 Rae1 Ned5 24 Nac5 Qc8 25 Ne5 Rb5 26 Ng6+ Kh7 27 Nxf8+ Bxf8 28 Rc1 Nd7 29 Bh3 g4 30 Bxg4 fxg4 31 Qd3+ 1-0

On October 22, 1989, at the New York Academy of Art, Deep Thought faced World Champion Kasparov in a two-game match for a purse of $10,000. Each side had ninety minutes to complete all his moves. This meant each game could last a maximum of three hours.

At a press conference just before the games, Kasparov said he had studied about fifty of Deep Thought's games in preparation for this match. He estimated the machine's strength as approaching 2500 FIDE and felt he would win nine points if they played a ten-game match.

Kasparov won both games easily. He played tentatively and positionally in the first but switched to confident aggressive play in the second.

Exhibition Game (1)
New York City, October 1989
Sicilian Defense

White: Deep Thought *Black: Garry Kasparov*

1	e4	c5
2	c3	

Kasparov certainly knew that Deep Thought would play this way against the Sicilian Defense.

2 . . . e6 3 d4 d5 4 exd5 exd5 5 Nf3 Bd6 6 Be3 c4 7 b3 cxb3 8 axb3 Ne7 9 Na3

Deep Thought varies from Short–Kasparov, Dortmund 1980, which continued 9 c4 Nbc6 10 c5 Bc7 11 Nc3 0–0 12 Bd3 Bf5 13 0–0 Qd7 with an equal position. White is embarking on a dubious plan of gaining space on the queenside by harassing Black's bishop.

9 . . . Nbc6 10 Nb5 Bb8 11 Bd3 Bf5 12 c4 0–0 13 Ra4?!

The audience laughed at this move, the only purpose of which seems to be to protect the b4-square. Kasparov ignores it and continues with his development.

13 . . . Qd7 14 Nc3 Bc7 15 Bxf5 Qxf5 16 Nh4? Qd7 17 0–0 Rad8 18 Re1 Rfe8 19 c5

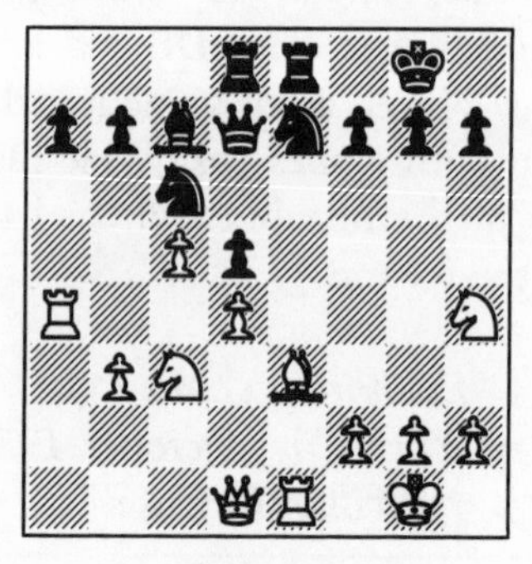

After 19 c5

19 . . . Ba5!

Kasparov plans to continue positionally by eliminating the c3-knight. Since computers consider bishops worth more than knights, Deep Thought must have been mystified.

20 Qd3 a6 21 h3 Bxc3 22 Qxc3 Nf5 23 Nxf5 Qxf5 24 Ra2 Re6 25 Rae2 Rde8 26 Qd2 f6 27 Qc3 h5

The game is strategically over; all that's left is the final breakthrough.

28 b4 R8e7 29 Kh1 g5 30 Kg1 g4 31 h4 Re4 32 Qb2 Na7 33 Qd2 R4e6 34 Qc1 Nb5 35 Qd2 Na3 36 Qd1 Kf7 37 Qb3 Nc4 38 Kh2 Re4 39 g3 Qf3 40 b5 a5 41 c6 f5 42 cxb7 Rxb7 43 Kg1 f4 44 gxf4 g3 45 Qd1 Rbe7 46 b6 gxf2+

The audience thought 46 . . . Nxe3 47 fxe3 Rxe3 was better.

47 Rxf2 Qxd1 48 Rxd1 Rxe3 49 Rg2 Nxb6 50 Rg5 a4 51 Rxh5 a3 52 Rd2 Re2 0-1

Exhibition Game (2)
New York City, October 1989
Queen's Gambit Accepted

White: Garry Kasparov *Black: Deep Thought*

1 d4 d5 2 c4 dxc4 3 e4 Nc6 4 Nf3 Bg4 5 d5 Ne5 6 Nc3 c6?! 7 Bf4 Ng6 8 Be3 cxd5 9 exd5 Ne5 10 Qd4

Kasparov turns on the afterburners.

10 . . .	**Nxf3 +**
11 gxf3	**Bxf3?**

11 . . . Bd7 is absolutely necessary, but computers are suckers for material.

12 Bxc4	**Qd6**
13 Nb5	**Qf6**

Not 13 . . . Qd7 14 Nxa7 threatening 15 Bb5.

14 Qc5	**Qb6**

If 14 . . . Bxh1 15 Nc7 + Kd8 16 Nxa8 Qd6 17 Qxa7 is overwhelming.

15 Qa3	**e6**

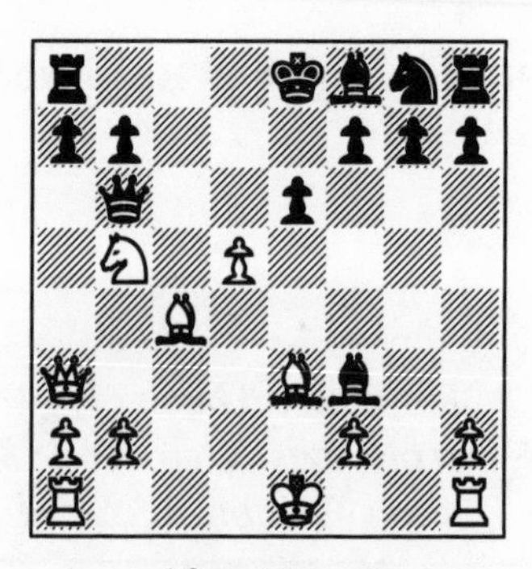

After 15... e6

Tantamount to resignation. Now 16 Qa4 is a simple way to win, but Kasparov wants a crowd-pleaser.

16 Nc7 + ! Qxc7 17 Bb5 + Qc6 18 Bxc6 + bxc6 19 Bc5 Bxc5 20 Qxf3 Bb4 + 21 Ke2 cxd5 22 Qg4 Be7 23 Rhc1 Kf8 24 Rc7 Bd6 25 Rb7 Nf6 26 Qa4 a5 27 Rc1 h6 28 Rc6 Ne8

29 b4 Bxh2 30 bxa5 Kg8 31 Qb4 Bd6 32 Rxd6 Nxd6 33 Rb8+ Rxb8 34 Qxb8+ Kh7 35 Qxd6 Rc8 36 a4 Rc4 37 Qd7 1-0

Since Kasparov won so easily and convincingly, was there any reason for the machine to play Karpov? Perhaps not, but a game was arranged at Harvard University. Due to travel problems, however, Karpov arrived in the United States exhausted. The organizers granted Karpov the white pieces as a concession, which had the most unexpected consequences for Deep Thought, aside from winning or drawing.

Exhibition Game
Harvard University, February 1990
Caro-Kann Defense

White: Anatoly Karpov ***Black: Deep Thought***

1 e4 c6

A surprise: the machine had never before played the Caro-Kann. I had spent the previous evening with Karpov and knew that preparing Deep Thought to play him wouldn't have mattered anyway. I showed him the first game he had ever seen played by Deep Thought! Kasparov, in contrast, treats every game seriously enough to prepare deeply for it.

2 d4 d5
3 Nd2

Karpov's specialty, designed to inhibit 3 . . . g6 by supporting the d-pawn with the c-pawn.

3	...	g6!?
4	c3	Bg7
5	e5	f6!?

After 5 ... f6

I was astounded when Deep Thought played this move, since computers normally don't like to "weaken" squares around their king. It shows profound positional understanding.

6	f4	Nh6
7	Ngf3	

GM Henley later criticized this move and suggested the more harmonious 7 Ndf3, intending Bd3 and Ne2. Deep Thought expected 7 Ndf3.

7	...	0–0
8	Be2	fxe5
9	fxe5	c5
10	Nb3	

Of course not 10 dxc5 Ng4.

10 . . . cxd4 11 cxd4 Nc6 12 0–0 Qb6 13 Kh1 a5! 14 a4 Bf5 15 Bg5 Be4 16 Nc5

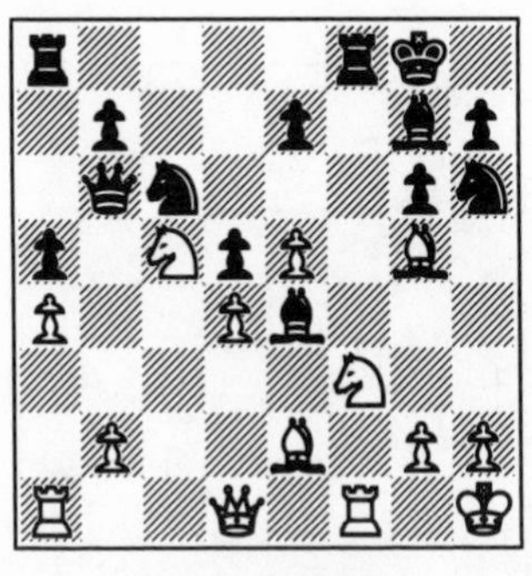

After 16 Nc5

Brave, but provocative. Safer is GM Patrick Wolff's 16 Bb5.

16 . . . Qxb2!?

True to the spirit of computerdom, Deep Thought snatches a pawn. Complications arising from 16 . . . Nf5!, however, are more in keeping with the demands of the position. If 17 Nd7, then 17 . . . Qxb2 18 Nxf8 Ncxd4!? creates unfathomable complications. Black, threatening 19 . . . Nb3, 19 . . . Nxe2, and recapturing the f8-knight, seems no worse and may even be better.

17 Nxe4 dxe4
18 Rb1 Qa3

Deep Thought has to be careful, since 18 . . . Qc3 drops the queen to 19 Rb3, and 18 . . . Qa2 fails to 19 Nd2. The computer evaluated the position as one-third of a pawn in Karpov's favor. Karpov was quite impressed when he heard that.

19 Bc1 Qc3 20 Bd2 Qa3 21 Bc1 Qc3 22 Rb3 Qa1 23 Bc4+ Kh8 24 Bxh6 Qxd1 25 Bxg7+ Kxg7 26 Rxd1 exf3 27 gxf3 Ra7!!

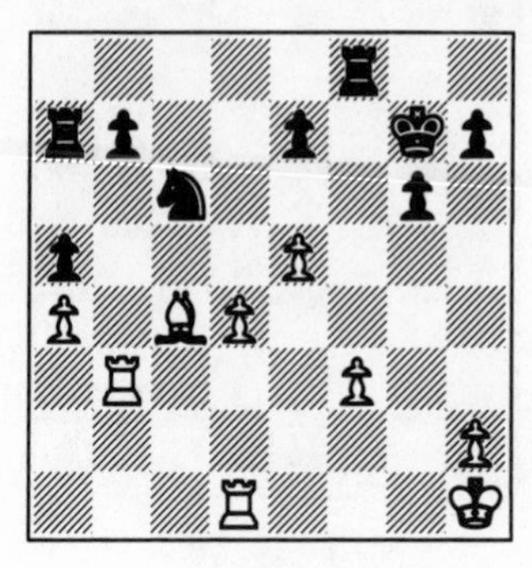

After 27 ... Ra7

Karpov later remarked that this was the best move of the game.

28 Bd5 Rd8 29 Rb5 Ra6 30 Be4 Ra7 31 Bd5 Ra6 32 Rc5 Rd7 33 Kg2 Rb6 34 Bxc6 bxc6 35 Kf2 Rd5 36 Rxd5 cxd5 37 Rc1 Rb4 38 Ke3 Rxa4

38 . . . Rb3+ 39 Ke2 Rb4, forcing repetition, also leads to a draw. But Deep Thought considered its position.

39 Rc5 e6 40 Rc7+ Kg8 41 Re7 Ra3+ 42 Kf4 Rd3 43 Rxe6 Rxd4+ 44 Kg5 Kf7 45 Ra6 a4?

Again, Deep Thought felt it was ahead. 45 . . . h6+ 46 Kxh6 Rh4+ 47 Kg5 Rh5+ 48 Kf4 Rf5+ followed by 49 . . . Rxe5 draws easily.

46 f4	**h6+**
47 Kg4	**Rc4?**

47 . . . g5! must be tried, with drawing chances.

48 h4	**Rd4**
49 Rf6+	**Kg7**
50 Ra6	**Kf7**
51 h5	**gxh5+**

The last chance for 51 . . . g5, though Karpov felt he would still have winning chances. Now it's all over.

52 Kf5 Kg7 53 Ra7+ Kf8 54 e6 Re4 55 Rd7 Rc4 56 Rxd5 h4 57 Rd3 Ke7 58 Rd7+ Kf8 59 Rh7 h5 60 Ke5 h3 61 f5 Kg8 62 Rxh5 a3 63 Rxh3 a2 64 Ra3 Rc5+ 65 Kf6 1-0

6

NEW YORK CITY, GAMES 1 THROUGH 6

In this section, annotations by the book's primary collaborators are given in the present tense, while on-site commentary during the games themselves is presented in the past tense to differentiate between considered opinion and "live" speculation. Unless otherwise noted, commentary can be ascribed to the primary analysts credited at the head of each game. Regularly used abbreviations for contributors and sources are: MR (GM Michael Rohde), LS (GM Leonid Shamkovich), SP (GM Semion Palatnik), RD (GM Roman Dzindzichashvili), RH (GM Ron Henley), European (the official match bulletin sponsored by The European *newspaper), CL (*Chess Life *magazine), PB (the press bulletin) and SC (*USA Today *Sports Center). Unattributed comments in the games analysis were made by Don Maddox.*

The fifth world championship match between Garry Kasparov and Anatoly Karpov began at the Hotel Macklowe in New York City with surprisingly little controversy. Both players seemed intent on chess and unwilling to squander energy on extraneous issues. Though Kasparov raised the specter of controversy by refusing to play under the Soviet flag, Karpov was slow to bite, remarking only at a pre-match press conference that Garry's "sudden" allegiance to the Russian republic, under whose flag he had decided to play, was of "rather recent and convenient vintage." The old animosity was evident, but the players came here to play chess.

On Monday, October 8, Karpov, dressed in a light gray suit and white shoes—matching the color of his pieces in Game 1—sat across from Kasparov, wearing a dark suit and black shoes, and pushed the first pawn in the first world championship played in the United States since 1907.

Kasparov answered Karpov's 1 d4 with the King's Indian Defense, surprising a sell-out audience by choosing the solid Byrne Variation, and soon took the game into unexplored territory. When Karpov declined to spice up the game, the world champion decided to play with fire himself. Though he emerged from his tightrope walk with a draw, Deep Thought, IBM's super-chessplaying computer, found a promising line for White in overnight analysis.

It became clear in subsequent games that Kasparov intended to continue his high-wire act. He seemed convinced that he was going to crush the challenger and justify his pre-match hype about the ratings gap between him and Karpov (2800 to 2730).

Match 5, Game 1
October 8, 1990
King's Indian Defense

White: Anatoly Karpov ***Black: Garry Kasparov***

Annotated by GM Leonid Shamkovich and GM Michael Rohde

1	d4	Nf6
2	c4	g6
3	Nc3	Bg7

The King's Indian Defense, nearly an innovation in K–K matches, had been essayed only once before by Kasparov—in Match 4, Game 17, Seville—when they played the Modern Classical system: 4 e4 d6 5 Nf3 0–0 6 Be2 e5 7 0–0 Nc6 8 d5 Ne7 9 Nd2. Still, its appearance was not unexpected. Kasparov has employed this dynamic defense frequently in tournaments, and his limited success with the Grünfeld Defense in previous encounters with Karpov had begun to pall on Kasparov and spectators alike.

Karpov and his seconds, of course, also expected the King's Indian and must have worked to fit him with a few comfortable lines and innovations—not an easy task in view of Karpov's limited experience with the King's Indian. (LS)

4 e4	**d6**
5 f3	

After 5 f3

The game's first surprise. Karpov selects the sharp Sämisch Variation. In Game 3, Karpov will revert to 5 Nf3, the Classical Variation. (MR)

5 . . .	0–0
6 Be3	c6

As a teenager, Kasparov preferred 6 . . . Nc6, but lately he has been experimenting with 6 . . . e5 7 d5 c6. (MR)

Against Gheorghiu (Thessaloniki Olympiad 1988) and Timman (Linares 1990), Kasparov chose the method Rohde cites, but against Gulko (Linares 1990), he tried the sharp 6 . . . c6 7 Bd3 e5 8 d5 b5!? (the game against Timman transposed to this position), and Kasparov went on to lose. Against Psakhis in their 1990 training match in Spain, Kasparov tried 6 . . . Nbd7 7 Bd3 c5. (LS)

7 Bd3 a6

The second surprise. Kasparov adopts the solid but unfashionable Byrne Variation, perhaps because he believes it is relatively unfamiliar to Karpov. This is *New York Times* chess columnist Robert Byrne's exclusive choice against the Sämisch. (MR)

This well-known plan, preparing . . . b5 before . . . e5, is new to both Kasparov's and Karpov's practices. (LS)

8 Nge2 b5
9 0–0

Naturally, Karpov chooses the solid strategic attack on the queenside rather than the sharper (and riskier) 9 0–0–0 followed by Qd2, Bh6, and h4–h5—a kind of dicey play that is not Karpov's style. (LS)

9 . . . Nbd7
10 Rc1

More to the point are 10 b3, to meet 10 . . . e5 with 11 d5, and 10 Qd2, preparing d-file pressure with 11 Rad1. (MR)

10 . . . e5
11 a3

This is a new move—unnecessarily slow, perhaps, since Black never threatens . . . b4. Probably best is the solid 11 Qd2 (MR).

Less convincing is 11 b3 exd4 12 Nxd4 Ne5 13 cxb5 axb5 14 Be2 d5, with an edge for Black (Diaz del Corral–Spassky, Palma de Mallorca 1969). (LS)

The press bulletin also cites 11 d5 (Razuvayev) and 11 b4 (GM Yasser Seirawan), but warned against 11 dxe5 Nxe5! (11 . . . dxe5 12 c5!).

Kasparov took twenty-four minutes for his next move.

11 . . . exd4
12 Nxd4 Bb7

A good alternative is 12 . . . Ne5 13 cxb5 axb5, or 13 . . . cxb5 14 Be2 Bb7. (LS)

At this point, Shamkovich gave Black a small edge, GM Larry Christiansen endorsed White—not the last time two grandmasters were to find themselves on opposite sides of a position during the heat of battle. Christiansen tempered his evaluation though, with an acknowledgment that "mere mortals have little understanding of Kasparov–Karpov games."

13 cxb5

Black can virtually force this exchange by playing . . . Ne5. (MR)

More logical, it seems to me, is 13 Qd2; e.g., 13 . . . Ne5 14 cxb5 cxb5! (14 . . . axb5 15 Be2, when White has a slight edge) 15 Be2 (15 Rfd1!?) 15 . . . d5, and the game is equal. White has a significant edge after 14 . . . Nxd3? 15 bxc6 Nxc1 16 cxb7 Rb8 17 Nc6 Nb3! 18 Qc2 Qc7 19 Nxb8 Nc5 20 b4! Rxb8 21 bxc5 dxc5 22 Rb1. Of course, White has no guarantee of a serious advantage after 13 Qd2. (LS)

13 . . . cxb5!

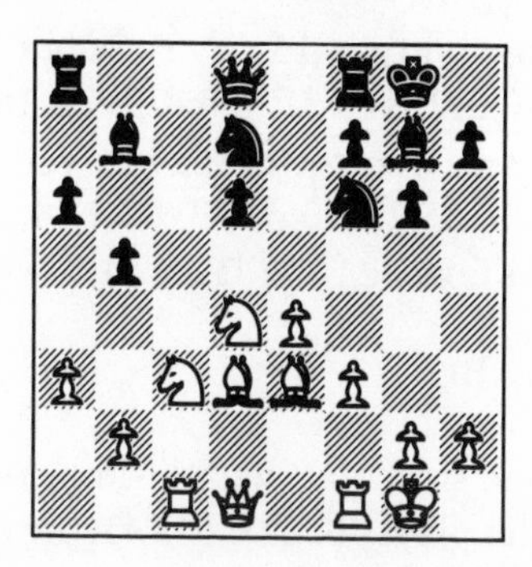

After 13 ... cxb5

Though it's more natural to capture toward the center with 13 . . . axb5, Kasparov's move is much stronger, ensuring himself at least a slight advantage with the coming break . . . d5. (MR)

14 Re1

This move sets the stage for a recurring Karpovian theme in this match: He prepares to "tuck in" his bishops with 15 Bf1 and 16 Bf2. Instead, there is little else for white to do in this position. (MR)

Karpov played this move after twenty-five minutes of thought. More interesting seems to be 14 Rf2, intending to double rooks after Rfc2 or Rfd2; e.g., 14 . . . Ne5 15 Bf1 d5 16 Qd2, with a considerable lead. Correct is 14 . . . Qe7! 15 Re2 Ne5. (LS)

14 . . . Ne5
15 Bf1 Re8

Kasparov prefers to pile on the tension, but it may have been stronger to cash in with 15 . . . d5 16 exd5 Nxd5 17

Nxd5 Qxd5, with undisputed advantage for Black. After the text move, the opposition of rooks along the e-file works in White's Favor. (MR)

Another possibility is 15 . . . Rc8, but White has a clear plus after 16 Qd2! Nc4 17 Bxc4 Rxc4 18 Rcd1 in view of the strong pressure on the d6-pawn. Very strong for White would be 16 . . . d5 17 Nxd5! Bxd5 18 Rxc8 Qxc8 19 exd5 Nxd5 20 Nf5! Qxf5 21 Qxd5. (LS)

16 Bf2

This strategic structure, with bishops on f1 and f2 (or f7 and f8 when he plays Black), is a favorite Karpov theme—very safe and promising for counterattack. (LS)

16 . . . d5

Black achieves little after 16 . . . Rc8 17 Rc2 Nc4 18 Bxc4 Rxc4 19 Rd2. (MR)

17 exd5 Nxd5

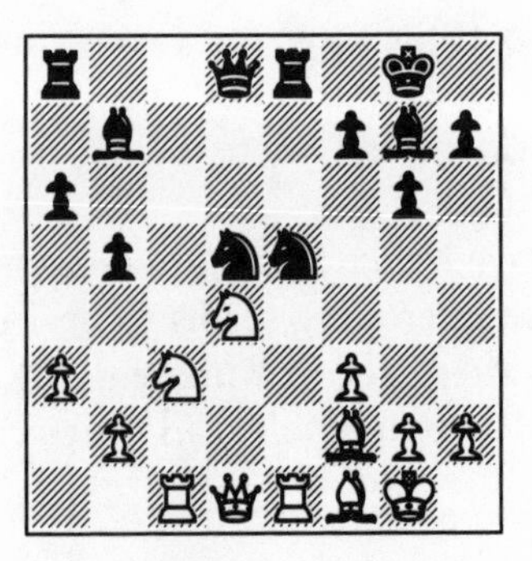

After 17... Nxd5

Seirawan declared that a younger Karpov would now have played 18 Ne4 without hesitation and that his twelve-minute pause here was a sign of "maturity."

18 Nxd5!

A letdown for the standing-room-only crowd, who wanted to see 18 Ne4 with ferocious complications: 18 . . . Nc4!! 19 Bxc4 bxc4 20 Rxc4 Nf4, with a dangerous initiative; or 18 . . . Nf4 19 Nc5! Qg5 20 g3 threatening 21 h4. (MR)

The alternative 18 Ne4?!, suggested by Seirawan in the analysis room and by de Firmian in the official bulletin, is questionable. De Firmian gives 18 . . . Nf4 19 Nc5 Qg5 20 Kh1 (not 20 Be3? Nh3+ 21 Kh1 Qxe3, and Black wins [LS]) 20 . . . Bd5 21 Be3, concluding "Black has kingside threats, but White has threats to win a piece." I agree wholeheartedly with the first half of this judgment—21 . . . Nc4!, as cited by Rohde above, gives Black a very strong counterattack; e.g., (A) 22 Bxf4 Qxf4 23 Rxe8+ Rxe8 24 Ne2 Qg5 25 Nd3 (25 f4 Bxg2+ 26 Bxg2 Qxc5, with a tremendous advantage for Black) 25 . . . Bh6!, threatening 26 . . . Ne3 with a good position for Black; or (B) 22 Rxc4 Bxc4 23 Qd2 Bxf1 24 Bxf4 (24 Rxf1 Rxe3!) 24 . . . Bxg2+, winning for Black. (LS)

18 . . . Qxd5
19 a4!

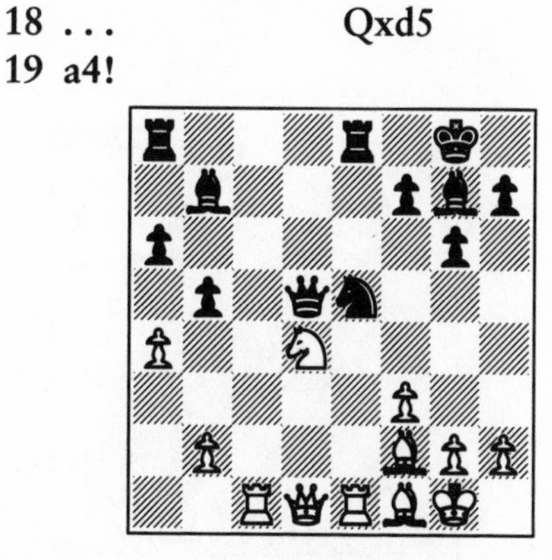

After 19 a4

19 . . . Bh6!

Kasparov could liquidate to equality with 19 . . . Nc4 20 axb5 axb5 21 Nxb5 Qxd1 22 Rexd1 Nxb2 23 Rd7 Bc8. (MR)

20 Ra1!

Karpov made this move instantly. I don't know if he even considered the romantic 20 Rc7!?, but his intuition did not let him down: 20 . . . Bf4! (with the idea 21 . . . Nxf3 +) 21 Rxb7 Qxb7 22 Re4 Bh6 23 Qe2 Qb8!—The only answer, but a strong one, repulsing 24 f4 with 24 . . . Nd7, with a fine game for Black. (LS)

20 . . . Nc4?? (MR)

Definitely an oversight, leaving White with a number of strong continuations. Kasparov should follow up logically with 20 . . . b4, closing the a-file. Then good for Black is 21 Qb3 Qa5. Much better for White is 21 Nb3, followed by 21 . . . Nd7! with a very unclear situation. (MR)

21 axb5 axb5

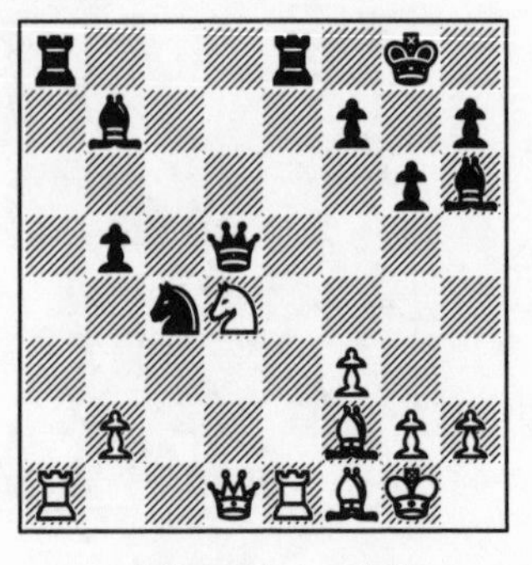

After 21 ... axb5

This is the most controversial position of the game. White has a wide range of options: 22 Rxa8, 22 Rxe8 +, 22 b3, 22 Nxb5, or both of the last two moves after a rook exchange. Which is White's best chance to obtain a real advantage?

Karpov tried 22 Rxa8 without success. Let's analyze the alternative 22 Rxe8 + Rxe8, and now:

(A) 23 b3 Nd2! 24 Bxb5 Rd8, and either 25 Ra7 or 25 Ra2 is met strongly by 25 . . . Ne4! (also confirmed by Deep Thought); e.g., 26 fxe4 Qxb5, with strong compensation. After 25 Ra7 Ne4! 26 Bc4, Black wins with 25 . . . Nxf2 26 Kxf2 Qc5!. Correct is 25 Qe2 (not 25 Qc2? Nxf3 + ! 26 gxf3 Bg7 27 Rd1 Qg5 + 28 Kf1 Bxd4 29 Rxd4 Qxb5 +, with advantage to Black) 25 . . . Nxb3 26 Nxb3 Qxb3 27 Bc4 Qc3 28 Re1 Bf8 29 Qa2 Qf6, and an equal game.

(B) 23 Nxb5 Qxd1? (23 . . . Qxb5? fails to 24 b3 Bd5 25 Ra4!) 24 Rxd1 Rc8 25 Rb1 Bg7 26 Bd4!, and White wins. Correct is 23 . . . Nxb2, when White has only a small plus. (LS)

22 Rxa8?

After being on the defensive for the whole game, Karpov suddenly has a shot at winning, but having several apparently strong continuations, he misses it! The correct move was identified by Deep Thought after the game: 22 b3!, with the following variations:

(A) 22 . . . Nd6 23 Rxe8 + Rxe8 24 Nxb5! Nxb5 25 Qxd5 Bxd5 26 Bxb5 Rc8 (26 . . . Rb8 27 Bc4) 27 Ba4 (27 b4 Rb8 28 Ra5) 27 . . . Bd2 28 Rd1 Rc2.

(B) 22 . . . Rxe1 23 Rxa8 + Bxa8 24 Qxe1 Nd2 (24 . . . Nd6 25 Nxb5! Nxb5 26 Qe8 + Kg7 27 Qxb5) 25 Bxb5 Nxb3 26 Qe8 + Bf8 (26 . . . Kg7 27 Nxb3 Qxb3 28 Bd4 +

f6 29 Qe7+ Kg8 30 Qd8+ Bf8 31 Bc5 Qf7 32 Bc4) 27 Nxb3 Qxb3 28 Bc5.

(C) 22 . . . Nd2 23 Rxe8+ (23 Rxa8 Rxa8 24 Bxb5 Bf4 [Wolff]) 23 . . . Rxe8 24 Bxb5 Rd8 25 Ra2 (25 Ra7 Rc8 26 Be2! Qd7 27 Ba6 Rc7 28 Bxb7 Rxb7 29 Ra8+ Kg7 30 Qa1 f6 31 Qa3 Kf7 32 b4 Rc7 33 b5 [Deep Thought]) 25 . . . Nxb3 (25 . . . Ne4 26 fxe4 Qxb5 [Deep Thought]) 26 Qxb3 Qxb3 27 Nxb3 Rd1+ 28 Bf1 Bd5 29 Ra3 Bc4 30 Ra8+ Kg7 31 Bd4+ f6 32 Ra7+ Kg8 33 Ra1 Bxb3 34 Rxd1 Bxd1 35 Bxf6.

(D) 22 . . . Ne3 23 Rxa8 Bxa8 24 Qd3. White seems to be winning in all of these lines. (MR)

22 . . . Rxa8
23 Qb3

Now 23 b3 Nd6 yields nothing for White. A good try is 23 Nxb5, looking for 23 . . . Qxb5? 24 b3 Bd5 25 Re5!. But Black has 23 . . . Qxd1 24 Rxd1 Nxb2 25 Rb1 Bg7 26 Bd4 Bxd4+ 27 Nxd4 Ra2 28 Ne2 Bc8! 29 Nc1 Bf5. (MR)

23 . . . Bc6

More accurate is 23 . . . Nd6 24 Qxd5 Bxd5 25 Nxb5 Nxb5 26 Bxb5 Bg7, continuing as in the game. Now 24 Nxc6! Qxc6 25 Qc2 (Seirawan) gives White a slight edge after 25 . . . Ra2 26 Bd4 (better than Seirawan's 26 Qd3 Bg5!, with equality) 26 . . . Bg7 27 Qc3 Bxd4+ 28 Qxd4 Ra8 29 Bd3 Nd6 30 Kf2. (LS)

24 Bd3?!

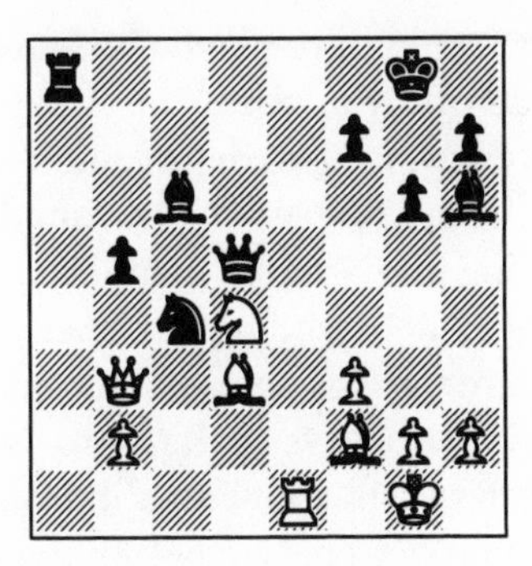

After 24 Bd3

24 . . .	**Nd6!**

Kasparov forces a drawish ending with a modern-style pawn sacrifice. (LS)

25 Qxd5	**Bxd5**
26 Nxb5	

Black draws also after 26 Re5 Bc4. (LS)

26 . . .	**Nxb5**
27 Bxb5	**Bg7**
28 b4	**Bc3**
29 Rd1	**Bb3**
30 Rb1	

According to de Firmian, Black wins after 30 Rc1 Bd2! 31 Rb1 Bc2 32 Rb2? Ra1+ 33 Bf1 Bd3. (European)

30 . . .	**Ba2**
Draw	

In conclusion, it seems that both 22 Rxe8+ and 22 Rxa8 demanded high-level acrobatics from Black to keep the balance. Kasparov could have played it safe, of course, with 19 . . . Nc4 instead of the adventurous 19 . . . Bh6, but he was evidently pressing for more than equality. (LS)

In Game 2, Kasparov shook the foundations of Anatoly Karpov's opening preparation, demolishing his pet variation in the Ruy Lopez and sending the challenger scurrying for extra time to shore up his defenses. In the press room, many observers began to believe in Kasparov's invincibility, and some even began to talk about an abbreviated match in New York (if either player were two points ahead after ten games, the whole show was scheduled to pack up for Lyon, France, and the second half of the match).

Later Karpov was to claim that Kasparov's sacrifice on move 25 was "home preparation," a tremendous achievement in itself, though not the same as calculating the combination over the board.

Match 5, Game 2
October 10, 1990
Ruy Lopez

White: Garry Kasparov *Black: Anatoly Karpov*

Annotated by GM Leonid Shamkovich and GM Michael Rohde

1 e4

Kasparov establishes very early that he wants to create complications. Although Garry's lifelong favorite has been 1 d4, he has done well with 1 e4 against Karpov. (MR)

1 . . . e5

Karpov's normal response. Like GMs Paul Keres and Boris Spassky, he prefers this classical move, although he has played the Caro-Kann once against Kasparov (Match 4, Game 14). (LS)

2	**Nf3**	**Nc6**
3	**Bb5**	**a6**
4	**Ba4**	**Nf6**
5	**0–0**	**Be7**
6	**Re1**	**b5**
7	**Bb3**	**d6**
8	**c3**	**0–0**
9	**h3**	**Bb7**

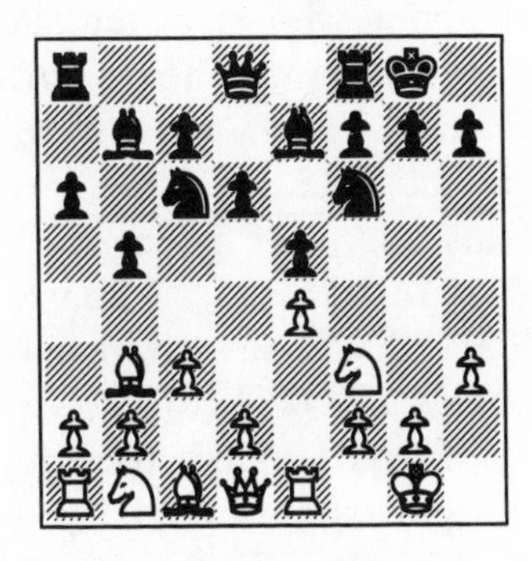

After 9 ... Bb7

10	**d4**	**Re8!?**
11	**Nbd2**	**Bf8**
12	**a4**	**h6**
13	**Bc2**	**exd4**
14	**cxd4**	**Nb4**
15	**Bb1**	**bxa4!?**

The counterblow 15 . . . c5 is more logical, as played in Match 3, Game 14: 15 . . . c5 16 d5 Nd7 17 Ra3 c4 18 axb5 axb5 19 Nd4 Rxa3 20 bxa3 Nd3 21 Bxd3 cxd3 22 Bb2 Qa5

23 Nf5 Ne5 (23 . . . g6!?—Kasparov) 24 Bxe5! dxe5 25 Nb3 Qb6 26 Qxd3 Ra8? (26 . . . Bc8!?—Kasparov) 27 Rc1 with a slight edge for White (the knights are actually stronger than Black's bishops); and in Match 3, Game 16: 18 Nd4 Qf6 19 N2f3 Nc5 20 axb5 axb5 21 Nxb5 Rxa3 22 Nxa3 Ba6 (Black sacrificed the pawn for the initiative, and he now threatens . . . Nd3) 23 Re3?! Rb8 (23 . . . Nbd3!?—Kasparov) 24 e5! dxe5 25 Nxe5 Nbd3?! (25 . . . Ncd3) 26 Ng4? (26 Qc2!—Kasparov) 26 . . . Qb6!, with an unclear position. Karpov later made some time-pressure blunders and could not save his king.

The variation has been examined countless times since then in international tournaments without reaching a definitive judgment about who is better and why. For many months afterward Karpov declined to participate in this critical debate. Against Hjartarson in Game 5 of his 1989 Seattle match, he chose 15 . . . bxa4 instead, ignoring the demolition of his queenside pawn chain in exchange for active piece play: 16 Rxa4 a5 17 Ra3 Ra6 18 Nh2 g6 19 Ng4 (19 f4 d5! 20 e5 Ne4 [Ivanchuk–Karpov, Linares 1989]) 19 . . . Nxg4 20 Qxg4 c5! 21 dxc5 dxc5 22 e5 Qd4. A year later, GM Jan Timman tried to improve White's game against Karpov with 18 Nh4?! Nxe4! 19 Nxe4 Bxe4 20 Bxe4 d5! 21 Rae3 Rae6 22 Bg6 Qxh4 23 Rxe6 Rxe6 24 Rxe6 fxe6 25 Be3 Qf6 26 Qg4? (26 Bb1!?—Karpov) 26 . . . Bd6, but lost in this dismal position.

That brilliant Karpov victory made a strong impression on the chess world, and Karpov himself was confident enough in the power of his new plan to repeat it here against Kasparov, even though he must have expected a prepared innovation from his opponent. (LS)

16 Rxa4	**a5**
17 Ra3	**Ra6**

18 Nh2	**g6**
19 f3!	

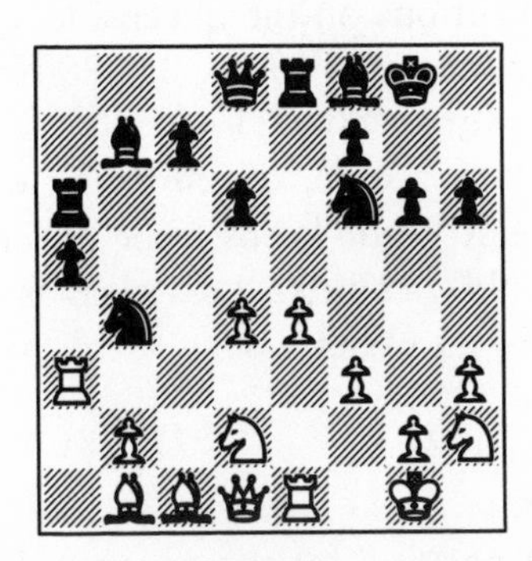

After 19 f3

According to Seirawan, "the novelty of the year." White overprotects the pawn at e4, freeing the knight on d2 for action and blunting Black's pressure on White's center. Previously played were 19 Ng4 and 19 f4. (MR)

This was a very unpleasant surprise for Karpov. White protects the pawn at e4 and deprives Black of his general plan, which is based on pressure against just this center pawn. The forming principle of the Zaitsev (10 . . . Re8) is to organize an immediate attack because the older 10 . . . h6 allows White to regroup with 11 Nbd2 Re8 12 Nf1 and then Ng3 with a slight edge.

By protecting the e-pawn, White consolidates his position and manages to attack Black's queenside pawns and the kingside at the same time. Black is obligated to find some active counterplay. (LS)

19 . . .	**Qd7?**

This move was criticized because the queen turns out to be inconveniently placed. Most logical is the simple 19 . . .

Bg7, asking to be shown: 20 Nc4 c6 21 Bd2 Nh5 is fine for Black; or if 20 Ndf1, Karpov will never have to bother with defensive contortions on the queenside. (MR)

Fedorowicz suggested 19 . . . Bg7 20 Nc4 Qa8, but White has a clear advantage after 21 d5! Nh5 22 Nf1. Deserving of more attention is 19 . . . c5 20 dxc5? d5!, with excellent counterplay; but White keeps some advantage after 20 d5! Bg7 21 Nc4 Nd7 22 Be3!. Less clear is 22 Bf4 Qh4!? 23 Bxd6 Nxd5 24 g3 Qxh3. (LS)

20 Nc4 Qb5

An inferior position for the queen. (LS)

21 Rc3

Now the positional threat of . . . d5 is met by Na3 followed by e5. (LS)

21 . . . Bc8

Preventing e5 followed by e6. (LS)

Najdorf suggested 21 . . . d5 22 Na3 Qb6 23 e5 c5 24 exf6 Rxe1+ 25 Qxe1 cxd4, with play for the piece.

22 Be3 Kh7? (MR)

White was threatening 23 Qc1 with the double attack 24 Bxh6 or 24 Na3, but the text is passive; obviously better is 22 . . . h5, denying White the g4-square. (MR)

De Firmian recommended 22 . . . h5, but White has a strong answer in 23 Qc1 c6 24 Bxh6!, attacking the weak d6-pawn. By playing 22 . . . Kh7, Black avoids forcing variations involving 23 Qc1 Kh7 (to protect h6) 24 Na3, seizing the c7-pawn. (LS)

23 Qc1 c6

Now the black pieces on the queenside and the kingside are completely disconnected. In the Bulletin, de Firmian noted: "23 . . . Qb8 would at least avoid the game continuation." This is true, but White's attack is still very strong after 24 Ng4 Ng8 25 Ra3 Qb5 26 Nxa5! Rxa5 27 Qxc7 Rxa3 28 Qxf7+ Kh8 29 bxa3. (LS)

Deep Thought, with its usual penchant for pawn-splitting, evaluated Karpov's position as a third of a pawn down.

24 Ng4

Najdorf, drawing his usual rapt audience, intoned, "Chess is a very difficult game. In boxing you win by points; in chess, you win only by knockout."

24 . . . Ng8?

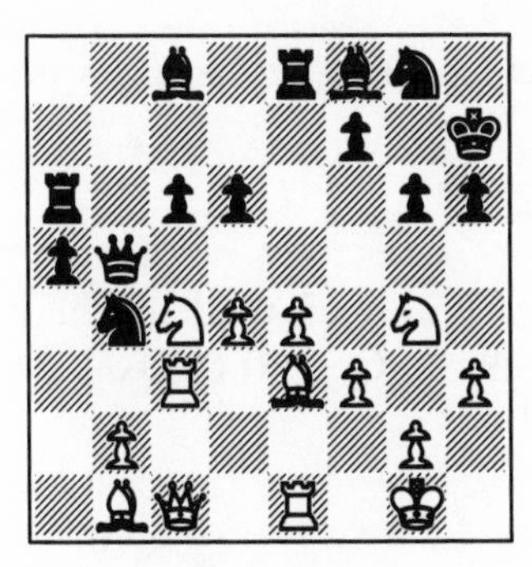

After 24 ... Ng8

Another horribly passive move. Black has to try 24 . . . Bxg4! 25 hxg4 Qb8!. If White answers 26 Kf2, threatening 27 Rh1, then Black gets strong central counterplay with 26 . . . d5!.White keeps an edge, though, with 26 g5. (MR)

25 Bxh6!!

This blow leaves Black disorganized. Kasparov could have played it safe with 25 Nf2 followed by f4. (MR)

25 . . .	**Bxh6**
26 Nxh6	**Nxh6**
27 Nxd6	**Qb6**
28 Nxe8	

Kasparov was responding casually now; Karpov's lips were moving incessantly as he calculated over the board.

Deep Thought, after siding with Karpov for several moves, was coming around to Garry's point of view. Dzindzichashvili thought Karpov was better here, but Christiansen and GM Patrick Wolff were declaring Black "crushed."

28 . . .	**Qxd4 +**

Karpov spent twenty-two minutes on this forced move.

29 Kh1

Also strong is 29 Qe3 to deny the black rook the a7-square. Then 29 . . . Qe5 30 f4 Qxe8 31 f5 leaves Black in sad shape. (MR)

29 . . .	**Qd8**

This snares White's Trojan horse. When this move appeared, most grandmasters decided that Kasparov's combination was flawed (the alternative was 29 . . . Qe5). Only Kasparov had foreseen his thirty-first move. (LS)

30 Rd1	Qxe8
31 Qg5!!	

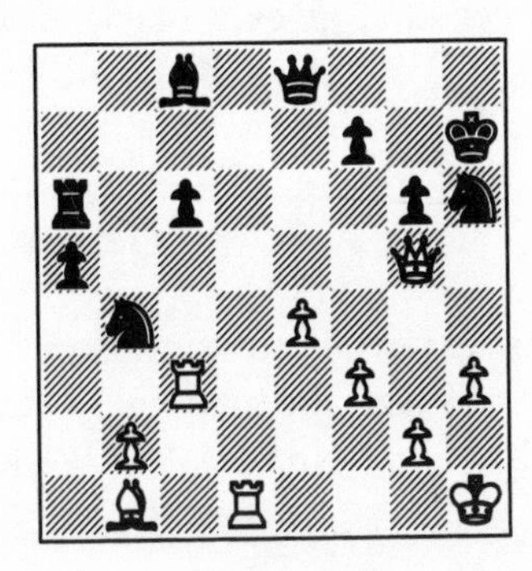

After 31 Qg5

This is the point of Kasparov's combination beginning with 25 Bxh6. Now Black cannot oppose the intrusion of White's queen and rook into his camp because his pieces are badly situated. (LS)

31 . . .	Ra7

Virtually forced: 31 . . . Ng8 32 Qh4+ Kg7 33 Rd8 is very strong; 31 . . . Bd7 32 Rc4; or 31 . . . Qe6 32 Rd8 f6 33 Rh8+ Kxh8 34 Qxh6+ Kg8 35 Qxg6+ Kf8 36 Rc5. (MR)

32 Rd8	Qe6
33 f4	Ba6

Roundly criticized, but there are no good moves; e.g., 33 . . . f6 34 Qc5 wins: 34 . . . Rd7 35 Rxc8! Rd1+ 36 Kh2 Qxc8 37 Qe7+ Kg8 38 Rg3, or 34 . . . Rg7 35 Qxa5. (MR)

34 f5	Qe7
35 Qd2	

GM Alexei Suetin suggested 35 Rh8+ Kxh8 36 Qxh6+ Kg8 37 fxg6 fxg6 38 Rxc6!? Nxc6 39 Ba2+, but IM Jon Tisdall, in *Chess Life,* gives a Black improvement: 37 . . . Qe5 38 Rc5 Qg7 39 gxf7+ Kxf7 40 Rf5+ Ke8 41 Qd6, "with a strong but not necessarily decisive attack."

35 . . .	**Qe5**

Karpov was in terrible time pressure. White is winning after 35 . . . c5 36 Rg3 threatening 37 Rh8+.

No better is 35 . . . Nd5 36 Rh8+! Kxh8 37 Qxh6+. (MR)

36 Qf2	**Qe7**
37 Qd4	**Ng8**
38 e5	**Nd5**

By now, even Deep Thought saw the error of its ways, and gave White a five pawn lead.

39 fxg6+	**fxg6**
40 Rxc6	**Qxd8**
41 Qxa7+	**Nde7**
42 Rxa6	**Qd1+**
43 Qg1	**Qd2**
44 Qf1	**1–0**

After two games Karpov was already down by one game. Kasparov's brilliant display against the challenger's favorite defense seemed to support his claim to a crushing win.

When Maddox visited the Karpov camp the following day to help with a computer problem, he left with a friendly, "If there's anything I can do to help, let me know."

"How about a defense to 1 e4?" Henley shot back.

The question was serious enough for Karpov to take his

first timeout of the match, a surprising development after only two games.

In the next game, Kasparov played with reckless abandon, leaving his queen hanging like ripe fruit for the plucking. Karpov hesitated, then snatched the forbidden apple, only to find himself forced to return it in the rising crescendo of time pressure. Kasparov emerged from the crisis with a tremendous game, but Karpov hung on with a stunning defense.

It was becoming clear to everyone that this match would be something special, an irresistible force encountering an immovable object.

Match 5, Game 3
October 15, 1990
King's Indian Defense

White: Anatoly Karpov — *Black: Garry Kasparov*

Annotated by GM Michael Rohde

	White	Black
1	d4	Nf6
2	c4	g6
3	Nc3	Bg7
4	e4	d6
5	Nf3	0–0
6	Be2	e5
7	Be3	

According to the press bulletin, Karpov last played this move against Quinteros in Malta 1980. Kasparov has also been known to play this alternative to 7 0–0. (MR)

7	...	Qe7
8	dxe5	dxe5
9	Nd5	Qd8

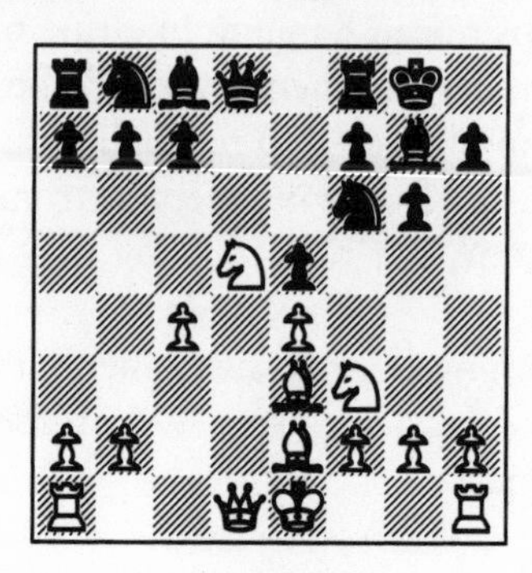

After 9 ... Qd8

Leading to a Karpovian position is 9 . . . Nxd5 10 cxd5 c6 (10 . . . Qb4+? turns out badly after 11 Nd2 Qxb2 12 0–0) 11 d6 Qe6 12 h4! (Sokolov–Djuric, San Bernardino 1988). The move Kasparov played leads to the edge of a precipice. (MR)

10	Bc5	Nxe4

Forced. Not 10 . . . Re8? 11 Be7! (Peet–Canfell, Dieren 1990). (MR)

11	Be7	Qd7
12	Bxf8	

Black has reasonable compensation for the exchange after 12 Qc2 Re8 13 Qxe4 Rxe7. (MR)

12	...	Kxf8
13	Qc2	

Tisdall asked out loud in the press room, "Isn't this a little extreme? Shouldn't they settle for a quiet game in here somewhere?"

IM Bjarke Kristensen shot back, "Kasparov wants to kill him—that's the point."

13 . . . Nc5

While Kasparov hunched in angry concentration, shaking his head from side to side as if he were trying to chase away a swarm of insects, Karpov sat quietly with his hands folded in front of his mouth. (SC)

14 Rd1

Karpov left the board, and Garry hunkered down even more intently.

14 . . . Nc6

Preparing to sacrifice the queen. This move is forced. In the press room, GM Robert Byrne jokingly informed reporters that wires had been crossed in the electronic feed: "This is a blitz game from the back room of the Manhattan Chess Club!"

"Beautiful," said GM Hans Ree. "I admire this. I don't know who is better, but it's beautiful."

Thus far, Karpov had used 1:09; Kasparov 0:21.

15 0–0

Karpov wisely declines the queen: 15 Nb6 axb6 16 Rxd7 Bxd7, and Black has ideas of playing . . . e4 and . . . Nd4, etc. After 15 Ng5, Black's best is probably 15 . . . Kg8 16

Nf6+ Bxf6 17 Rxd7 Bxd7 18 Ne4, and White wins the queen undet better circumstances. An alternative is 16 b4 Qd8 17 Nxf7 Kxf7 18 bxc5 Nd4 19 Qa4. (MR)

15 . . . Ne6!!

Kasparov continues his string of forced moves. Disastrous are 15 . . . Nd4 16 Nxd4 exd4 17 Qc1 Qd8 18 Rfe1 Bd7 19 Qf4 (de Firmian); and 15 . . . e4 16 Ng5 Qf5 17 Nxh7+ Kg8 18 Nxc7. The puzzling aspect of this game is that, although Kasparov had obviously prepared the line, his position never inspired confidence. (MR)

16 Nb6?

Karpov finally succumbs to temptation. Better is 16 Qd2 threatening 17 Ng5. Black then has 16 . . . Ncd4 17 Nxd4 Nxd4 18 f4, or 16 . . . h6 17 Rfe1. (MR)

16 . . . axb6
17 Rxd7 Bxd7

The smoke has cleared and Black has two minor pieces, a pawn, and a central initiative for the queen. White should now simply play 18 a3 with a small advantage. If Black trades knights on d4, fine; if Black tries 18 . . . f5 to threaten 19 . . . e4, White counters strongly with 19 Rd1. (MR)

18 Qd2??

A horrible blunder: After Black's reply, White's a-pawn is threatened and he loses control over e4. (MR)

18 . . . Be8
19 b3

More active is 19 a3. (MR)

Dzindzichashvili said he thought Black was OK; Wolff preferred White. Deep Thought still clung to its evaluation of the position in White's favor, but less enthusiastically.

19 . . .	**e4**
20 Ne1	

Najdorf felt Black was "much better." IM Victor Frias thought White was winning. Tisdall responded, "Even if Black is worse, I'd rather be Black."

20 . . .	**f5**
21 Bd1	

According to IM John Grefe, "Anatoly is playing a new kind of chess here—all his pieces are on the back rank again!"

21 . . .	**Ne5**

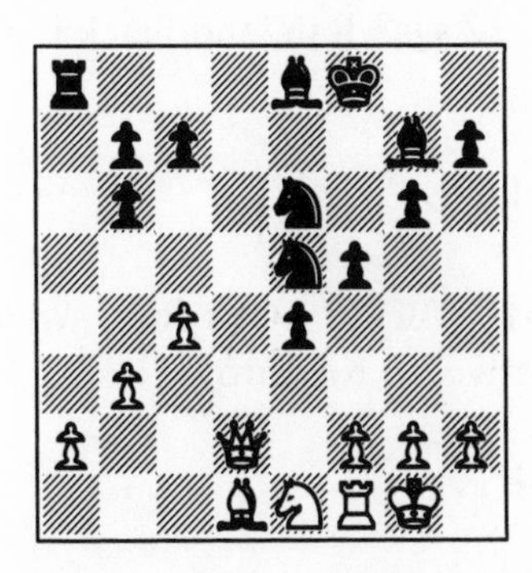

After 21 ... Ne5

Christiansen and Seirawan both recommended 21 . . . Rd8 22 Qc1 Ncd4.

22 Nc2

White sacrifices the pawn at a2 in a desperate bid for freedom. (MR)

GM William Lombardy asked sharply, "If this is his best, why did he take the queen?"

22 . . . Rxa2

Rejecting the sacrifice with 22 . . . Rd8 23 Qe3 Rd3 24 Qe1 is unclear. (MR)

23 Qd5

Deep Thought preferred 23 f3.

23 . . . Ke7

Karpov gives 23 . . . Ra5! and 24 Qxb7 Bc6 25 Qb8+ (25 Qc8+ Kf7 26 Nb4 Ra8, with a Black plus) 25 . . . Kf7 26 Nb4 Nd7! 27 Qc8 Ra8, and Black is ahead; or 24 Qxe6 Bd7. (RH)

24 Nb4

Not 24 Qxb7? Bc6 25 Qc8 Ra8. After the text, 24 . . . Ra7 is too passive, so Kasparov wins back the queen. (MR)

24 . . . c6

Portisch offered 24 . . . Bc6! as stronger.

25 Qxe6+ Kxe6
26 Nxa2 Nf7!

An excellent regrouping—the knight gets to d6 to support the e-pawn. Kasparov has a big endgame advantage. (MR)

Deep Thought gave Black .6 of a pawn edge: "Of course Kasparov is a better endgame player than the machine." (Hsu)

27 Be2	**Nd6**
28 Nb4	**Bc3**
29 Nc2	**f4**
30 Rd1	**h5**
31 f3	**e3**
32 g3	**g5**
33 Bd3	**h4**
34 Kf1!	

Karpov maneuvers his king to e2 so that his rook can later occupy the g-file. Both players were in time pressure here. (MR)

34 . . .	**c5**
35 Ke2	**b5??**

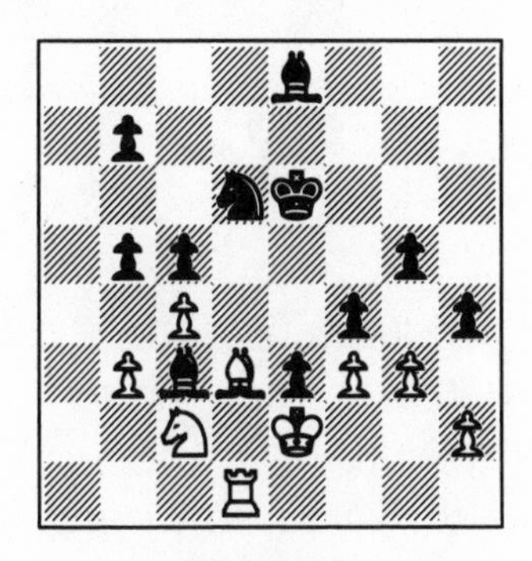

After 35 ... b5

Too hasty. Black should prepare this move with 35 . . . Bf6!. (MR)

36 cxb5 Nxb5

Drawish is 36 . . . Bxb5 37 Bxb5. (MR)

37 Bc4+ Ke7
38 Rd5

Karpov wins back the pawn. (MR)

38 . . . Bf6

Black gets nowhere after 38 . . . fxg3 39 hxg3 h3 40 Kf1, according to de Firmian. (European)

39 Rxc5 Nc3+
40 Kf1 Bg6
41 Ne1

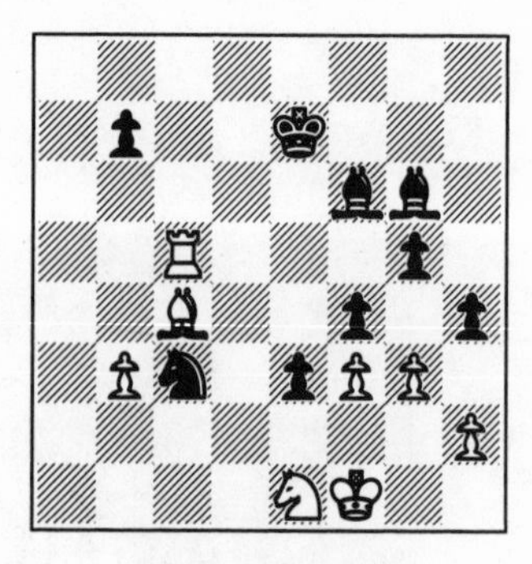

After 41 Ne1

Kasparov sealed. Some grandmasters still thought Kasparov was winning.

Unless otherwise noted, the annotations from this point on are by GM Ron Henley and the Karpov team.

41 . . . Kd6

A major alternative is 41 . . . b6!, which creates more problems for White.

42 Ra5

Not 42 Rc8 Bf5, when White has problems. (MR) Deep Thought analyzed 42 Rc8 as leading to a draw.

42 . . . fxg3!?

Black also has 42 . . . h3 43 gxf4 gxf4 44 Ra8 and now:

(A) 44 . . . b5 45 Ra6+ Ke7 46 Ra7+ Kf8 47 Ra8+ Kg7 48 Ra7+ Kh6 49 Bd3! Bxd3+ (49 . . . Bh4? 50 Ra6, and White wins) 50 Nxd3 e2+ 51 Ke1 Bh4+ 52 Kd2, winning.

(B) 44 . . . Nb1 45 Ke2 Nd2 46 Ra5! Bh4 47 Nd3 Bxd3+ 48 Kxd3 Nxf3 49 Rd5+, and: 49 . . . Kc6 50 Rh5 (50 Ke4? Nd2+ 51 Kxf4 Nxc4 52 bxc4 e2, and Black wins) 50 . . . Ne1+ 51 Ke4 Ng2 52 Kf3, with the idea Bf1 and a plus for White; or 49 . . . Kc7 50 Rh5 Bg3 51 hxg3 fxg3 52 Rxh3 g2 53 Rg3, drawn.

43 hxg3 hxg3

Or 43 . . . h3.

44 Ng2 b5

Karpov gives 44 . . . g4:

(A) 45 Be2!? gxf3 46 Bxf3 Bd3+ 47 Ke1 Bd4 and 48 Rg5? Ne4! 49 Bxe4? (49 Rg6+) 49 . . . Bc3+! 50 Kd1 e2+ 51 Kc1 Bxe4, with a definite edge for Black; or 48 Nf4! with the idea Nxd3, Rg5, or Bxb7.

(B) 45 fxg4 Bd4 (45 . . . e2 + 46 Bxe2 Nxe2 47 Kxe2 Be4 48 Rf5! Bd4 49 Rf3!, with a draw) 46 Nf4 Be4 47 Ne2 b5 48 Nxd4 g2 + 49 Kg1 bxc4 50 bxc4 e2 51 Ra1 Ke5 (51 . . . Kc5 52 Nxe2 Nxe2 + 53 Kf2 Nf4 54 Ke3 Nh3 55 Kxe4 g1Q 56 Rxg1 Nxg1 57 g5 Ne2 58 g6 Ng3 + 59 Ke5 Nh5, drawn) 52 Nxe2! Nxe2 + 53 Kf2 Nf4 54 Kg3! Bd3 55 Re1 +, drawn (55 Rg1 Bf1 56 c5 Ne2 + 57 Kf2 Nxg1 58 Kxg1 Kd5 59 g5, drawn).

45 Ra6 +

White loses after 45 Rxb5? Nxb5 46 Bxb5 Bd4 (46 . . . Kc5 47 Bc4 Kd4 48 Ke2 Bf5 49 Nxe3 Bh3 50 Bd3 g2? 51 Nxg2 Bxg2 52 Bf5 Ke5 53 Bg4, with equality) 47 Ke2 Bf5 48 Nxe3 Bh3 49 Be8 (49 Bd3 Ke5!) 49 . . . g2.

White also has 45 Nxe3 bxc4 (45 . . . Bd4) 46 Nxc4 + Ke7 (46 . . . Kd7 47 Ne5 + Bxe5 48 Rxe5 g4 49 fxg4; or 46 . . . Kc7 47 Ra6 Bd3 + 48 Kg2 Bxc4 49 Rxf6, with a draw) 47 Ne5!, and 47 . . . Bxe5 48 Rxe5 + Kf6 49 Rc5 (49 Re3); or 47 . . . Bf5.

45 . . .	**Ke7**
46 Ra7 +	**Ke8**

White can win after 46 . . . Kd8 47 Be2 (47 Be6!? Bd3 + 48 Ke1) 47 . . . Bd4 48 Ra6; or 46 . . . Kf8 47 Ra8 + Kg7 (47 . . . Be8 48 Bd3 Bd4 49 Bg6 e2 + 50 Ke1 Bf2 + 51 Kd2) 48 Ra7 + Kh6? 49 Nxe3! bxc4 50 Ng4 + Kh5 51 Nxf6 + Kh4? 52 Ra8 g4 53 f4.

47 Ra8 +	**Bd8**

White is definitely in the lead after 47 . . . Kd7 48 Ra7 + Kc8 49 Ra6! bxc4 50 Rxf6 Bd3 + 51 Ke1 cxb3? 52 Rc6 + Kb7 53 Rxc3 Bc2 54 Rc4.

48 Nxe3	**bxc4**
49 Nxc4	**g4**

Kasparov plays for a few last tricks, but careful play by White liquidates to a draw.

50 Kg2

Black creates complications after 50 fxg4 Bd3+ 51 Ke1 Ke7.

Not 50 Ne5? gxf3 51 Nxg6 (51 Nxf3 Be4 with an edge for Black) 51 . . . Nd1! 52 Nh4 Ne3+ and Black is ahead. (MR)

50 . . .	**Ne2**
51 Ne5	**gxf3+**
52 Kxf3	**g2**
53 Rxd8+	**Draw**

After 53 Kxg2?! Be4+ 54 Kf2 Bxa8 55 Kxe2 Black can play for a while.

In Game 4, rather than risk Kasparov's prepared analysis Karpov chose a relatively unexplored possibility on move 19 after fifty-three minutes' thought. According to de Firmian, "The game instantly became a wilderness of complications." (European)

Karpov emerged with a winning advantage, but Kasparov's continuing pressure and the relentless clock gave him a last-minute reprieve when Karpov blundered into a draw by perpetual check just before time control.

Whispers began to circulate among Kasparov supporters that he was underestimating Karpov and flirting with disaster by pressing too recklessly for a crushing victory.

Despite the rumbles, however, he emerged from Game 4 with a 2.5–1.5 lead.

Match 5, Game 4
October 17, 1990
Ruy Lopez

White: Garry Kasparov *Black: Anatoly Karpov*

Annotated by GM Michael Rohde and GM Semion Palatnik

1 e4

Karpov arrived first on stage, made his move, and waited three minutes for Kasparov.

1 ...	e5
2 Nf3	Nc6
3 Bb5	a6
4 Ba4	Nf6
5 0–0	Be7
6 Re1	b5
7 Bb3	d6
8 c3	0–0
9 h3	Bb7

Karpov again heads for the Zaitsev Variation.

10 d4	Re8
11 Nbd2	Bf8
12 a4	h6
13 Bc2	exd4
14 cxd4	Nb4
15 Bb1	c5

This is the first deviation from Game 2. Karpov tried this move twice in Match 3, losing both games. (MR)

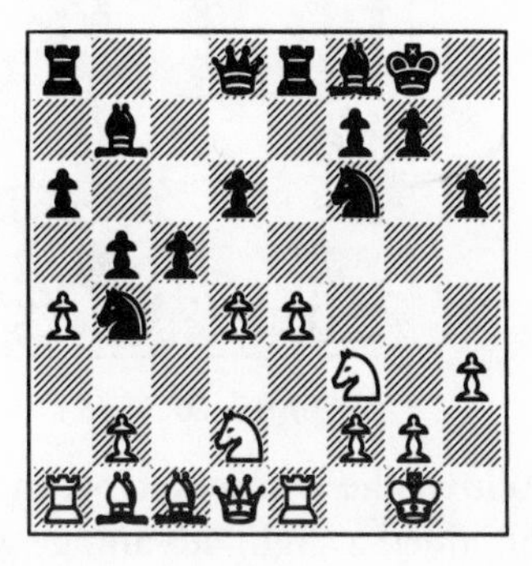

After 15 ... c5

16 d5	**Nd7**
17 Ra3	**f5**

In one of the analysis rooms, GM Arthur Bisguier said, "Black's game is a little loose, but all of his pieces are very active."

"Good for White?" asked a spectator.

"*Very* good?" answered Bisguier. "I doubt it."

18 exf5	**Nf6**
19 Ne4	**Bxd5**

Karpov thought nearly an hour before playing this move, dismissed as dubious by IM Alexander Ivanov in his notes to de Firmian–Ivanov in *Informant 49*. Ivanov gave the line 20 Nxf6 + Qxf6 21 Bd2, with an attack brewing for White. He actually played 19 . . . Nbxd5. (MR)

20 Nxf6 +

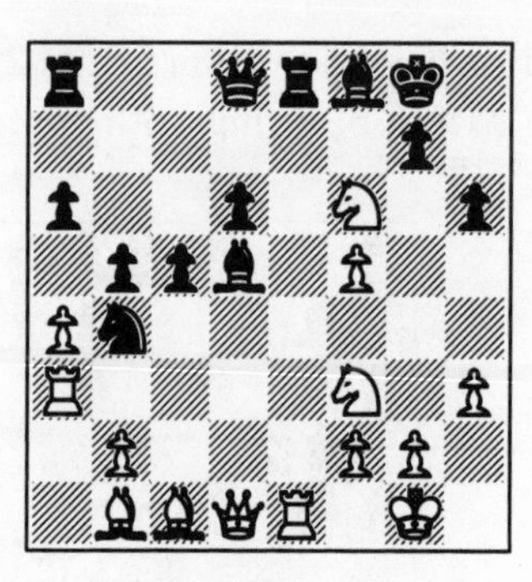

After 20 Nxf6+

Kasparov follows the Ivanov recipe. In Horvath–Zobisch 1988, White obtained a slight advantage with 20 Rae3 Bxe4 21 Bxe4 d5 22 Bb1 Rxe3 23 Rxe3 d4 24 Re6 d3 25 Ne5 c4 26 Qf3 Rc8 27 Qg3 (Balatonberenyi). (MR)

20 . . . Qxf6

Former World Champion Boris Spassky preferred Kasparov's position here.

21 Bd2

Black is fine after 21 Rae3 Bf7. (SP)

21 . . . Qxb2!

The trap has been sprung. (MR)

22 Bxb4

GMs Dlugy, Palatnik, and Boris Gulko preferred 22 Rae3.

After the text, Shamkovich and Suetin were busy exploring 22 . . . Bxf3 23 Rxf3 Qxb4 24 Re6.

As usual, Deep Thought could find no compensation for White's pawn.

22 . . . Bf7!!

The point. Black avoids trading the light-squared bishops and regains the piece with an advantage. (MR)

23 Re6!?

Typically, Kasparov comes up with an amazing concept at the critical juncture. The rook bottles Black up, since if Black captures, he will have problems on the b1–h7 diagonal. A safer course for White is 23 axb5 Qxb4 24 Rxa6 Qxb5 25 Rxa8 Rxa8 26 Be4, etc. (MR)

There was stunned silence in the press room. Deep Thought gave Black slightly more than a pawn lead: 23 . . . Bxe6 24 fxe6 Qxb4 25 Qd3 Rxe6 26 axb5 Rae8 27 bxa6 c4 28 Qh7+ Kf7 29 Qf5+ Ke7 30 Nd4 Re1+.

23 . . . Qxb4

Not 23 . . . cxb4? 24 Rb3 Qa1 25 Nd4! bxa4 26 Nc2. (MR)

24 Rb3

Less committal, according to the press bulletin, is 24 Rae3 d5 25 Ba2 (25 Rxe8 Rxe8 26 Rxe8 Bxe8 27 Qxd5+ Bf7) 25 . . . c4 26 Nd4.

24 . . . Qxa4?

A weak move played quickly. After the correct 24 . . . Qc4, Black threatens to open a queenside file with 25 . . . bxa4, and after 25 Bd3 Qd5, White is in bad shape. (MR)

25 Bc2

Korchnoi thought White was better at this point; Najdorf uncharacteristically declined comment; and even Dzindzichashvili, always willing to throw out an opinion, was undecided.

25 . . .	Rad8
26 Rbe3	Qb4

The queen maintains an active post. If now 27 Qe2 Qc4 28 Rxe8 Qxe2 29 Rxf8+ Kxf8, Black stands well. (MR)

27 g3

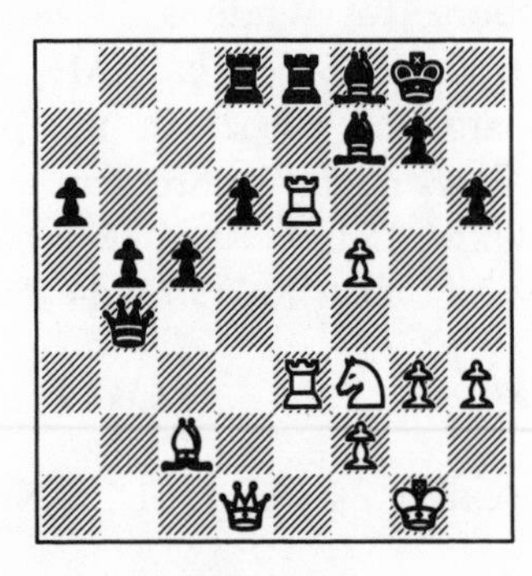

After 27 g3

Kristensen noted an eerie reluctance on the part of commentators to side against Kasparov: "They seem slow to realize or admit that Karpov is better."

27 . . . a5

GMs Christiansen and Korchnoi suggested a promising line for Black: 27 . . . d5 28 Ne5 d4 29 Rb3 Bxe6! 30 Rxb4 Bxf5! 31 Bxf5 Rxe5. (European)

In *Chess Life,* Tisdall debated Christiansen and Korchnoi's suggestion, concluding that White may "stay afloat" after 27 . . . d5 28 Rxe8!? Rxe8 29 Rxe8 Bxe8 30 Qxd5+ Bf7 31 Qa8, "with ideas like Ne5-d7 and Be4-d5." "Black must be better," he concludes, "but perhaps not winning."

Karpov appeared on the monitors to be smiling to himself; Kasparov looked worried.

28 Nh4	**d5**

Now that the knight cannot go to e5, Black finally advances the d-pawn, threatening . . . d4-d3. (MR)

Deep Thought recommended 29 Qe2, giving White a 1/100th of a pawn edge: 29 Qe2 Qc4 30 Rxe8 Qxe2 31 Rxf8 + Kxf8 32 Rxe2.

29 Qe2	**Qc4**
30 Bd3	**Qc1 +**
31 Kg2	**c4**
32 Bc2	**Bxe6**
33 Rxe6	

Black answers 33 fxe6 with 33 . . . d4. (MR)

33 . . .	**Rxe6**
34 Qxe6 +	

Or 34 fxe6 Qg5. (MR)

34 . . .	**Kh8**
35 Ng6 +	**Kh7**
36 Qe2!	

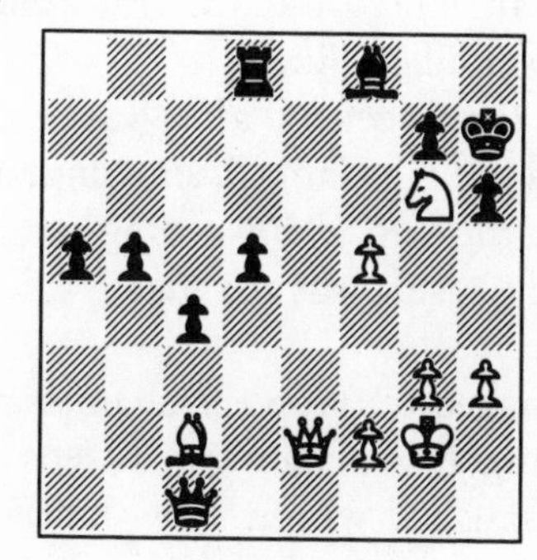

After 36 Qe2

Both 36 Ne5 Rd6 and 36 Nxf8+ Rxf8 37 Qg6+ Kg8 38 Qe6+ Kh8 lose. (MR)

36 . . . Qg5!

Not 36 . . . d4 37 Be4?, but Palatnik though White could draw after 37 f6! d3 38 Qe4 gxf6.

37 f6 Qxf6
38 Nxf8+ Kg8
39 Ng6 Qf7?

In time pressure, Karpov threatens 40 . . . Re8 but allows perpetual check. Black wins after 39 . . . d4 40 Bf5 Qc6+ (Najdorf) and 41 . . . Re8; or 40 Be4 d3.

40 Ne7+ Kf8

Kasparov sealed. Karpov offered a draw just after midnight, and Kasparov accepted at 10:44 the next morning.

41 Ng6+ Draw

The next game was delayed by an unexpected Kasparov timeout, later attributed by NM Eric Schiller to the world champion's unspecified illness.

In spite of a long weekend after Kasparov's timeout, both players seemed tired in Game 5, showing signs of the tension resulting from the knock-down-drag-out fights of the first four games. The result was the match's first relatively quiet draw.

Karpov managed to wrap the champion in the coils of a drawish opening by exchanging queens early, but Kasparov was not satisfied with a slow dance to the grave and shook himself free with 21 . . . f5, creating some imbalance at the end.

Kasparov entered Game 6 with a 3–2 lead.

Match 5, Game 5
October 22, 1990
King's Indian Defense

White: Anatoly Karpov ***Black: Garry Kasparov***

Annotated by GM Michael Rohde

1	d4	Nf6
2	c4	g6
3	Nc3	Bg7
4	e4	d6
5	Nf3	0–0
6	Be2	e5
7	Be3	Na6

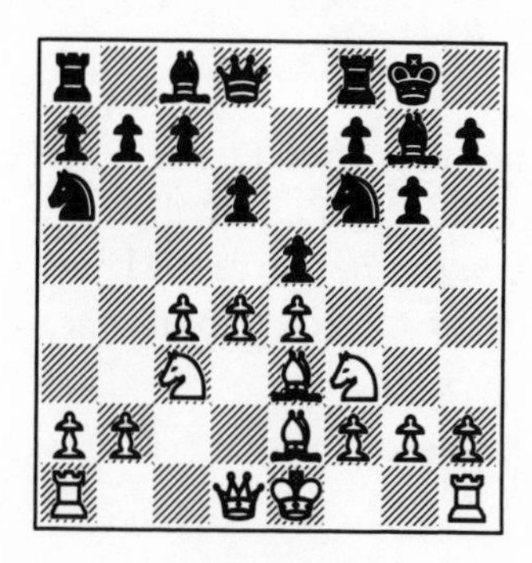

After 7 ... Na6

Kasparov varies from the dubious 7 . . . Qe7 of Game 3. In Shirov–Bonsch, Stockholm 1989, Black gained the initiative after 7 . . . Na6 8 dxe5 dxe5 9 Nd2 c6 10 c5 Qe7 11 Bxa6 bxa6. (MR)

8 0–0 c6

Previously played were 8 . . . Ng4 9 Bg5 Qe8 (Novikov–Glek, Odessa 1989; and Browne–Chekhov, Palma 1989) and 8 . . . Qe8 9 dxe5 Ng4!? (Garcia-Palermo–Ermolinski, Forli 1989). (MR)

9 dxe5

Karpov plays for a slight endgame advantage. Dlugy suggested that 9 d5 Ng4 10 Bg5 f6 11 Bd2 Nh6 was unclear, and the press bulletin cited 9 Qc2 as possible. (MR)

"Typical Karpov," said GM Ljubo Ljubojevic. "Dead even."

9 . . . dxe5
10 Qxd8 Rxd8
11 Rfd1

White has nothing after 11 Nxe5!? Nxe4 12 Nxe4 Bxe5 13 Bg5 (Dlugy) 13 . . . Re8. (MR)

Tisdall, in *Chess Life*, gives GM Joel Lautier's 11 h3! as White's surest way to a clear plus.

11 . . . Re8
12 h3

Dlugy's 12 c5 Ng4 13 Bxa6 Nxe3 14 fxe3 bxa6 15 Rd6 seems antipositional. (MR)

GM Pal Benko thought White was slightly better here.

12 ...	Bf8
13 Nd2	

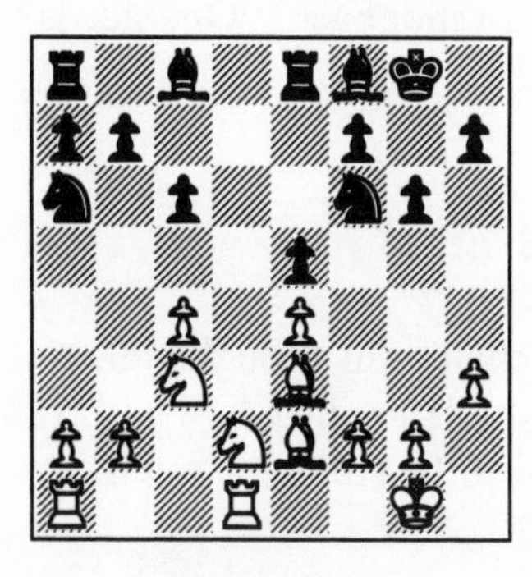

After 13 Nd2

Ljubojevic and Shamkovich began a running argument, Shamkovich defending Black, Ljubo White. At first, Ljubojevic seemed to be on the short end of the discussion, but eventually gained enough ground to sway spectators in his favor. Dzindzichashvili thought the position was dead even.

13 ...	b6
14 a3	Nc5

At this point Shamkovich decided that 13 ... b6 may have been too slow, and he conceded White a slight edge.

15 b4	Ne6
16 Nb3	Ba6

Now the position is equal. Good for White is 16 ... c5 17 Nd5. (MR)

GM Valery Salov, visiting New York, offered the unclear variation 16 ... a5!? 17 bxa5 bxa5 18 Na4 Nxe4 19 Bf3 f5 20 Bxe4 fxe4 21 Nbc5.

In Dzindzichashvili's analysis room, a spectator asked, "Do you think both sides are equal?"

"No," Roman shot back. "One side is equal, the other has an advantage."

17 f3	Nh5
18 Bf2	

Dzindzichashvili still thought the position was a draw. Both he and Rohde predicted 18 . . . f5. At times, Kasparov almost seemed to be stifling a yawn.

18 . . .	Red8
19 Bf1	Nhf4

Trying to drum up something from nothing. (MR)

Best, according to the press bulletin, is 19 . . . Bg7. Dlugy gave White a solid edge after 19 . . . Rxd1 20 Rxd1 Rd8 21 Rxd8 Nxd8 22 c5! Bxf1 23 cxb6! Ba6 24 bxa7 Bb7 25 Na5 Ba8 26 Na4.

20 g3	Nh5
21 Kg2	f5

Black tries to create a target at e4. (MR)

22 Rab1	Rac8
23 Rxd8	Rxd8
24 Rd1	

"A draw offer," announced Dzindzichashvili.

24 . . .	Rxd1
25 Nxd1	fxe4

26	**fxe4**	**c5**
27	**bxc5**	

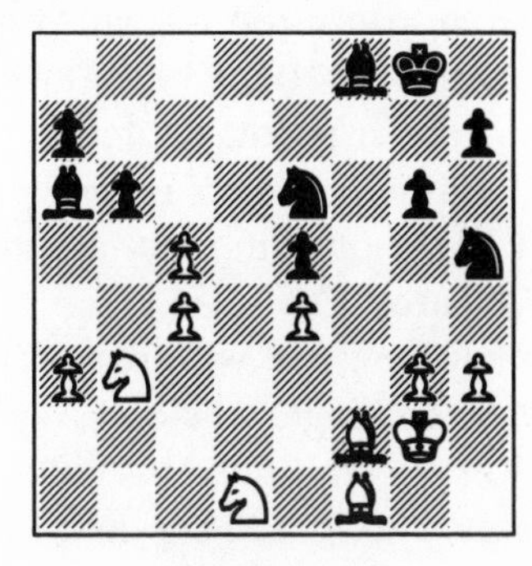

After 27 bxc5

According to de Firmian, "Play remains interesting after 27 b5 Bb7 28 Nc3 Nd4, but then Black is probably better." (European)

27	. . .	**Nxc5**
28	**Nxc5**	**Bxc5**
29	**Bxc5**	**bxc5**
30	**Nc3**	**Nf6**
31	**Kf3**	**Bb7**
32	**Bd3**	**Kf8**

Tisdall offered a prayer for time pressure to liven things up.

33	**h4**	**h6**
34	**Bc2**	**Ke7**
35	**Ba4**	**a6**
36	**Ke3**	**Draw**

On Wednesday, October 24, Karpov seemed on the verge of taming Kasparov for the first time and knotting the match at 3–3 after six games. But Kasparov once again found a dynamic pawn sacrifice (move 25) to throw the game into the sort of creative confusion on which he thrives. Karpov slipped into time trouble trying to deal with the labyrinth of complications, and Kasparov tightened the screws. In the final minutes, with both players in time pressure, the world champion let Karpov off the hook, and the score remained plus-one for Kasparov (3.5–2.5).

Both camps left the game with reason for concern. Kasparov seemed to be coming ever closer to paying for his reckless style, and Karpov continued his bouts against the clock. The question was who would slip first.

Match 5, Game 6
October 24, 1990
Ruy Lopez

White: Garry Kasparov *Black: Anatoly Karpov*

Annotated by GM Michael Rohde

1	e4	e5
2	Nf3	Nc6
3	Bb5	a6
4	Ba4	Nf6
5	0–0	Be7
6	Re1	b5
7	Bb3	d6
8	c3	0–0
9	h3	Nd7

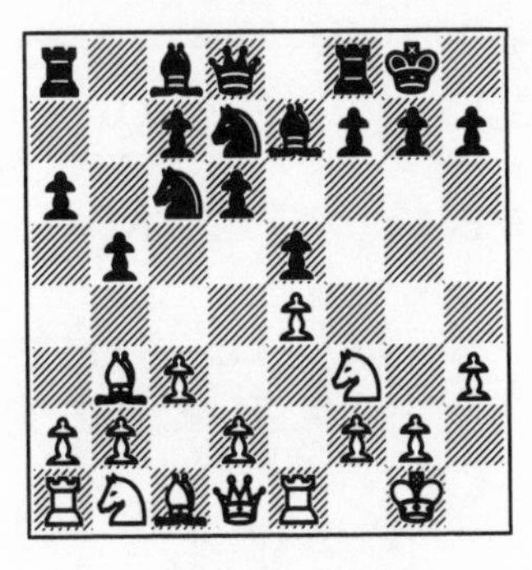

After 9 ... Nd7

Karpov gives up the Zaitsev and adopts the solid but passive Ragozin variation in its place. (MR)

For the first time since Game 2, Karpov seemed fairly relaxed and confident.

10 d4	**Bf6**
11 a4	**Bb7**

Kasparov is on record as preferring 11 . . . Rb8 12 axb5 axb5 13 Be3 Ne7 14 d5 g6 (14 . . . Nc5 15 Bc2 c6 16 b4 Na6 17 dxc6 Nxc6, Nunn–Karpov, Rotterdam 1989, lost by Karpov) 15 Na3 Bg7 16 Qe2 Nf6 17 Nd2 Bd7 18 Nc2 c6 19 dxc6 Nxc6 20 Bg5, with a slight plus for White (Arnasson–Hecht, Thessaloniki 1984). An alternative is 14 Nbd2 (Georgiev–Karpov, Reggio Emilia 1989), and White got a quick draw after 14 Ng5 h6 15 Bxf7+ in Sax–Karpov, Skelleftea 1989. (PB)

12 axb5

Probably more accurate is 12 d5 first; then after 12 . . . Na5 13 Bc2 Nc4 14 b3 Ncb6 White has the option of a5. (MR)

12 . . .	axb5
13 Rxa8	Qxa8
14 d5	Na5
15 Bc2	Nc4

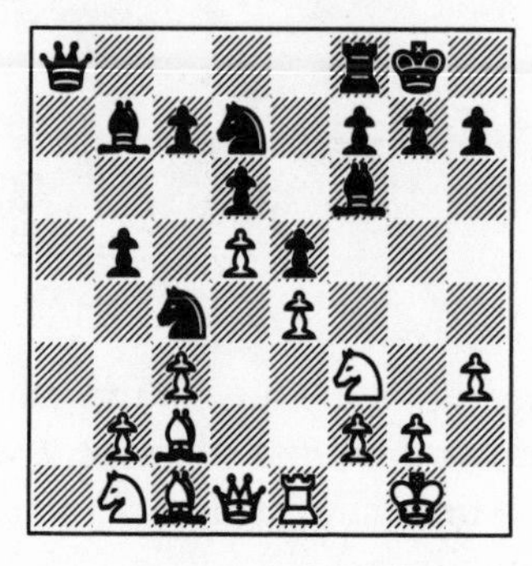

After 15 ... Nc4

16 b3	Ncb6
17 Na3	Ba6

Karpov has obtained dynamic equality. He will break White's center with 18 . . . c6, and his bishop at a6 is no weaker than White's knight at a3.

An alternative is the immediate 17 . . . c6!?. (MR)

18 Nh2

Another inventive Kasparov move. The knight will annoy Black on the kingside. (MR)

18 . . . c6

Deep Thought liked 18 . . . Bd8, giving Black a quarter-pawn advantage. Shamkovich gave White a very clear plus here. Byrne said, "I'm pretty sure Black is *not* ahead. This is a typical Ruy—someone has to *do* something before we can figure a leader."

19 dxc6	**Qxc6**
20 Bd2	**Be7**
21 Ng4	**Ra8**

Missing a good chance to gain space with 21 . . . f5! 22 exf5 Bb7, when Black is ready to play . . . d5 (23 Ne3 d5). (MR)

22 Ne3	**Nf6**
23 Nf5	**Bf8**
24 Bg5	**Nbd7**

More active is 24 . . . d5, with a good position. (MR)
Karpov's team gives 24 . . . d5 25 exd5 Nbxd5 26 Nxb5 Bxb5 27 c4. (RH)

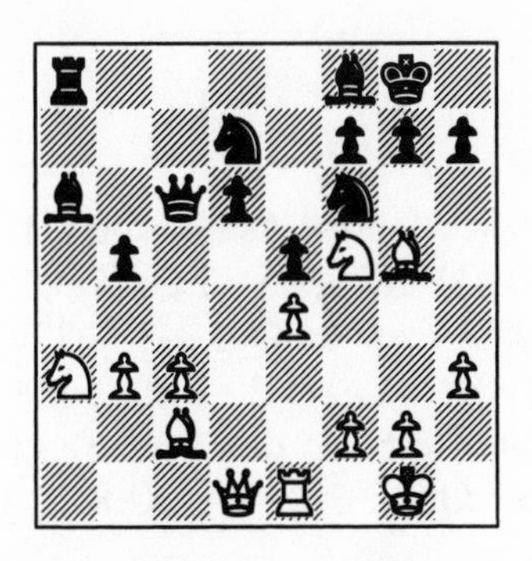

After 24 ... Nbd7

25 c4!

A brilliant pawn sacrifice designed to liquidate the entire queenside and eliminate Black's hopes for activity. (MR)

25 . . . bxc4
26 bxc4 Bxc4?!

An uncharacteristically incautious move by Karpov. Instead, he should test the waters with 26 . . . h6 (also endorsed by Karpov later with an "!"). (MR)

27 Nxc4 Qxc4
28 Bb3 Qc3

"I'm sure White has a win," said Wolff; "I just can't find it."

29 Kh2!

White leaves the first rank so that he can play Re3 without worrying about . . . Qa1, forcing the exchange of queens. Perhaps Karpov should have played 28 . . . Qb4. (MR)

29 . . . h6

Lautier and NM Maurice Ashley suggested 29 . . . g6 30 Re3 Qa1 31 Qd2 (31 Qf3 gxf5 32 Qxf5 Bg7 33 Rg3 Kf8 34 Bxf6 Nxf6 35 Rxg7 Kxg7 36 Qg5 + Kf8 37 Qxf6 Qa7, with equality [Wolff]) 31 . . . gxf5 32 Bxf6 Nxf6? (32 . . . f4 33 Re1 is unclear, according to de Firmian) 33 Rg3 + Bg7 34 Qg5 Ne8 35 Qe7 Qa7 36 Bxf7 + Kh8 37 Qf8 + Bxf8 38 Rg8 mate. (European)

"Karpov must be happy," said Valvo.

30 Bxf6 Nxf6
31 Re3 Qc7

Necessary to prepare the defense of f7 or f6. (MR)

32 Rf3

Wolff said Black had few winning chances here: "All of White's pieces are better."

GM Pal Benko declared the position a draw.

32 . . . Kh7

Forced, although Ljubojevic suggested 32 . . . Qd8 33 Rg3 Kh8 34 Bxf7 Nxe4. (MR)

33 Ne3!

Now White threatens 34 Rxf6. (MR)

33 . . . Qe7

Good for White is 33 . . . Re8 34 Rxf6 gxf6 35 Qh5. (European)

34 Nd5	**Nxd5**
35 Bxd5	**Ra7**

Cold-blooded defense! The endgame is drawn after 36 Rxf7 Qxf7 37 Bxf7 Rxf7. (MR)

36 Qb3	**f6**
37 Qb8	**g6**

Lautier said White was winning; Deep Thought gave two-tenths of a pawn to White.

38 Rc3??

After 38 Rc3

This obvious move throws away the win that is White's after 38 g4!!. The idea is to stop Black's expansionary 38 . . . h5, leaving him with no good defense against Rc3-c8, leading—after . . . Bg7—to Rh8+ and Qg8 mate. For example, 38 . . . Rd7 39 Rc3 Rd8 40 Qb6 Bg7 41 Rc7 Rd7 42 Rc8, etc. If Black tries . . . h5, then after the trade on h5 the f5-square is fatally weak. (MR)

38 . . .	**h5**
39 g4	

Black defends easily after 39 Rc8 Bg7 40 Rh8+ Bxh8 41 Qg8+ Kh6 42 Qxh8+ Qh7. (European)

39 . . .	**Kh6!**
40 gxh5	**Kxh5!**
41 Rc8	**Bg7**

Kasparov sealed after thirty minutes' thought.

42 Re8	**Draw**

Anticipating, perhaps, 42 . . . Qc7 43 Qxc7 Rxc7 44 Rd8. Chief Arbiter Gert Gijssen received Kasparov's draw offer at 11:00 A.M. the Thursday morning. Two hours later Karpov accepted.

ADJOURNMENT ANALYSIS

by GM Ron Henley

Kasparov selected the safest method to force a draw, by regaining the d-pawn in the ending. Our analysis, below, shows that White had compensation for the pawn, but no more.

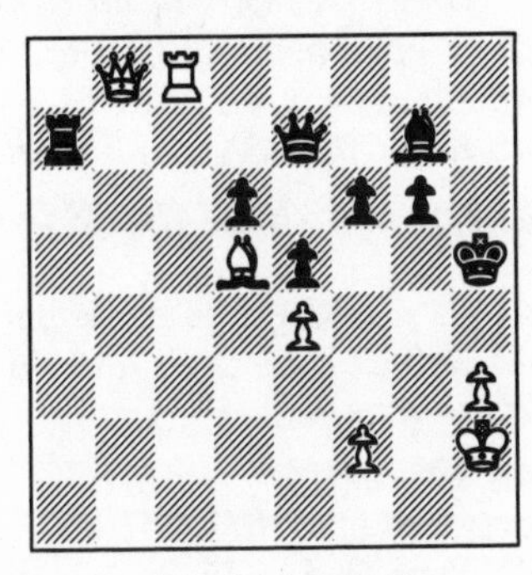

After 41 ... Bg7

Kasparov sealed **42 Re8**. Karpov's team also analyzed the following possibilities:

A *42 Rc3 f5 43 h4*

A1 *43 . . . Kh6 44 Rg3 (44 exf5 e4) 44 . . . f4 45 Rg4 Rd7, drawn;*

A2 *43 . . . Kxh4? 44 Rh3+ (44 Rg3 f4 45 Rxg6 Kh5 46 Qxd6, drawn) 44 . . . Kg5 45 Rg3+ Kf6 46 Qg8 fxe4 47 Qh7 g5 48 Qxe4 Qe8 49 Qe3 Qh5+ 50 Rh3 Qd1 51 Rf3+, with a win for White.*

B *42 Be6 Qxe6 (42 . . . Qb7! draws) 43 Qxa7 Qxc8 44 Qxg7*

B1 *44 . . . Kg5? 45 h4+ Kf4 (45 . . . Kxh4?? 46 Qh6+ Kg4 47 Qh3+, and White wins; or 45 . . . Kg4 46 Qxf6 Qc2 47 Qg5+ Kf3 48 Qe3+ Kg4 49 Qg3+ Kh5 50 Qg5+ mate) 46 Qxg6;*

B2 *44 . . . Qc2 45 Qh8+ Kg5 46 h4+ Kg4 (46 . . .*

Kf4 47 Qxf6+ Kg4 48 Qg5+ Kf3 49 Qe3+ Kg4 50 Qg3+ Kh5 51 Qg5+ mate) 47 Qxf6 Qd2! (47 . . . Qxe4?? 48 f3+ Qxf3 49 Qg5+ mate; or 47 . . . Qd3 48 f3+ Qxf3 49 Qg5+ mate) 48 Kg2 Qf4, drawn;

B3 *44 . . . f5 45 h4 fxe4 46 Qh7+ Kg4 47 h5 g5 (47 . . . Qf5 48 Qxg6+ Qg5; not 47 . . . gxh5?? 48 Qg6+)*

C *42 Qb6 f5 43 Qe3 f4 44 Qf3+ Kh6 45 Rc1 (45 Qg4 Qg5, drawn) 45 . . . Rc7 46 Rg1 Rc2? (either 46 . . . Qh4 or 46 . . . Bf8 draws) 47 Qg4 Rxf2+ 48 Kh1 Qf6 (48 . . . g5 49 h4) 49 Bf7! g5*

D *42 Rc1 f5 43 Rg1 (43 Qg8 Qh4 44 Qh7+ Bh6 45 Qxa7 Qf4+, drawn) 43 . . . Ra3!, with the idea of 44 . . . Rxh3+ and perpetual check (43 . . . f4? 44 Bc6 Qc7 45 Qg8! Kh6 46 Be8 g5 47 h4 and White wins)*

D1 *44 exf5 e4 (44 . . . Rxh3+ 45 Kxh3 Qh4+ 46 Kg2 Qg4+ 47 Kf1 Qd1+ 48 Kg2 Qg4+, drawn) 45 Rxg6 Qe5+ 46 Rg3 Qxf5! (46 . . . Rxg3? 47 fxg3 Qxd5 48 Qe8+ Kg5 49 Qg6+ mate)*

D1a *47 Rxa3 Qxf2+ 48 Kh1 Qf1+ 49 Kh2 Be5+ 50 Rg3 Bxg3+! 51 Kxg3 Qd3+ 52 Kg2 (52 Kf4 Qf3+ mate) 52 . . . Qxd5;*

D1b *47 f3 Be5 48 Qe8+ Kh6 49 f4 Rxg3, and Black wins;*

D1c *47 Qxd6 Qxf2+ 48 Rg2 Rxh3+ 49 Kxh3 Qh4+ mate;*

D1d *47 Rxg7 Qxh3+ 48 Kg1 Ra1+, and Black wins;*

D1e *47 Qe8+ Kh6 48 Qxe4 Qxf2+ 49 Qg2 (49 Rg2 Be5+ 50 Qxe5 Qxg2+, and Black wins) 49 . . . Qxg3+ 50 Qxg3 Be5, and Black wins;*

D2 *44 Qb1 Qh4 45 Qd1+ Kh6 46 Qc1+ Qf4+, drawn;*

D3 *44 Bb3*

D3a *44 . . . Qh4 45 Rg3 (with the idea Bd1+) 45 . . . Qf4 46 Qe8? (with the idea 47 Qxg6+) 46 . . .*

Qxf2+ 47 Rg2 Qf4+ 48 Rg3 (48 Kh1 Ra1+) Qxg3+! 49 Kxg3 Rxb3+ 50 Kg2 fxe4 51 Qe6 Rb2+ 52 Kg3 Kh6;

D3b *44 . . . d5!? 45 exd5 (45 Bxd5 Rxh3+ 46 Kxh3 Qh4+ 47 Kg2 Qg4+ 48 Kf1 Qd1+, drawn) 45 . . . e4;*

D4 *44 Qb4 Rf3 45 exf5 Rxf2+ 46 Kh1 Rf4 (46 . . . Qh4 47 Qxh4+ Kxh4 48 Rxg6 Bf8 49 f6 Kxh3 50 Be6+ Kh4 51 f7) 47 Bf3+ Kh6 48 Rxg6+ Kh7 49 Qb3 e4 50 Bg4 (50 f6 Rxf6, drawn) 50 . . . e3 51 Qd3 Qb7+ 52 Kh2 Qb2+ 53 Be2 Rf2+ 54 Rg2 Be5+*

D4a *55 Kh1? Qc1+ 56 Rg1 (56 Qd1 Qc6 57 Bf1 e2, and Black wins) 56 . . . Rh2+ mate;*

D4b *55 Kg1 Qc1+ 56 Bf1 (56 Qd1 draws) 56 . . . e2 (56 . . . Rxg2+ 57 Kxg2 Qd2+, drawn) 57 Rxf2 e1Q 58 f6+ Kh6 59 f7 Qg5+ 60 Rg2 Qee3+ 61 Kh1! Qxd3 62 f8Q+ Bg7 63 Rxg5 Bxf8 64 Bxd3 Kxg5, drawn.*

Now we analyze the move Kasparov actually sealed: **42 Re8:**

42 . . . Qd7 43 Rd8

Or 43 Bc6 Qxc6 44 Qxa7, and now:

A) *44 . . . Qxe8 45 Qxg7 f5 46 f3! Qd8! (46 . . . fxe4 47 h4 exf3 48 Kg3, and White wins; or 46 . . . Qe6 47 h4 fxe4 48 Kg3, White wins) 47 Qh7+ Kg5 48 Kg3 f4+ 49 Kg2 Kf6 50 Qh4+ g5 51 Qh6+, drawn;*

B) *44 . . . Qxe4 45 Qxg7 Qf4+ 46 Kg2 Qg5+ 47 Kf1 Qc1+ 48 Ke2 Qc2+ 49 Kf3*

B1) *49 . . . Qc6+?? 50 Kg3 Qxe8 (50 . . . Qc3+ 51 Kh2, and White wins) 51 Qh7+ Kg5 52 Qh4+ Kf5 53 Qg4+ mate;*

B2) *49 . . . Qf5+! 50 Kg3 Qg5+ 51 Kf3 Qf5+ 52 Ke3 Qf4+ 53 Kd3 Qd4+, drawn.*

43 . . . Qc7 44 Qxc7 Rxc7 45 Rxd6 Draw

7

NEW YORK CITY, GAMES 7 THROUGH 12

By Game 7, many commentators were beginning to wonder out loud about Kasparov's reckless disregard for his own safety against a seasoned challenger noted for his defensive prowess. Even the world champion's staunchest supporters were concerned that he was pushing too hard, "playing Russian roulette with a loaded gun." (de Firmian, European)

On move 27, the hammer fell on a live chamber. Karpov evened the match after what may have been the grossest blunder of Kasparov's career.

Match 5, Game 7
October 26, 1990
King's Indian Defense

White: Anatoly Karpov — *Black: Garry Kasparov*

Annotated by GM Michael Rohde

	White	Black
1	d4	Nf6
2	c4	g6

3 Nc3 Bg7
4 e4 d6
5 Nf3 0-0
6 Be2 e5
7 Be3 Na6

Kasparov sticks with the Game 5 continuation.

8 0-0 Ng4

In Game 5, Kasparov had no problems after 8 . . . c6 9 dxe5 dxe5. (MR)

9 Bg5 f6

Also possible is 9 . . . Qe8, leaving the knight on a6 to protect c7 in the event of 10 Nd5. (MR)

10 Bc1 Kh8

According to de Firmian, this is a novelty: "Previously played was 10 . . . Qe8 11 h3 Nh6 12 dxe5 dxe5 13 b3 Be6 14 Ba3 Rf7 15 Qc2 Bf8 16 Bxf8 Qxf8 17 a3 Rd7 18 Rfd1 Rxd1 19 Nxd1 Nf7 (Cebalo–Sokolov, Yugoslavia 1989), with an equal game." (European)

11 h3 Nh6
12 dxe5 fxe5?!

More natural is 12 . . . dxe5, with a resilient formation for Black. With the text, Black accepts a positional disadvantage—White pressure on the d-file—in return for vague hopes of kingside counterplay. (MR)

Tal, saying 12 . . . fxe5 "is simply wrong," gave Black the edge after 12 . . . dxe5!. (PB)

In a commentary room, Dzindzichashvili announced, "Garry knows this is worse, but not much worse. The biggest surprise of the match."

Watching the game by remote from the Hotel Regency, Kasparov's team was elated: "This is the kind of position we like to play."

13 Be3	**Nf7**
14 Qd2	**Nc5**

Seirawan and Dzindzichashvili argued over which side had the easier game, with Seirawan defending Black's position.

15 Ng5!

After 15 Ng5

This fine move exchanges Black's useful defensive knight on f7 for the static white steed on f3. Karpov is not tempted by 15 Bxc5 dxc5 16 Qe3 (Tal and Geller) b6 17 Rad1 Bd7, when Black follows up with . . . Qc8, . . . Be6, etc. (MR)

15 . . .	**Nxg5**
16 Bxg5	**Bf6**
17 Be3	

Spurning the tacit draw offer 17 Bh6 Bg7 18 Bg5 Bf6 19 Bh6. (MR)

17 . . . Ne6

Byrne declared the game even.

18 Bg4 h5

In the press room, Alburt chose this moment to declare, "Kasparov is toying with Karpov the way I would play with an opponent rated two hundred points below me in an open tournament."

19 Bxe6 Bxe6
20 Nd5

Shamkovich thought, at the time, that this was premature.

20 . . . Bh4?!

A truly bizarre bishop placement. If White now tries 21 Bxa7?! threatening 22 Qh6+, Black has 21 . . . Bxd5, when White is forced to take perpetual check with 22 Qh6+ to avoid losing a piece. (MR)

21 Rac1

Another try is 21 f4!? c6 22 fxe5 cxd5 23 cxd5 Bg8 24 e6, when the game is unclear. (MR)

21 . . . Kh7
22 Rc3 Rf7
23 b3 c6

24 Nb4	**Rd7**
25 Rcc1	

Karpov, giving up on the plan involving 25 Rd3, retreats to connect his rooks in preparation for f4. (MR)

25 . . .	**Bf6**
26 f4	**exf4**
27 Bxf4	**Qa5??**

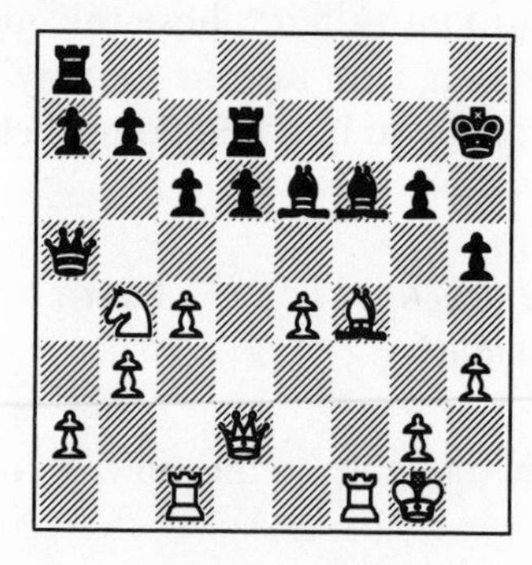

After 27 ... Qa5

The blunder of the match. Instead, Kasparov could have played the dynamic 27 . . . Qh8!. Everyone in the house saw White's next shot coming. (MR)

"Well, bust my bird!" exclaimed Byrne as soon as the move was played.

28 Nd5

Wolff criticized Karpov for wasting thirteen minutes on this move.

28 . . .	**Qc5 +**

Not 28 . . . Qxd2? 29 Nxf6 +. (MR)

29 Kh1!

Black has better drawing chances after 29 Be3 Bg5 30 Nf6+ Kh6! 31 Bxc5 Bxd2 32 Rcd1 Rdd8!, so White tries to win a pawn after 32 Nxd7 Bxc1 33 Rxc1 Bxd7 34 Bxd6, with opposite-colored bishops as penalty. (MR)

29 ...	**Bxd5**
30 cxd5	**Qd4**

Good for White is 30 . . . Qb5 31 a4! Qxb3 32 dxc6 bxc6 33 e5!, so Black is forced into a hopeless pawn-down endgame. (MR)

31 dxc6	**bxc6**
32 Rxc6	**Re8**
33 Rc4	**Qxd2**
34 Bxd2	**Be5**
35 Be3	**Bg3**
36 Rf3	**h4**
37 Bf2	**Bxf2**

Dzindzichashvili gave 37 . . . Rde7 38 Bxg3 hxg3 39 Rxg3 Rxe4 40 Rxe4 Rxe4 41 Rg5, and White wins. (PB)

38 Rxf2	**Rde7**
39 Rf4	**g5**
40 Rf6	**Rxe4**
41 Rxe4	**Rxe4**
42 Rxd6	**Re7**
43 Ra6	**Kg7**

Karpov sealed his next move . . .

44 Kg1	**1-0**

Kasparov resigned without resumption.

With the score even and Kasparov's illusion of invincibility shattered, Karpov unveiled his own unexpected novelty on move 14 of Game 8. But the world champion consolidated and launched a roller-coaster kingside attack, and Karpov found himself with a delicate defense in time pressure.

Instead of putting Karpov away, Kasparov seemed seduced by the lure of Karpov's clock, playing hastily and inaccurately as the time control approached. Trying to increase the pressure, Kasparov blundered for the second game in a row, entering the adjournment a pawn down in a position he fully expected to lose.

But Kasparov's superhuman defense saved the half-point and kept the match level. Kasparov's supporters were relieved at having narrowly averted disaster; Karpov's were visibly encouraged by having missed Kasparov's scalp by only the narrowest of margins.

Match 5, Game 8
October 29, 1990
Ruy Lopez

White: Garry Kasparov ***Black: Anatoly Karpov***

Annotated by GM Michael Rohde and GM Semion Palatnik

1	e4	e5
2	Nf3	Nc6
3	Bb5	a6
4	Ba4	Nf6
5	0-0	Be7
6	Re1	b5
7	Bb3	d6

8	c3	0-0
9	h3	Nd7
10	d4	Bf6
11	a4	Bb7
12	Be3	Na5
13	Bc2	Nc4
14	Bc1	d5!

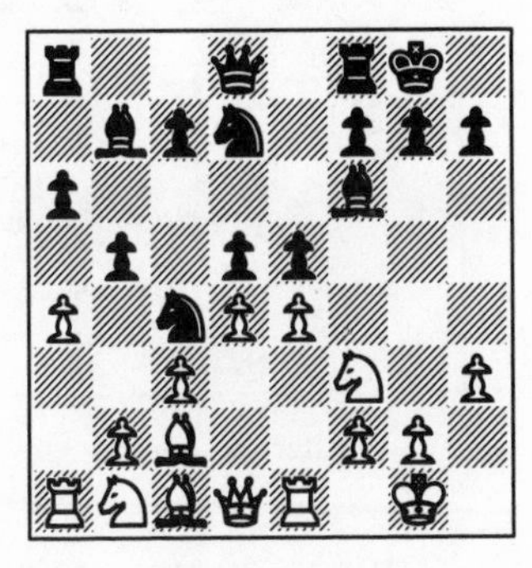

After 14 ... d5

This move elicited an audible gasp from the auditorium. Black takes advantage of White's temporary lag in development and gives the knight at c4 a good retreat square on d6. (MR)

15 dxe5

Black is at least equal after 15 exd5 Bxd5 16 b3 Bxf3 17 Qxf3 Nd6 or 15 b3? dxe4. (MR)

15	...	Ndxe5
16	Nxe5	Nxe5
17	axb5	axb5

White has a strong position after 17 . . . dxe4 18 Qxd8 Rfxd8 19 bxa6 Nd3 20 Bxd3 exd3 21 a7!, but 19 . . . Rxa6

20 Rxa6 Bxa6 21 Bxe4 Nd3 22 Bxd3 Bxd3 23 Nd2 is only slightly better for White. (SP)

18 Rxa8 Qxa8?

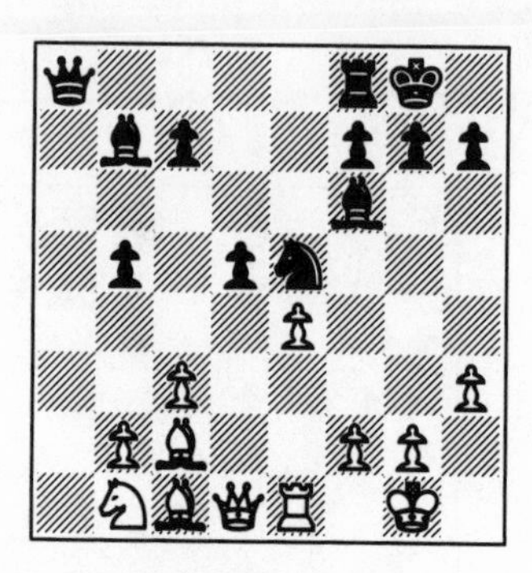

After 18 ... Qxa8

For the sake of temporary pressure on e4, Karpov seriously misplaces his queen. The obvious 18 . . . Bxa8 leads to equality; e.g., 19 f4 Nd7! 20 e5 Bh4 with a good game for Black after . . . Nc5 and . . . Ne4. (MR)

19 f4 Ng6

Black is now obliged to place his knight passively. Black loses after 19 . . . Nd7 20 e5 Bh4? 21 Qh5 (with the black queen on d8, this doesn't work). Black gets smashed after 19 . . . Nd7 20 e5 Be7 21 f5, so the text is forced. (MR)

20 e5 Bh4
21 Rf1 Be7

White answers 21 . . . d4 with 22 Qg4.

22 Nd2 Bc5 +

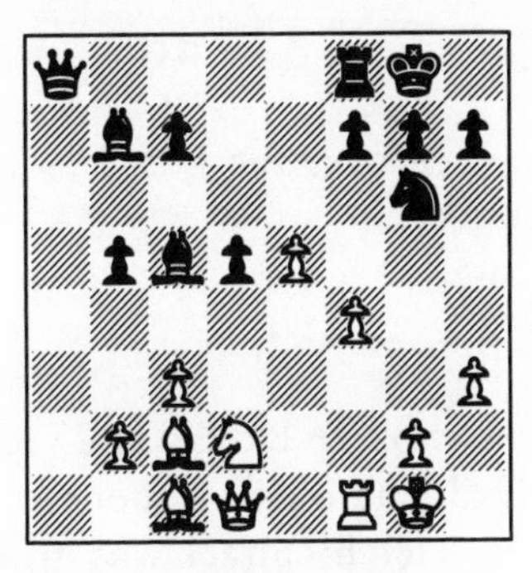

After 22 ... Bc5+

Not very impressive. Why use up a potentially valuable check? More logical is 22 . . . d4. (MR)

De Firmian (European) gives three continuations after 22 . . . d4:

A) 23 Qe2 dxc3 24 bxc3 Ba3, winning the queen after 25 f5? Bc5+ 26 Kh1 Nxe5 27 Qxe5? Bxg2+ 28 Kh2 Bd6;

B) 23 cxd4 Bxg2 24 Rf2 Nh4 25 f5 Bg5, with a good game for Black (26 Qg4 Bx2d 27 Qxh4 Bxc1 28 Rxg2 Rd8 [28 . . . Kh8? 29 Rxg7 Kxg7 30 f6+, followed by Qxh7 mate] 29 Rxg7+!? Kxg7 30 f6+ Kf8 31 Qxh7 Be3+ 32 Kh2 Bf4+ 33 Kg1, with equality [SP]);

C) 23 Nf3 dxc3 24 bxc3 Be4, with equality.

23 Kh2 **d4**

Not 23 . . . Be3 24 Nf3 Bxf4+ 25 Bxf4 Nxf4 26 Bxh7+! Kxh7 27 Ng5+, etc. (MR)

Tal here gave White a considerable edge, "possibly winning." Shamkovich thought White's position was "crushing." Meanwhile, Kasparov analyzed alone onstage.

24 Qe2!

Defending g2 and threatening Ne4. Black is fine after 24 Nb3 Bb6 25 cxd4 Bxg2 26 Rg1 Be4. (SP)

24 . . . dxc3

Kasparov leaned in over the board as if sensing a kill; Karpov sat impassively.

25 bxc3

Better is 25 Ne4! cxb2 26 Bxb2 Ba6 27 Ra1 b4 28 f5 Nf4 29 Qf3 Nd5 30 Qg3, and Black is about to be blown away. Apparently Kasparov felt his attack was strong enough without risking a pawn sacrifice. (MR)

25 . . . Rd8
26 Ne4

A mistake is 26 f5? Nxe5 27 Qxe5 Bd6. (SP)

Deep Thought recommended 26 e6 with a half-pawn advantage, which prompted de Firmian to remark, "This computer makes such strange moves."

26 . . . Ba3

The start of a desperate but brilliant defensive sequence. Having Kasparov's kingside pawns roll, Karpov wakes up in his own time pressure.

27 Bxa3 Bxe4!

Not 27 . . . Qa6 28 e6 fxe6 29 Ng5 Nf8 30 Bxh7+!. (MR)

28 Qxe4 Qxa3
29 f5 Ne7!

Black tries to set up a dark-square blockade. He has obvious problems after 29 . . . Nf8 30 e6. (MR)

30 Qh4	

Better is 30 Rf3, defending the c-pawn and joining the attack. (MR)

30 . . .	**f6**
31 Qg3?	

Much more active is 31 Rf3. Trouble is 31 exf6? Qd6+!. (MR)

31 . . .	**Kf8**
32 Kh1	

Better is 32 exf6 gxf6 33 Qxc7 Qd6+ 34 Qxd6. (SP)

32 . . .	**Qc5!**

This strong centralizing move equalizes. Kasparov, however, still pursues the attack. (MR)

33 exf6	**gxf6**
34 Bb3	**Nd5**
35 Qh4	**Kg7**
36 Rd1	**c6**
37 Rd4?	

White gets no compensation for the c-pawn. Necessary is 37 Rd3 Qe7 with equality. (MR)

37 . . .	**Qxc3**
38 Rg4+	**Kh8**
39 Bxd5	**Qa1+**
40 Kh2	**Qe5+**

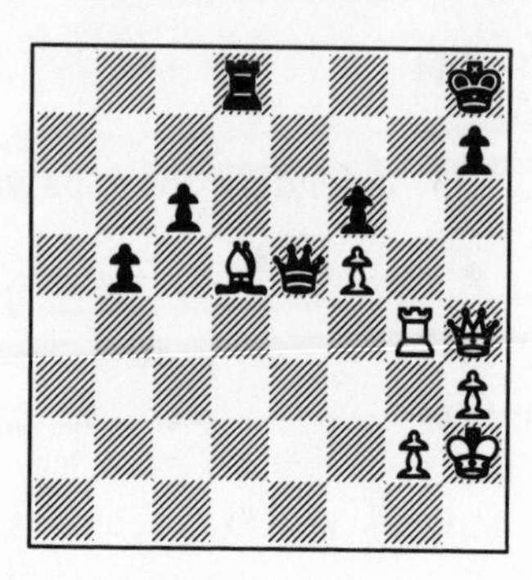

After 40 ... Qe5+

Karpov sealed. Most observers felt Karpov had good chances to make progress. Kasparov later admitted he thought he was losing when the game resumed.

Calculating seventeen moves deep, Deep Thought gave Black a .69-pawn edge. From grandmaster to grandmaster estimates of Karpov's chances for a win varied: Dzindzichashvili 40 percent, Ljubojevic 50 percent, Shamkovich 30 percent. Lautier gave Karpov a win, and Seirawan seemed close to agreeing.

41 Rg3	**cxd5**

A mistake is 41 . . . Rxd5?? 42 Qg4 and Black is mated after 41 . . . Qxd5??. (SP)

42 Qg4	**Qc7**
43 Qd4	**Qd6**
44 Kh1!	

The point is that 44 Qg4 is met by 44 . . . Qd7!, threatening 45 . . . d4. (MR)

44 . . .	**Re8**
45 Qg4	**Qd7**

46	Rd3	Re1+
47	Kh2	Re4

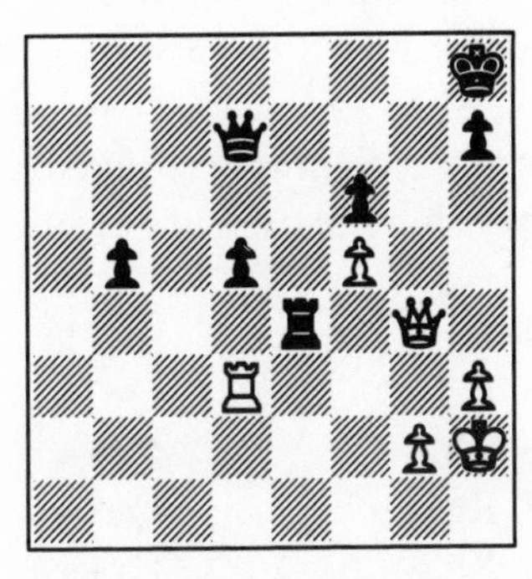

After 47 ... Re4

Karpov is making significant progress, but he has used a lot of time on his clock, indicating that his adjournment analysis had concentrated on other lines. Now White loses after 48 Qxe4? Qc7+. (MR)

48	Qg3	Re5
49	Ra3	Re8
50	Qf4	

Alburt gave White a fifty-fifty chance to hold a draw.

50	...	Qb7!

Karpov's move prevents Ra6 and threatens 51 . . . Qb8 or 51 . . . b4. On 50 . . . Rd8 White intended 51 Ra6. (MR)

51	Kh1	Qb8
52	Qh4	Qb6
53	Qb4	d4?

This was Karpov's only opportunity for 53 . . . Qf2!!. White then loses after 54 Qxb5? Re1+ 55 Kh2 Qf4+ 56 Rg3 Re3, and White has no checks while Black threatens 54 . . . Qe1+. It is curtains for White also after 54 Kh2? Rg8. So he has to try 54 Ra1 Rg8 55 Rg1, but Black has a dominating position after 55 . . . Qe2 56 Qd6 Qe5. (MR)

Roshal, Karpov's biographer, joked sardonically, "Karpov can only play in time pressure or under threat of mate."

54 Rg3 Qc7!
55 Rd3 Qc1+
56 Kh2 Qf4+
57 Kg1 Qc1+
58 Kh2 Qf4+
59 Kg1 Rc8?!

De Firmian recommends 59 . . . Kg7! 60 Rxd4 Re1+ 61 Qxe1 Qxd4+ 62 Kh1 b4 63 Qe7+ Kh6. (European)

60 Rd1

Suddenly the white queen is very well placed at b4, hitting black pawns and soon controlling b8. Karpov sacrifices the b-pawn to get the d-pawn moving, but the win is no longer there. (MR)

60 . . . Rd8

Dzindzichashvili thought this was a mistake, giving 61 Qxb5 Qe3+ 62 Kh1 d3, draw.

61 Qxb5 Qe3+
62 Kh1 d3
63 Qa5 Qd4
64 Qa1

"What a move!" (Tisdall)

64 . . .	Qb6
65 Qa2	Kg7
66 Qd2	

According to Dzindzichashvili, the best Karpov had left at this point was "to wiggle for a mistake."

66 . . .	Qc5
67 Rf1	Rd4
68 Rf3	Qd6
69 Re3	Ra4
70 Re1	h5

Lautier still thought Black was winning. Deep Thought gave Karpov less than .1-pawn lead—"the lowest I've ever seen," said Murray Campbell.

71 Rb1	Qd7
72 Qd1	Kh6
73 Qd2+	Kg7
74 Qe3!	

Much better than 74 Qd1 Qd4! 75 Qxh5 Ra1 76 Rxa1 Qxa1+ 77 Kh2 Qd4 or 77 . . . Qe5. (SP)

74 . . .	h4
75 Qf3	Kh6
76 Qe3+	Kg7
77 Qf3	d2
78 Qh5	Qf7
79 Qxf7	+ Kxf7
80 Rd1	Rd4
81 Kg1	Rd5

82	Kf2	Rxf5 +
83	Ke2	Rg5
84	Kf2	Draw

Many people expected a timeout after Game 8's adjournment marathon; it was just a question of who would break down and call before the noon deadline. Tal predicted, "They will wait until 11:59 to call, and the line will be busy."

No one called.

Having gotten nowhere with the King's Indian, for Game 9 Kasparov switched to the Grünfeld, an old favorite but one that has never been very successful for him against Karpov. His luck was no better this time. Karpov quickly established an advantage and seemed to be on the verge of converting it to a win when a transposition of moves over the board permitted Kasparov to escape with a draw. The score after nine games: 4.5–4.5.

Match 5, Game 9
October 31, 1990
Grünfeld Defense

White: Anatoly Karpov ***Black: Garry Kasparov***

Annotated by GM Ron Henley and GM Roman Dzindzichashvili

1 d4

With this game something strange begins to happen. Portions of Games 9, 10, and 11 seem to be contested by players of very different levels. (RD)

1 . . .	Nf6
2 c4	g6
3 Nc3	d5

The match's first Grünfeld. Karpov's eyes registered surprise when Kasparov pushed the d-pawn.

4 cxd5	Nxd5
5 e4	Nxc3
6 bxc3	Bg7
7 Be3	c5

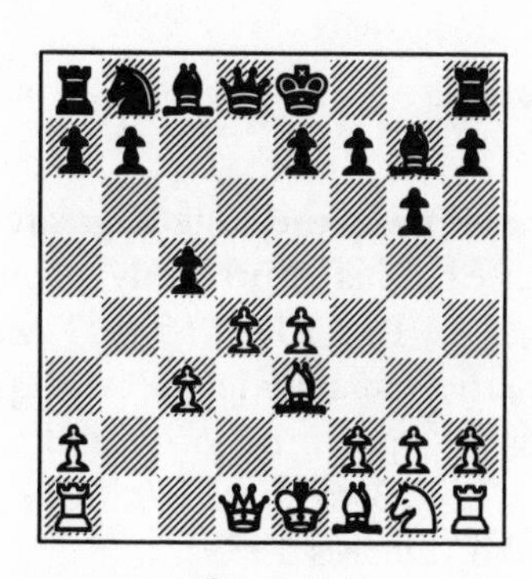

After 7 ... c5

8 Qd2!?

Dlugy has played this line fairly regularly: "I gave it up though. It doesn't give White much." (European)

Karpov postpones theoretical discussion of the sharp variation 8 Bc4 0-0 9 Ne2 Nc6 10 0-0 Bg4 11 f3 Na5 12 Bxf7+, which has been tested by these two players many times before. (RD)

8 . . .	**cxd4**
9 cxd4	**Nc6**
10 Rd1	**Qa5!**

Kasparov realizes that Black's best chances to equalize lie in the endgame. White was already threatening 11 d5 followed by a possible kingside attack.

11 Qxa5	**Nxa5**

This approximately equal position is better suited to Karpov's style. (RD)

12 Nf3

Karpov's move gives the knight greater activity than it would have on e2. This is probably stronger than 12 Bd3 0-0 13 Ne2 Bd7 14 Rc1 Rfc8! 15 Kd2 e6, when Black has reached a thematic, equal endgame with queenside counterplay due to his 2–1 pawn majority and the possibilities of . . . f5 and . . . Bf8-a3 to force White to give up the c-file (Yusupov–Gulko, Linares 1989).

12 . . .	**0-0**
13 Be2	

"No problem for Black," Palatnik repeated, "but White's center makes it difficult for Kasparov to attack." Karpov seemed happy at the board; Kasparov was leaning in like a vulture.

13 . . .	**Bd7?!**

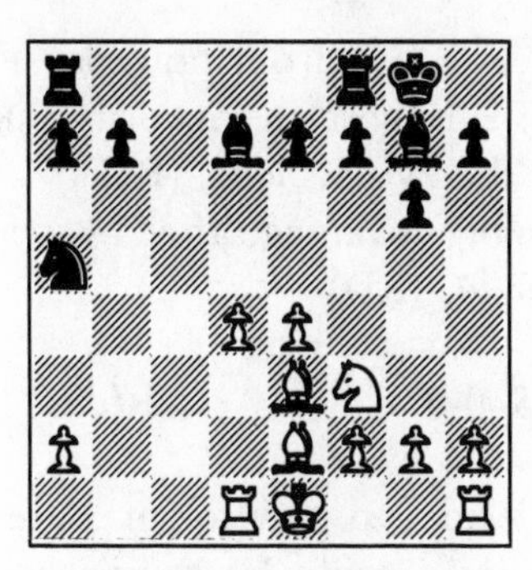

After 13 ... Bd7

Perhaps better is 13 . . . Bg4, recommended by Christiansen, after which both sides have many choices; e.g., 14 h3 Bxf3 15 Bxf3 Nc4 16 e5!? Nxe3 17 fxe3 Rab8 18 Rc1 Rfc8 19 Ke2 b6, when Black probably has good chances to equalize, but nothing more.

A thematic development for Black is 13 . . . b6 followed by . . . Bb7, but Garry wants to occupy the c-file as quickly as possible. (RH)

14 Bd2!

Much stronger than the routine 14 0-0 Rfc8 15 Rc1 Rxc1 16 Rxc1 Rc8 17 Rxc8+ Bxc8 18 d5 b6 19 Nd4 Bd7 20 f4, which does not offer White sufficient chances to win. With rooks on the board, his central dominance offers mating chances. (RH)

This very strong move was probably overlooked by Black. (RD)

14 . . . b6

White now has the option of altering the pawn structure with Bxa5, a possibility that has to be considered by both players at every move from now on. The capture would cripple Black's 2-1 queenside majority, but Black would gain the b-file and the two bishops. (RH)

White has a big advantage after 14 . . . Nc6 15 d5 Ne5 16 Nxe5 Bxe5 17 f4. (RD)

15 0-0 Rfd8?!

Kasparov decides to play for pressure against d4. However, 15 . . . Rfc8 would be consistent with his previous play; e.g., 16 Rc1 Bg4, recommended by Seirawan in *Inside Chess* magazine. The idea is to pressure the white pawn at d4 (16 . . . Rxc1 17 Rxc1 Rc8 18 Rxc8+ Bxc8 19 Bxa5 bxa5 20 h3!, preventing . . . Bg4 and . . . Bxf3 which leads to opposite-colored bishops. White would then have some chances for a significant advantage with no risk, always a desirable situation in match play:

A) 17 Be3 Rxc1 18 Rxc1 Rc8 19 Rxc8+ Bxc8 20 Nd2 f5 21 f3 e6 leaves White with a minimal edge at best;

B) 17 Ba6 Rxc1 18 Rxc1 Bxf3 19 gxf3 Bxd4 20 Rc7 e6, and White has compensation for the pawn, but not more (Seirawan);

C) 17 e5?! Be6 18 Bxa5 bxa5 19 a4 (19 Ba6 Rxc1 20 Rxc1 Bxa2 21 Ra1 Bd5 22 Rxa5 Bxf3 23 gxf3 Rd8, with equality) 19 . . . Bd5, and Black has excellent activity since 20 Nd2? allows 20 . . . Bh6! 21 f4?, losing to 21 . . . Rxc1 22 Rxc1 Bxf4;

D) 17 d5 Bb2!? 18 Rb1 Bg7 (not 18 . . . Rc2? 19 Bd3, and 18 . . . Bc3 19 Bg5! may offer White some chances for an edge) 19 Rfc1, with the typical advantages White aims for in the central exchange variation, where Black has yet to solve his problems and find meaningful counterplay. (RH)

16 Rc1 Bg4
17 d5 Nb7

An excellent idea, relocating the knight to c5 now that the white d-pawn has advanced.

Black has chances to defend successfully after 17 . . . Rac8 18 Bb4 Kf8 19 Ba6 Rxc1 20 Rxc1 Bxf3 21 gxf3 Be5, but his knight will remain a passive bystander until White decides to release it. In addition, if the dark-squared bishops are exchanged, the white rook will penetrate to c7. (RH)

After 17 . . . f5? 18 h3 Bxf3 19 Bxf3 fxe4 20 Bxe4, Seirawan says the weak black pawn at e7 and the two bishops give White a clear edge.

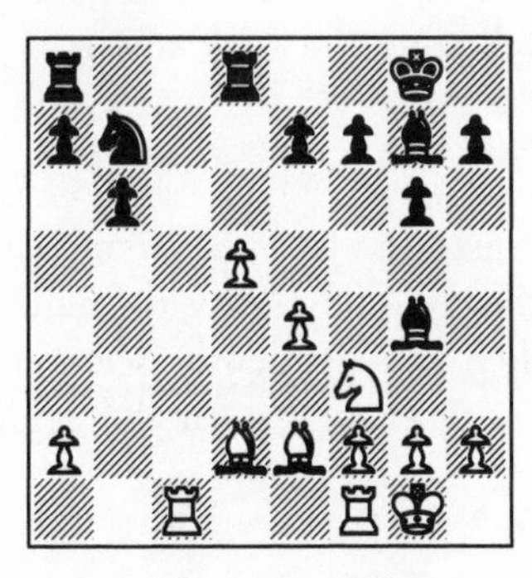

After 17 ... Nb7

18 h3!

Karpov thus secures the bishop-pair for a lasting advantage.

The white pawn at d5 is weak after 18 Rc7?! Nc5 19 Rxe7 Bf6 20 Rc7 Nxe4, and not much better is 18 Bb4 e6! 19 Rc7 exd5!, and now:

A) 20 Rxb7 dxe4 21 Bc4 exf3 22 Rxf7 Kh8 23 gxf3 Rd4! 24 Rc1 (not 24 fxg4? Rxg4+ 25 Kh1 Rxc4, or 24 Rxg7 Rxc4, or 24 Bc3 Rxc4 25 Bxg7+ Kg8 26 Re7 Bxf3, with a slight edge for Black) 24 . . . Rxc4 25 Rxc4 Be6 26 Rcc7 Bxf7 27 Rxf7 equalizes;

B) 20 exd5 Nd6 leads to equality: 21 h3 Ne8!? 22 Rc4 Bc8 23 Rd1 Ba6 24 Rc2 Bxe2 25 Rxe2 Rd7 26 Ne5 Bxe5 27

Rxe5 f6 28 Re7 Rad8 29 Rde1 Nc7 30 d6 Nd5 31 Rxd7 Rxd7 32 Ba3 Kf7, when Black has succeeded in blockading the passed d-pawn, which could now become a weakness. (RH)

18 . . .	**Bxf3**
19 Bxf3	**Nc5**
20 Be3	**Rac8**

White has a slight edge because of the two bishops and his strong pawn center. Black, however, has good chances of defending by blockading the dark squares. (RD)

21 Bg4!

This and the next few moves exemplify what Karpov brings to chess theory—his ability to make small, probing moves which taken independently seem insignificant, yet which create ongoing problems for the defender. (RH)

21 . . . Rb8

More accurate is 21 . . . Rc7. (RD)

"Isn't this 'The Big Grovel'?" interjected Tisdall. Kasparov seemed very unhappy over the board.

22 Rc4!

Excellent play. The rook protects the pawn at e4 and prepares the possibility of Rfc1 or lateral action along the fourth rank. Black gets full compensation for the pawn after 22 Bxc5?! bxc5 23 Rxc5 Rb2 24 Ra5 h5 25 Bf3 Bd4 26 Ra4 Rd2. (RH)

22 . . . h5

In this typical Karpov squeeze, solving one problem often creates another. Kasparov chases the bishop away from g4, where it controls c8, but the h5-pawn becomes a lever for Karpov to use to open the h-file. (RH)

23 Bf3 e6
24 Rd1

The opposite-colored bishops would force a clear draw after White snares the pawn by Bxc5 and then Rxc5. (RD)

24 ... exd5
25 exd5

"Karpov could play this forever," Valvo remarked in the press room.

25 ... Be5

On the surface, Black looks OK since he is preparing to bolster the barricading knight at c5, and the position on the queenside and in the center appears stable. But ... (RH)

26 g4!

Karpov starts action in a new sector of the board. Once the h-file is open, the black bishop will face a tough choice: whether to continue on to d6 to blockade the d-pawn and support the knight at c5, or to try to maintain control of the a1-h8 diagonal. (RH)

26 ... hxg4
27 hxg4

In the press room, someone asked what would happen now. Without blinking, Tisdall summed up the situation succinctly with, "Karpov will try to increase his advantage by getting into time trouble."

27 ... Nb7?

This terrible blunder should have cost Kasparov the point. After the game, Karpov and Portisch analyzed defenses for Black based on . . . Kg7 and . . . f6, but White can continue with Kg2, Be2, and f4, when White's pressure on the king-side combined with his two bishops and passed d-pawn should prove decisive. (RH)

28 Ra4!

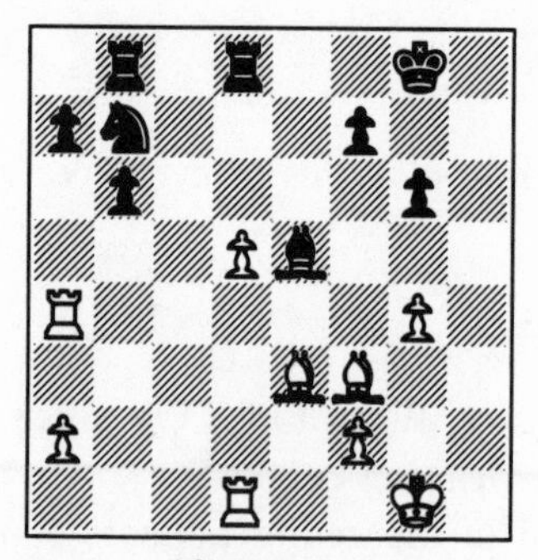

After 28 Ra4

Kasparov overlooked this simple move, which diverts his knight from d6. (RH)

28 . . . Na5

Unpleasant but forced, since 28 . . . Ra8 29 d6! is decisive for White. Rather lame play by the world champion. (RH)

29 g5?

A serious mistake, which went virtually unnoticed in the press room. The main problem is that this takes the important g5-square from White's bishop, so now he can't play Bg5 attacking Black's rook and helping to pave the way for the passed d-pawn.

Krogius pointed out the correct continuation during the game: 29 Re4!, putting the question to Black's bishop: 29 . . . Bd6 30 Be2! (an important finesse, after which Black's position is overrun by one white bishop on b5 and the other on g5 or d4; this idea was discovered by Karpov and Portisch) 30 . . . Nb7 31 Bb5 Nc5 32 Rc4, when the passed d-pawn and threats of mating attacks along the h-file should prove decisive. (RH)

29 . . .	**Rbc8**
30 Be2	

White still has a clear edge since the black knight is still a problem. (RH)

30 . . .	**Bd6**

In one of the analysis rooms, Benko thought Kasparov was worse "and will have to suffer for a draw."

31 Kg2	**Bc5!**

If Black can exchange dark-squared bishops he can bring his king to d6 and play for the advantage. (RH)

32 Bd2??

After the game, Karpov explained that he intended 32 Bf4 Bd6 and then 33 Bd2, but simply forgot to insert 32 Bf4 first. (RH)

According to Tisdall in *Pergamon Chess* magazine, Ljubojevic moaned in disbelief, "I have known Karpov all my life, and I've never seen him give away a *square*—and here he gives away a *pawn!*"

32 . . .	**Rxd5**

Kasparov could not believe his good fortune!

33 Bf3

While Kasparov was thinking about his last move, Karpov realized what he had done, and now he responded almost immediately with no emotion, as though everything were okay. (RH)

33 . . .	**Rdd8**
34 Bxa5	**Draw**

Here Karpov offered a draw, which was immediately accepted by Kasparov. Completely drawn is 34 . . . bxa5 35 Rxd8 + Rxd8 36 Rxa5 Bb6 37 Rd5, leading to bishops of opposite colors. (RH)

In Game 10 the two players finally took a timeout by "running in place" with an eighteeen-move draw. Karpov switched to the Petroff Defense and offered a novelty on move 8 that seemed to disarm the world champion. The score: 5.0–5.0.

Match 5, Game 10
November 2, 1990
Petroff Defense

White: Garry Kasparov ***Black: Anatoly Karpov***

Annotated by GM Ron Henley

1 e4	**e5**
2 Nf3	**Nf6**

3 d4	**exd4**
4 e5	**Ne4**
5 Qxd4	**d5**
6 exd6	**Nxd6**
7 Nc3	

The other continuations—7 Bd3, 7 Bg5, and 7 Bf4—do not promise White much. (RH)

7 . . .	**Nc6**
8 Qf4	**Nf5!**

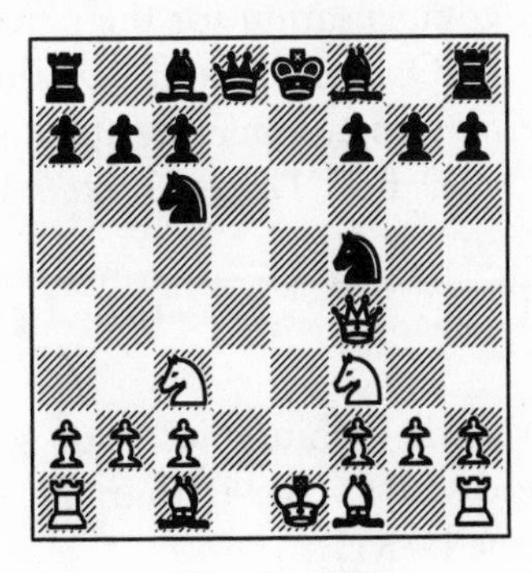

After 8 ... Nf5

An important theoretical novelty prepared by Karpov and Zaitsev. Previous practice includes 8 . . . Be6, 8 . . . Bf5, 8 . . . Qe7+, 8 . . . Be7, and 8 . . . g6, none of which gives Black complete equality. (RH)

9 Bb5	**Bd6**
10 Qe4+	**Qe7**

Kasparov had used a full hour at this point, compared with Karpov's eighteen minutes. Considering the time used, Benjamin felt Kasparov was not playing with the same confidence he had at the beginning of the match.

Dzindzichashvili proved correct here when he said Kasparov was not happy with the opening: after 10 . . . Ne7 11 Bxc6+ bxc6 12 0-0 0-0 13 Rd1, Black's two bishops compensate for his fractured queenside pawns (not 13 Bf4? Bf5 14 Qa4 Bxc2!). He predicted that this position would not be repeated in the match—"not to Kasparov's taste." (RH)

11 Bg5

Kasparov decides to provoke . . . f6 instead of playing 11 Bd2 immediately. Dzindzichashvili felt that Black would have sufficient compensation for the pawn after 11 0-0 0-0 12 Bxc6 bxc6 13 Qxc6 Rb8, and Benjamin gave Black adequate counterplay to compensate for his queenside weaknesses after 11 0-0 Bd7 12 Bxc6 bxc6 13 Re1 0-0. (RH)

11 . . . f6

This deprives the white pieces of g5 and e5 in the endgame. The disadvantage is that the a2-g8 diagonal is severely weakened. (RH)

12 Bd2 Bd7

Dzindzichashvili felt that Karpov was in no danger, while Dlugy thought Kasparov might still have some chances for an advantage.

Dzindzi declared solemnly, "If you want to beat Karpov, this is not the kind of position you want."

"If you want to draw with Kasparov," Dlugy shot back, "this is not the kind of position you want."

13 0-0-0

Black achieves full equality after 13 0-0 Qxe4 14 Nxe4 Be7, followed by 15 . . . 0-0-0. (RH)

13 . . . Qxe4
14 Nxe4 Be7!

I was happy to see Karpov play this move. After 14 . . . 0-0-0 15 g4 Nfe7 16 Nxd6+ cxd6 17 Rhg1, Dzindzichashvili saw no problems for Black, but I thought it could prove unpleasant. Later Karpov agreed, though he said Black should be able to hold. (RH)

15 g4!

The only attempt to maintain some initiative. Otherwise Black completes his development with 15 . . . 0-0-0 and White has nothing. (RH)

15 . . . a6!

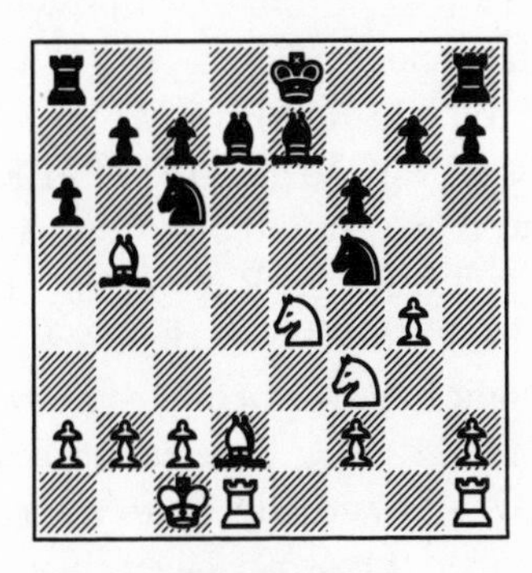

After 15 ... a6

Karpov often spends long thinks on seemingly forced moves. Byrne and I were analyzing 15 . . . Nh6 16 Bxh6 gxh6 17 h3 h5! 18 gxh5 (Mednis pointed out 18 g5 fxg5! 19

Nexg5 h6, with a beautiful position for Black) 18 . . . f5, when the black bishops were about to come to life and the extra white pawn at h5 would not be very relevant.

Even so, Karpov's solution is the most solid. (RH)

16 Bc4

Also drawn is 16 Bxc6 Bxc6 17 Rhe1 Bxe4 18 Rxe4 Nd6 19 Re6 Kf7 20 Rde1 Rhe8. (RH)

16 . . .	**Nd6**
17 Nxd6+	**Bxd6**
18 Rde1+	**Draw**

Karpov was mildly surprised when Kasparov offered a draw here, since Black still has to play correctly. One try is 18 Rhe1+ Be7 19 Bd5 0-0-0 20 Bxc6 Bxc6 21 Rxe7 Bxf3, with a draw.

Black draws in the present position with 18 . . . Be7! (not 18 . . . Ne7?! 19 Rhg1 0-0-0 20 Nd4, when the invasion at e6 gives White a clear advantage) 19 Bd5 0-0-0 20 Bxc6 Bxc6 21 Rxe7 Bxf3 22 Rg1 Rd7. White gets an edge after 18 . . . Kf8?! 19 Rhg1 Re8 20 g5 Rxe1+ 21 Rxe1 Ne5 22 Nxe5 Bxe5 23 f4, but Black should also draw after 18 . . . Kd8 19 Rhg1 Re8 20 g5 Rxe1+ 21 Rxe1 f5, or 21 . . . Ne5 22 Nxe5 Bxe5 23 f4 Bd4! 24 Bb4 c5 25 Ba5+ Kc8. (RH)

Game 11 might have seemed like another rest stop for the two K's after the grueling pace set early in the match, but this short draw was actually quite tense. Kasparov's 13th move opened a can of worms; sacrificing the exchange for at best vague compensation. Karpov threaded his way through a laborious defense, and the game sputtered to an early draw in a shower of harmless fireworks: 5.5–5.5.

Everyone was asking the same question: Would Kasparov be satisfied to leave New York with the match deadlocked, or would he pull out the stops with the white pieces and press for a win before the two-week break? Some argued that since the early pace had drained both players a safe draw was likely, but most thought the world champion would put all of his energy into leaving New York with a bang. Kasparov's supporters may have been secretly praying for a quiet draw—his reckless play was taking its toll on them.

Match 5, Game 11
November 5, 1990
King's Indian Defense

White: Anatoly Karpov ***Black: Garry Kasparov***

Annotated by GM Ron Henley

1 d4	Nf6
2 c4	g6
3 Nc3	Bg7
4 e4	d6
5 Nf3	0-0
6 Be2	e5
7 Be3	exd4

Kasparov deviates from earlier games, trying to keep Karpov off balance by switching moves.

8 Nxd4	Re8
9 f3	

A major alternative that Gata Kamsky used to defeat former world champion Mikhail Tal in the 1990 NY Open is 9 Qc2. (RH)

9 . . .	c6
10 Qd2	d5
11 exd5	cxd5
12 0-0	Nc6
13 c5	

The sharpest continuation. Alternatives are 13 Nxc6 bxc6 14 Rad1 Ba6 15 cxd5 Bxe2 16 Qxe2 Nxd5 17 Nxd5 cxd5 18 Qf2 Bxb2 19 Bxa7 Qd7, with equality (Portisch–Bouaziz, Szirak Interzonal 1987); and 13 Rad1 Nxd4 14 Bxd4 dxc4 15 Bxc4 Be6 16 Bb5 Rf8 17 Qf2 Qa5 18 Qh4 a6, with equality (Tal–Yurataev, USSR 1983). (RH)

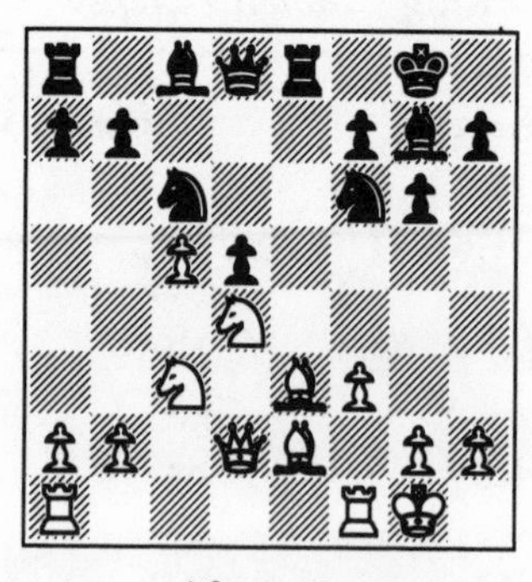

After 13 c5

13 . . .	Rxe3!?

Probably dubious from a theoretical point of view, but you have to admire Kasparov's nerve to play this in a world championship match. Known moves are 13 . . . Qe7 and 13 . . . Bd7. Since Kasparov played this move without hesitation, it was probably part of his prematch preparation. (RH)

Shamkovich expressed concern that Black's compensation was inadequate for the exchange.

14 Qxe3	Qf8

Black threatens 15 . . . Ng4 winning immediately. (RH)

15 Nxc6 **bxc6**
16 Kh1

Karpov had used fifty-three minutes to Kasparov's five, and de Firmian remarked that Kasparov may have been willing "to take a dubious position to reach a wildly complicated game." He went on to observe, "[Kasparov] has consistently outplayed Karpov in obscure positions, while Karpov has outplayed him in technical positions." (European)

16 . . . **Rb8**

Deep Thought recommended 16 . . . Bf5, with compensation.

17 Na4

After the game, Karpov suggested that 17 Nd1 was an improvement, but Black always has some compensation. (RH)

17 . . . **Rb4**
18 b3 **Be6**

White had used fifty-nine minutes; Black only eleven.

19 Nb2?!

White still has chances for an advantage after 19 Rad1!. The text loses too much time and allows Kasparov to build up a dangerous kingside initiative. (RH)

19 . . .	Nh5
20 Nd3	Rh4
21 Qf2	

By telephone, Murray Campbell reported, "Deep Thought sees something funny happening here. It thinks that Garry has a forced draw in hand after 21 . . . g5, but with a single inaccuracy Karpov will be crushed. There are some rook sacs on h2 in the forcing variations."

21 . . .	Qe7!

According to Karpov, the remaining moves are forced. Kasparov was not tempted by Deep Thought's 21 . . . g5?! 22 g4 Bxa1 23 Rxa1 Qg7 24 Rg1 Nf6 25 Qd4, which Karpov felt led to a clear plus for White because of the black rook's awkward location at h4 and the weak pawn at c6. (RH)

22 g4

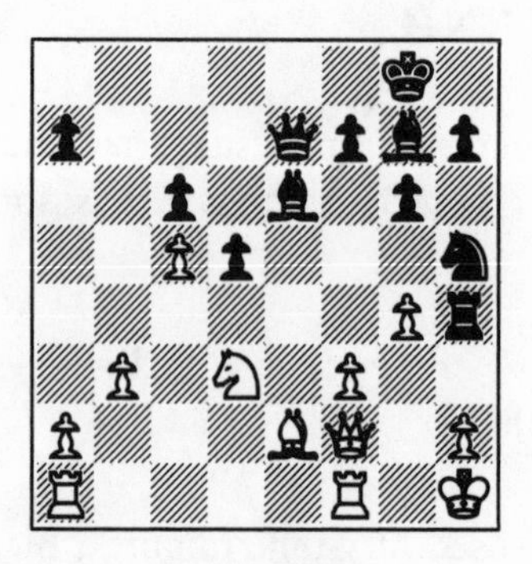

After 22 g4

22 . . .	Bd4!
23 Qxd4	

Forced. Black is better after 23 Qg2? Bxa1 24 Rxa1 Qf6 25 Re1 Nf4 26 Nxf4 Qxf4. (RH)

23 . . .	Rxh2 +
24 Kxh2	Qh4 +
Draw	

Black has a perpetual check.

As expected, Kasparov pressed for the win with White against Karpov's Ruy Lopez in Game 12. He built what seemed to be a promising position early, but Karpov dug in and, as usual, constructed a workable defense, though at some expense on the clock.

After a short nap in the middlegame, Kasparov awoke just in time to put enough pressure on Karpov to force him to accept a draw in the waning moments of time pressure. Analysis after the game seemed to demonstrate an advantage for Black, but Karpov was happy—he had managed to escape New York with an even score: 6.0–6.0.

Match 5, Game 12
November 7, 1990
Ruy Lopez

White: Garry Kasparov ***Black: Anatoly Karpov***

Annotated by GM Ron Henley

1 e4	e5
2 Nf3	Nc6
3 Bb5	a6
4 Ba4	Nf6
5 0-0	Be7
6 Re1	b5
7 Bb3	d6
8 c3	0-0
9 h3	Nd7

10 d4	Bf6
11 a4	Bb7
12 Na3	exd4

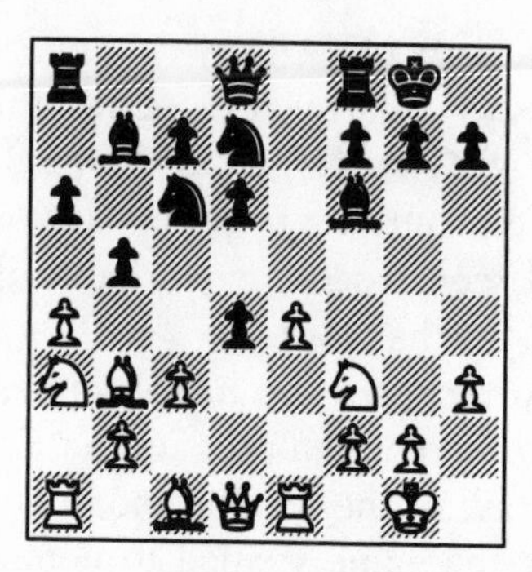

After 12 ... exd4

13 cxd4	Na5

This theoretical innovation is by Podgaets, a very strong specialist in the 9 . . . Nd7 Spanish. (RH)

14 Ba2	b4
15 Nc4	Nxc4
16 Bxc4	Re8

An original Podgaets idea, surrendering the f7-pawn to get White's e4-pawn and break up his central pair. (RH)

17 Qb3

Kasparov accepts the invitation. Otherwise, Black has active play; e.g., 17 Qd3? d5 18 exd5 Rxe1+ 19 Nxe1 Nb6, with good play; or 17 Bd3 c5 18 d5 Ne5, and Black has a good Benoni formation. (RH)

17 . . .	Rxe4
18 Bxf7+	Kh8
19 Be3!	

Most commentators expected 19 Bd2, to contest the e-file. Kasparov shuts off the e-file and begins operations in the center and on the queenside. (RH)

19 . . .	Re7
20 Bd5	c6?

An ugly move that received universal condemnation. Most people expected 20 . . . Bxd5 21 Qxd5 a5 with a difficult position to assess. Karpov said he simply forgot that the bishop could go to e6! After the text, Black has a cramped position without prospects. (RH)

21 Be6!

A balanced game is reached by 21 Bc4 d5 22 Bd3 a5. (RH)

21 . . .	Nf8
22 Bg4!	

Preventing 22 . . . c5 23 dxc5 Bxf3, since 24 Bxf3 avoids doubled pawns. Meanwhile, the bishop on g4 keeps Black's rooks off the c8-square. (RH)

22 . . .	a5
23 Rac1!	

Excellent play. Kasparov clamps down on the Black position. (RH)

23 . . .	Ng6

Karpov later said, "It was easy to find the right move here, since I only had one piece that could move!" (RH)

24 Bh5?!	Rc8

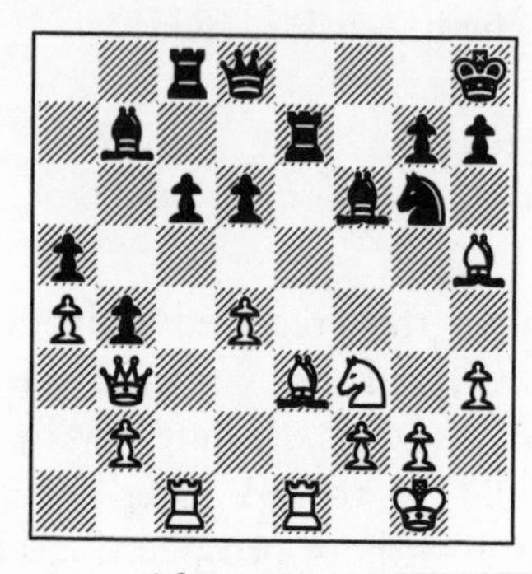

After 24 ... Rc8

25 Bg4!	Rb8
26 Qc2	Rc7
27 Qf5	Ne7!
28 Qd3	

Here Kasparov really plays violently out of character. One would certainly expect full steam ahead with 28 Qh5 g6 29 Qh6 (Salov gave 29 Bg5 gxh5 30 Bxf6+ Kg8 31 Be6+ Kf8 32 Ng5 with an exciting attack, but Karpov says Black is ahead after 32 . . . Bc8! 33 Nxh7+ Ke8) 29 . . . Ng8 30 Qf4 Bc8, when White has the advantage but Black is defending well.

A big mistake is 28 Qxa5?? Nd5 29 Bd2 Ra8 30 Bxb4 Rxa5 31 Bxa5 Qa8 32 Bxc7 Nxc7. (RH)

28 . . .	Nd5
29 Bd2	c5!

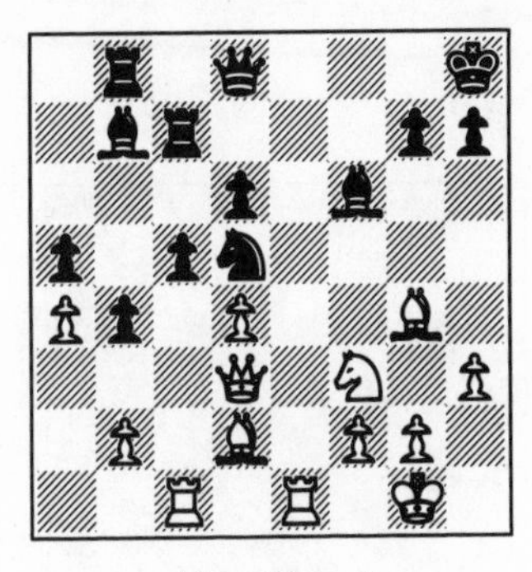

After 29 ... c5

White has made little progress in the last six moves, while Black has reorganized his troops and executed the liberating advance . . . c5!. In the press room, we sense a definite shift in momentum toward Karpov. (RH)

30 Be6	**Nb6**
31 dxc5	**dxc5**
32 Qxd8+	

An interesting try is 32 Qf5!? Bxf3 33 Bf4, and now:

A) 33 . . . Bb7 34 Red1 Qe7 (34 . . . Bd4? 35 Bxc7 Qxc7 36 Rxd4, with a win for White) 35 Bxc7 Qxc7 36 Rxc5 Qe7 37 Rxa5 Bxb2.

B) 33 . . . Bc6 34 Bxc7 Qxc7 35 Qxc5 Bxb2 36 Qxc6 Qxc6 37 Rxc6 Nxa4 38 Bc8 g6 39 Re8+ Kg7 40 Rc7+ Kf6 41 Rxh7, with a big edge for White (Karpov). (RH)

32 . . .	**Rxd8**
33 Bf4!	

Suddenly Kasparov wakes up, and tremendous complications arise with both players down to about fifteen minutes on the clock.

33 . . .	**Re7**
34 Ng5!	**Bd5!**

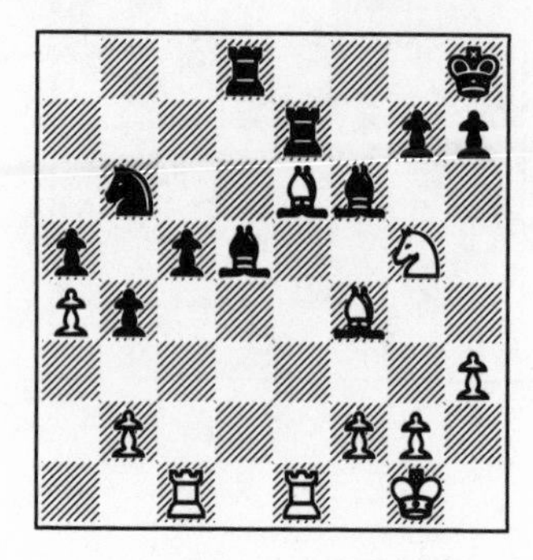

After 34 ... Bd5

Karpov fans were hoping he would sacrifice the exchange on f7 or e6 to capture the a4- and b2-pawns, but Karpov decides not to gamble. (RH)

Kasparov finds a forced continuation to maintain some initiative. If White sits back and does nothing, Black's queeenside pawn majority will roll over him in the endgame. (RH)

35 Bxd5	**Rxd5**
36 Rxe7	**Bxe7**
37 Re1!	**Draw**

Kasparov offered a draw with four minutes left on Karpov's clock. After thinking for two minutes, Karpov accepted in view of 37 . . . Nc8 38 Re6!, when White is slightly better.

The best reply, 37 . . . Bf8!, later showed a clear edge for Black; e.g., 38 Re8 Kg8:

A) 39 Rb8 Nd7 40 Rd8 Nb6 (40 . . . Nf6 41 Bc7!);

B) 39 Nxh7? Kxh7 40 Rxf8 c4!, when Black will secure

two connected passed pawns on the queenside, which will suffice to win;

C) 39 Ne6 Kf7 40 Rxf8+ Kxe6 41 Bc7, and now:

C1) 41 . . . Nd7 42 Re8+ Kf7 43 Ra8 (43 Rd8 Ke7 44 Rg8 Kf7 45 Rd8 Ke7 46 Bxa5 Rd1+ 47 Kh2 Rb1, and equality) 43 . . . Rd1+ 44 Kh2 Rb1 45 Bxa5 Rxb2, when the black pawns should be more dangerous than White's a-pawn.

C2) 41 . . . Nxa4 42 b3! Nc3 (42 . . . Nb2 43 Bxa5 c4 44 Bxb4 cxb3) 43 Bxa5 Rd1+ 44 Kh2 Rb1 45 Rc8 Kd5 46 Bb6 Rxb3 (46 . . . Ne4 47 f3) 47 Rxc5+ Kd6 48 Rc4 Nd5 49 Bc5+ Ke6. (RH)

8

INTERMISSION

New York had been an uncomfortable experience for the challenger, at least psychologically. But a few days after Game 12 he appeared as relaxed and comfortable as I have ever seen him, feeling that drawing the first half of the match had been a moral and practical victory.

As he prepared to leave for France, he had good reason to be optimistic. Kasparov had opened the match like gangbusters, challenging Karpov from the opening bell to trade blows in the center of the ring. After the world champion's brilliant demolition of Karpov's pet Ruy Lopez in Game 2, many observers in New York were ready to believe that Kasparov had indeed outstripped his perennial rival and was now virtually untouchable. With every Kasparov move in the early stages, spectators held their breaths, waiting for lightning to strike. For a while, even Karpov seemed to be ducking.

But soon whispers about the world champion's "recklessness" and "overconfidence" began to surface. In Game 6 it looked like his recklessness had finally caught up with him, but a last-second mistake by Karpov let him off the hook with a draw. Even the few loyal Kasparov supporters who still believed Garry was so strong he could virtually get away with anything were sobered—Karpov had had him dead to rights.

Within ten minutes of Lev Alburt's condescending characterization of Karpov's play, Kasparov had finally found the disaster he had been courting, hanging his queen out to dry in an inexplicable middlegame blunder in Game 7. Karpov had leveled the match score at 3.5–3.5. The young world champion had escalated the tension beyond the level even he was equipped to control.

Then, in Game 8, Kasparov seemed to come back—only to let a promising position get away in a time scramble and falling into an apparently losing position at adjournment. Sobered, and convinced that his position was lost, Kasparov managed to save the half-point, but no one could pretend anymore that Karpov had come to New York as Kasparov's patsy. If anyone had wilted under the match's brisk early pace, it was the world champion.

Showing signs of unsteadiness, he decided to put the brakes on in Game 9, reverting to the staid Grünfeld Defense instead of his earlier frenetic King's Indian. Even the relatively quick draws in Games 10 and 11 generated enough sparks to remind the audience that both players packed a wallop, and Game 12 proved that neither player was going to flinch from the fight.

Kasparov shrugged off a scheduled press conference—"I don't see why I should discuss strategy in the middle of the match"—so we don't know what he was thinking. But spectators in the closing days of the New York leg sensed a slight thaw between the two players. Kasparov and Karpov had begun to analyze briefly together on stage after the games.

During Game 11, the organizers had announced a press conference to close the New York leg of the match. Most journalists, including me, made plans to attend, but at the start of Game 12 we were told that "one of the players" had declined to participate. It turned out to be Kasparov.

On Thursday, Karpov agreed to meet with me, Jon Tisdall, and Robert Byrne the next day and then set out to arrange his own meeting with the press for the next morning. He seemed a little miffed that he had not been told that Kasparov had refused to attend the press conference. All of us would have preferred talking with both Garry and Anatoly, but we were eager to know Karpov's state of mind as he left the United States and to hear what he had to say about the match.

He entered the room filled with journalists accompanied by Ron Henley and a translator. He looked happy and relaxed, perhaps relieved not to be sharing the stage with his charismatic rival. Bob Burkett of Interscope, the match sponsor, introduced him, and the questions began. What follows are highlights of the press conference and our private interview with Anatoly.

PRESS CONFERENCE

Q: What will you be doing for the next two weeks?

AK: I will rest. I need two weeks to adjust to the change in climate and time, and it is no secret that both Kasparov and I will be doing a lot of chess work.

Q (Byrne): What can you say about the quality of the match so far?

AK: In Seville, I remember two serious mistakes, which cost me the title of world champion. First, I blundered a rook while leading the match; then I lost the last game when I should have drawn. In any world championship match, there are mistakes resulting from the tension and responsibility, and from time pressure. These games have all been very complicated—sharp and interesting struggles—except perhaps for Game 10. So it is only natural for the participants, who are human beings, to make mistakes. But I would not say the quality of the match is low.

Q (BYRNE): What do you consider your best game of the match? For example, you might single out the way you conducted the early part of the Grünfeld Defense.

AK: Yes, if I had won this game, I would have said it was my best. But I think the most interesting game for both sides was the fourth.

Q (BYRNE): What would you say was your worst?

AK: I can tell you my worst mistake, but not my worst game. The game that I lost was home preparation, so I can't blame myself. I think Kasparov has officially said somewhere that he found this combination at home. It is very important to find such a win at home—especially in the world championship—but not a big achievement. Still, Kasparov played this game very nicely, even at home.

Q: What have you and Kasparov been saying to one another at the end of the last three games?

AK: We discuss the final position—just exchanging a final opinion.

INTERVIEW

Q (BYRNE): When we talked six weeks ago, you were confident. But since then, I have heard many predictions of three to four points difference for Garry.

AK: Of course, in any match or tournament, you find something, you lose something, you miss something. Probably, I missed more than Kasparov. The first game, then the fourth game, then the ninth game, the sixth. If you count, I think I had real chances to win eight games out of twelve.

Q (BYRNE): Can you rattle off the numbers of those games?

AK: No, I don't remember exactly. I had no chances in the second game. I had no chances in the tenth game, the Russian [Petrov]. In most of the games, I had very good chances—all White games, first of all, except probably the eleventh.

Q (TISDALL): Game 3, with the queen sacrifice, also?

AK: Yes, not just the beginning. I shouldn't have given away the a2-pawn. When I took his queen, I made three mistakes in a row. After this I was in an even worse position if he had come back with a rook to a5.

Q (TISDALL): I also heard that you would be happy to leave here tied. That New York gave a "home court advantage" to Kasparov.

AK: Yes, Seirawan actually apologized to me on behalf of Americans for the situation in the match and the organization. But I must say that Bob Burkett was correct in his behavior toward me. I have no questions for Bob Burkett, but I have many questions for other people involved. Of course this created an unequal situation.

Yasser said, "We Americans are not always as neutral as we pretend to be."

When I lost Game 2, Seirawan said, "If you escape New York with minus-one, I will consider you one of the greatest chess players of all times."

9

LYON, GAMES 13 THROUGH 18

Chess in Lyon, France, was a far cry from chess in New York City. According to International Master Andrew Martin, Kasparov and Karpov seemed almost drowsy on opening night, as if their metabolisms had turned down a notch or two to accommodate the quiet lifestyle in Lyon. But both were ready to play chess when the time came.

The rash of tension-driven errors and near misses in the closing games in New York, combined with apparently warmer relations between the two players, had given rise to a conspiracy theory: "Maybe it is to the advantage of both players and the organizers for the match to leave New York 6.0 to 6.0."

The truth is much simpler. Under pressure, the mind plays tricks. In Game 7, according to Jonathan Tisdall and Spanish journalist Leontxo Garcia, Kasparov simply decided to exchange queens and shoved his queen to a5 without much thought, then left the stage to relax. He noticed his mistake, to his horror, on the electronic monitor and found himself skewered. No conspiracy, no backstage machinations. Just human error, well within standard deviation.

Later, Ljubojevic stared in disbelief when Karpov dropped

his passed pawn and gave Kasparov an unexpected respite in Game 9—a simple inversion of moves, no cloak-and-dagger visits in the dead of night.

Kasparov had left New York unhappy with his results as Black, and he decided to open Game 13 in Lyon with the Grünfeld Defense, abandoning for the moment the problematic King's Indian. The switch was successful in that it gave Kasparov the kind of position he loves to play: tense and full of tactical complexity.

Although the chess in the second half of the match continued to be of high quality, the draws were beginning to take their toll in the press. Less attention was being paid to the tense details of the struggle and more to the monotony of the results.

Knowledgeable fans knew that Kasparov was in for the fight of his life—again. Karpov had left New York feeling that an even score after the first twelve games was a tremendous success. He had not flinched from the fight in New York; he wasn't about to back down in Lyon.

A sellout crowd of a thousand spectators in Lyon crossed their fingers against a short draw, and the players did not disappoint them, wrestling for more than five hours to a drawn rook-and-pawn endgame.

Match 5, Game 13
November 24, 1990
Grünfeld Defense

White: Anatoly Karpov — *Black: Garry Kasparov*

Annotated by GM Leonid Shamkovich

1 d4 Nf6
2 c4 g6

3 Nc3	d5
4 cxd5	Nxd5
5 e4	Nxc3
6 bxc3	Bg7
7 Be3	c5
8 Qd2	

This variation, with Be3 and Qd2, prepares Bh6 and avoids the pin after Nf3 and . . . Bg4. (LS)

8 . . .	0-0
9 Rc1	Qa5
10 Nf3	e6

This makes White's d5 advance more difficult, but whether this is the best move is unclear. (LS)

11 d5

Spassky didn't like this move, preferring 11 Bd3 or 11 Bh6.

11 . . .	exd5
12 exd5	Re8

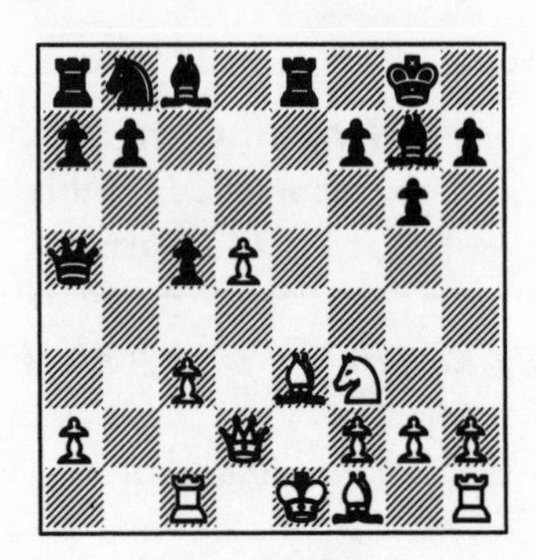

After 12 ... Re8

Interesting is 12 . . . Na6!? with the idea 13 c4 Nb4 14 a3 (14 Be2 b6) 14 . . . Qxa3 15 Bxc5 Nc2+ and a complicated equality. Promising for Black is 13 Be2 b5!? (LS)

13 Be2	**Bf5**
14 0-0	**Nd7**

GM William Watson gave Black a big plus after 15 Nh4 Be4 16 f3 Bxd5! 17 Qxd5 Rxe3 18 Qxd7 Rxe2. (SC)

15 h3	**Nb6**
16 g4	**Bd7**
17 c4	**Qxd2**
18 Nxd2	**Na4**
19 Bf3	**Nc3**

This is a very attractive and natural invasion, but perhaps more accurate is 19 . . . f5, preventing Ne4. (LS)

20 Rxc3!	**Bxc3**
21 Ne4	**Rxe4!**

This countersacrifice is virtually forced. In White's favor is 21 . . . Bg7 22 Nxc5 with a pawn and active pieces for the exchange. (LS)

22 Bxe4	**Re8**
23 Bd3	**b6**
24 Kg2	**f5**
25 gxf5	**Bxf5**
26 Bxf5	**gxf5**

Kristensen, in Lyon, still gave Black the edge.

27 Rd1	Kf7
28 Rd3	Bf6
29 Ra3	a5!

The new weakness at b6 is relatively unimportant since Black's bishop can defend it. The pawn at c4 is also a target after . . . Re4. (LS)

30 Rb3	Bd8
31 Rc3	Bc7
32 a4	Kf6
33 Kf1	

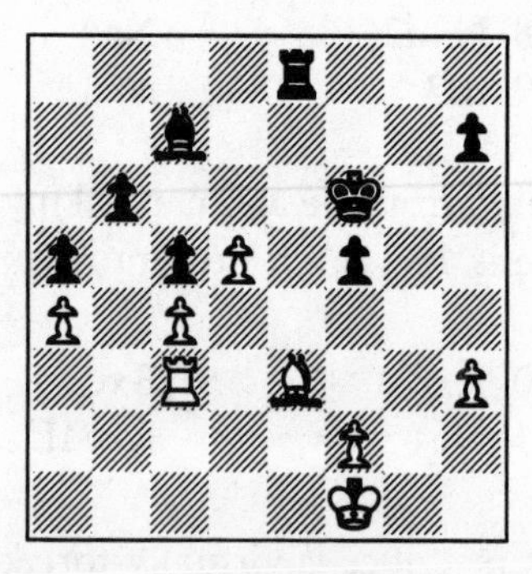

After 33 Kf1

But not 33 Kf3? because of 33 . . . Re4!, followed by . . . Ke5 and . . . f4. By playing 33 Kf1, White prepares to meet 33 . . . Re4 with 34 f3. (LS)

33 . . .	f4
34 Bc1	Kf5
35 Rc2	Rg8
36 Re2	Be5
37 Bb2	Bd4!

38 Bxd4	**cxd4**
39 Re7	**d3**

With the idea 40 . . . Rg1+! (LS)

40 Ke1	**Rc8**
41 Kd2	**Rxc4**

Karpov sealed.

42 Kxd3	**Draw**

The draw is simple after 42 . . . Rxa4 43 d6 Ra3+ or 43 . . . Ra1 44 Kc2 Ra4.

Kasparov lit the fuse on another major surprise in Game 14, switching from the Ruy Lopez to the Scotch Opening, with its reputation for drawish stolidity due to the early release of central tension. With the match deadlocked at 6.5–6.5, the world champion was ready for a change of pace.

At move 10 Kasparov played a new line, and Karpov quickly fell behind on the clock—at least until Kasparov spent fifty-three minutes on 19 Na3. By move 26 Karpov was visibly pleased with his position and Kasparov appeared to be squirming. But Kasparov fought back and Karpov was forced to thread his way to a draw as his time ticked away.

The game may have been tense for the players, but from the moment Kasparov unveiled his opening surprise, it was even more so for the spectators, few of whom were prepared for this unfamiliar territory.

"It's a win!" shouted Roshal at one point, according to IM Andrew Martin in the bulletin.

"For whom?" shot back British GM Joe Gallagher.

No answer.

The match remained tied, at 7.0–7.0.

Match 5, Game 14
November 26, 1990
Scotch Opening

White: Garry Kasparov *Black: Anatoly Karpov*

Annotated by GM Ron Henley

1	e4	e5
2	Nf3	Nc6
3	d4	

This ancient opening, considered drawish, was a surprise. The last time it reared its head in world championship play was in Steinitz–Chigorin, 1892. (Kristensen-SC)

3	...	exd4
4	Nxd4	Nf6
5	Nxc6	bxc6
6	e5	Qe7
7	Qe2	Nd5
8	c4	Ba6
9	b3	0-0-0
10	g3	

A novelty, according to Spassky. Previous tries were 10 Qb2 Nb6 11 Be2 (Ljubojevic–Seirawan, 1986) and 10 Bb2 (Hort–Unzicker, 1983).

10	...	Re8

After 10 ... f6?! 11 e6! dxe6 12 Bh3 Re8 13 0-0, the weakened pawn structure around the black king gives White excellent compensation for the pawn. According to Karpov, that is probably what Kasparov had in mind. (RH)

11 Bb2	**f6**
12 Bg2	

Kasparov had used only eight minutes to Karpov's fifty-five.

12 . . .	**fxe5**
13 0-0	**h5**
14 Qd2	**Nf6**
15 Qa5	**Bb7**
16 Ba3	**Qe6**

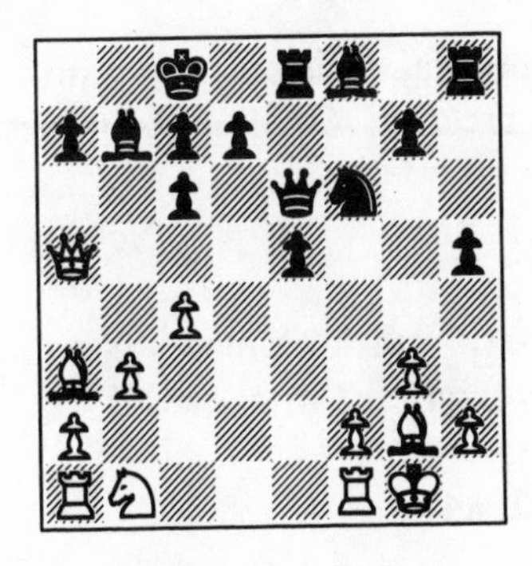

After 16 ... Qe6

Also possible is 16 . . . Qf7 17 Bxf8 Qxf8 18 Qxa7 Qb4!?, when Black may have . . . Qb6 at some point to halt White's attack. (RH)

17 Bxf8	**Rhxf8**

Spassky preferred 17 . . . Rexf8, but Karpov, feeling he had no real attack on the h-file, chose to centralize. (RH)

18 Qxa7

White had used twenty-eight minutes; Black an hour twenty-three minutes. Valvo noted Karpov glancing at his clock nervously, apparently disturbed at the growing gap.

18 . . . Qg4

Kasparov spent fifty-three minutes on his next move. Valvo was skeptical of the result: "not a fifty-three minute move."

19 Na3 h4
20 Nc2 h3

A very committal decision, giving up any chance to open the h-file but creating mating possibilities on g2. (RH)

21 Bh1 Ne4

Another sharp attacking move. Now 22 f3?? loses to 22 . . . Nxg3! 23 fxg4 Ne2 mate. (RH)

22 a4

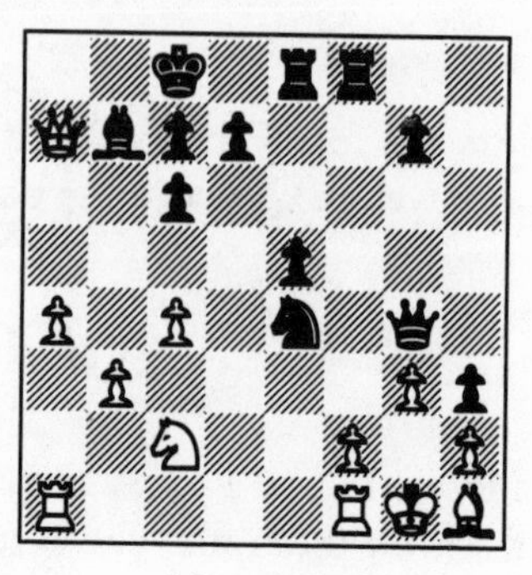

After 22 a4

Karpov says Black has tremendous compensation after 22 Ne3 Nc3!? 23 Qxb7+! Kxb7 24 Bxc6+ Kxc6 25 Nxg4 Rf3. (RH)

22 . . .	Nc3
23 Rae1	Ne2+

After 23 . . . Qe2? 24 Nb4, White is several valuable tempi ahead of the game. (RH)

24 Rxe2	Qxe2
25 Nb4	d5
26 cxd5	cxd5!

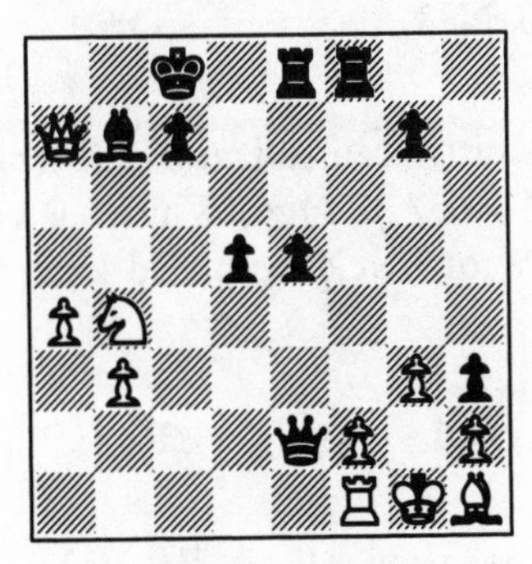

After 26 ... cxd5

Karpov broke into a broad smile, and Kasparov fidgeted nervously at the table. The champion's advantage on the clock had melted to less than twenty minutes. (SC)

For several minutes, Karpov considered 26 . . . c5 27 d6! e4 28 Qxc5 Rf7 29 Nd5 Bxd5 30 Qxd5 Ref8. Short of time, he was unable to reach any conclusion. (RH)

27 Bxd5

After 27 Rcl Qd2 28 Qc5, Spassky gave 28 . . . Re7 29 Nxd5 (29 Bxd5! is unclear, according to Karpov) 29 . . . Bxd5 30 Bxd5 Rxf2, with a Black advantage. Karpov, however, gives 28 . . . Rf7! 29 Bxd5 Bxd5 30 Nxd5 Rd8, with a solid advantage for Black; e.g., 31 Nb6+ Kb8, or 31 Nb4 Qd1+ 32 Rxd1 Rxd1 mate. (RH)

27 . . .	**Bxd5**
28 Nxd5	**Qc2!**

A forced move to prevent 29 Rc1 and to defend against 29 Qxc7 mate. (RH)

29 Qa6+	**Kd7**
30 Ne3	**Qe4!**

Excellent intuitive centralization. After the weaker 30 . . . Qxb3 31 Rd1+ Ke7 32 Qg6, White has very good practical chances in view of Black's exposed king and his time trouble. (RH)

31 Rc1	**Rb8!**

Much stronger than 31 . . . Rf6?! 32 Qb5+, or 31 . . . Re6?! 32 Rxc7+ Kxc7 33 Qxe6 Qb1+ (33 . . . Qf3? 34 Nd5+) 34 Nf1 Qf5 (34 . . . Qe4? 35 Qxh3), with an unclear position. (RH)

32 Qf1!

Now Black must surrender his trump h3-pawn, since 32 . . . Rh8 33 Qd1+ Kc8 34 Rc4 would destroy the coordination of the black pieces (Karpov). (RH)

32 ...	Rxb3
33 Qxh3+	Kd8

Not 33 ... Kd6? 34 Nc4+ and 35 Nd2 (Karpov).

34 Qh5!

Preventing both 34 ... Rxe3?? 35 Qg5+, and 34 ... Rb1?? 35 Qd1+ winning for White.

Weaker is 34 Rd1+?! Rd3 35 Qh4+ Qxh4 36 Rxd3+ Qd4!. (RH)

34 ...	Kc8!

Karpov, with less than two minutes on his clock, played this move instantly.

35 Qd1	Rxe3!

The right choice, to secure at least a draw and make the time control at move 40.

36 fxe3	Qxe3+
37 Kh1	Qe4+
38 Kg1	Qe3+
39 Kh1	

Kasparov wanted to claim a draw by repetition, but would have risked time forfeit if his claim were invalid.

39 ...	Qe4+
40 Kg1	Rd8

Adjourned.

41 Qc2	**Draw**

The Fidelity Elite 10 recommended 41 Qe1 as another way to draw.

Azmaiparashvili called our villa directly to offer a draw. About 11:30 the next morning, Karpov instructed me to phone Chief Arbiter Geurt Gijssen and accept provided a legal move was sealed.

Now it was Karpov's turn to drop a bomb—11 Bh6!. Kasparov repeated the Grünfeld only to walk into a prepared line and to find himself staging a desperate defense. Then suddenly Karpov seemed to lose control of the position and the game erupted into real fireworks. But at the critical moment, with both players running out of time, Kasparov offered a draw: 7.5–7.5.

For journalists, this game represented the ultimate torture—raising expectations to the maximum and then ending in an abrupt, unexpected draw. After seven straight draws, a few more cynical voices began to wonder out loud whether either player really wanted to win. That question would be answered soon enough.

Match 5, Game 15
November 28, 1990
Grünfeld Defense

White: Anatoly Karpov ***Black: Garry Kasparov***

Annotated by GM Leonid Shamkovich

1	d4	Nf6
2	c4	g6
3	Nc3	d5

4 cxd5	Nxd5
5 e4	Nxc3
6 bxc3	Bg7
7 Be3	c5
8 Qd2	0-0
9 Nf3	Qa5
10 Rcl	e6
11 Bh6!	

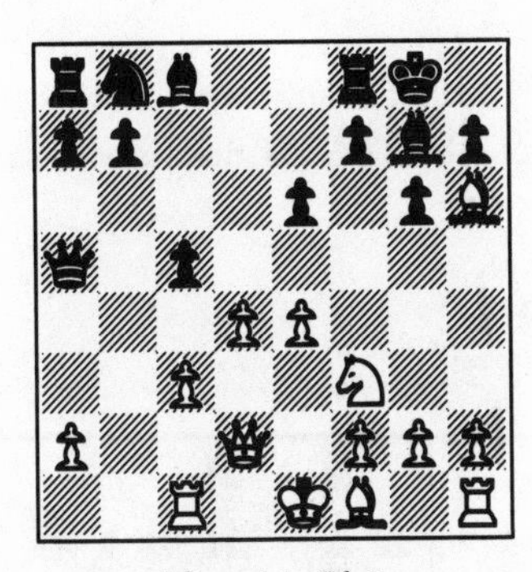

After 11 Bh6

A novelty. Watson gave White a big plus after 11 . . . cxd4 12 Bxg7 Kxg7 13 cxd4 Qxd2+ 14 Kxd2 Nc6 15 Ke3. (SC)

11 . . .	Nc6
12 h4!	

Very strong. The threat h5 is unpleasant even after the queen trade. (LS)

12 . . .	cxd4
13 Bxg7	Kxg7
14 cxd4	Qxd2+
15 Kxd2	Rd8
16 Ke3	Bd7

Black does not have time for the prophylactic 16 . . . h6 17 Rb1 (17 h5 g5) 17 . . . Rb8 18 Bb5 Bd7 19 Rhc1, with the idea 20 d5. (LS)

17 Rb1 Rab8

Unpleasant is 17 . . . b6 18 Ba6. (LS)

18 Bd3 Ne7

Black spent thirty-two minutes on this move. Still dubious is 18 . . . h6 19 Rhc1 b6 20 Bb5 Rbc8 21 Ba6, with strong queenside pressure. (LS)

19 h5!

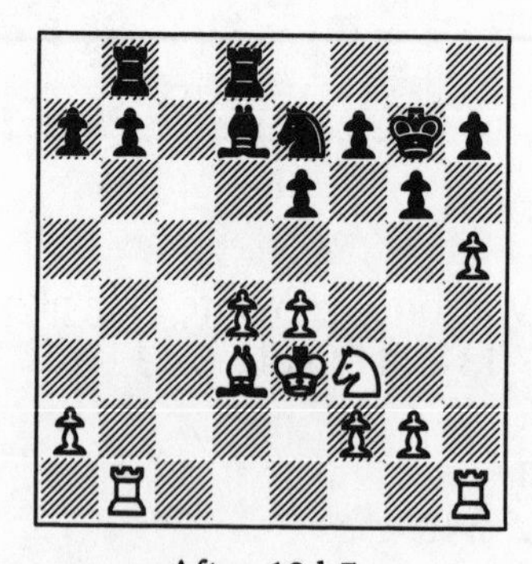

After 19 h5

Just in time! The threat hxg6 is still quite unpleasant for Black. (LS)

19 . . . f6
20 hxg6 hxg6
21 Rh2

More accurate is 21 g4 g5, but Karpov was hoping to create threats along the h-file. (LS)

21 . . . b6
22 g4

Not dangerous for Black is 22 Rbh1 Rh8. The text threatens g5, weakening the key e5 square. (LS)

22 . . . e5!?

"This is suicide," exclaimed Spassky.

Not quite. Risky, yes; suicide, no. White has a slight lead after the trivial 22 . . . Rh8 23 Rxh8 Rxh8 24 g5. But probably the safest is 22 . . . g5 23 e5 Nd5+ 24 Kd2 Rh8 25 Rbh1 Rxh2 26 Rxh2 Rh8, when Black holds. (LS)

23 dxe5 Bxg4
24 exf6+

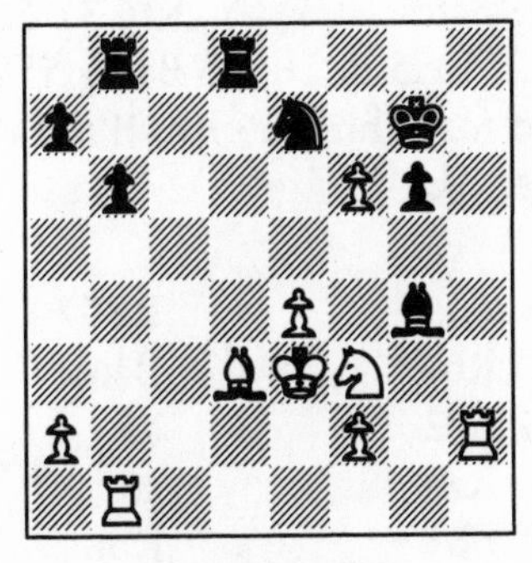

After 24 exf6+

Also extremely strong is 24 Rbh1 Bxf3 25 Rh7+ Kf8 26 Rh8+ Ng8 27 Bc4! with a strong attack. But after 24 . . .

Rxd3+! Black is all right; e.g., 25 Kxd3 Bxf3 26 Rh7+ Kf8 27 exf6 Ng8 28 f7 Bxh1 29 fxg8Q+ Kxg8 30 Rxh1, with a very slight edge for White. (LS)

24 ...	**Kxf6**
25 Nd4	**Rb7?**

This quite natural move turns out to be a critical error. Correct is 25 . . . Re8! 26 f3 Be6, when White is only slightly better. (LS)

26 f3

Very soon after the game, Fidelity's computer suggested the brilliant winning move 26 Rh4!!. Likely variations are 26 . . . Rbd7 27 e5+! Kxe5 28 Rb5+! (better than 28 Rxg4 Rxd4 29 Rxd4 Rxd4 30 f4+ Rxf4 31 Rb5+ Nd5+ 32 Rxd5+ Kxd5 33 Kxf4 Kd4, with a draw in spite of White's extra piece) 28 . . . Nd5+ 29 Rxd5+ Rxd5 30 Nc6+ (the point of White's attack) 30 . . . Kf6 31 Nxd8, winning; and 26 . . . Nf5+ 27 exf5 Re7+ 28 Be4 gxf5 29 f3 Kg5 30 Rh2, with a big lead for White. 26 Rh4!! is a triumph of modern electronic chess. (LS)

26 ...	**Rbd7**
27 Rb4	**Be6**
28 Rc2	**a5**
29 Ra4	**g5**
30 Bb5	**Rd6**
31 Be2	**Bd7**
32 Rac4	**Re8**
33 Rb2	**Nd5+**
Draw	

After 33 ... Nd5+

With this move Kasparov offered a draw, which was immediately accepted by Karpov. The position clearly favors Black; e.g., 34 Kf2 Nf4 35 Bf1, followed by two attractive alternatives: 35 . . . Rh8 36 Kg1 Ke5, or 36 . . . Ng6 with the idea 37 . . . Ne5; and 35 . . . Re5 36 a4 Rc5! 37 Rxc5 bxc5 38 Nb5 (38 Nb3 Rb6) 38 . . . Nd3+ 39 Bxd3 Rxd3 40 Rc2 Ke5 41 Rxc5+ Kf4, with a pull for Black.

So why did Kasparov offer a draw? This remains one of the match's mysteries. Apparently he was not convinced of his advantage and chose to conserve energy for his next game with White. (LS)

If either player's will to win was ever really in doubt, Game 16 put the lie to the skeptics—a three-session, 102-move marathon that tested both players to their limits. Despite some second-session mistakes by Kasparov and heroic defense by Karpov, the world champion notched a full point to take the match lead 8.5–7.5.

Kasparov repeated his experiment with the Scotch, forcing Karpov to sacrifice a pawn after the challenger deviated from Game 14 with 8 . . . Nb6. After the first session, most experts thought Karpov was finished; after the second, many thought he was holding the draw. Overnight analysis by both teams uncovered winning plans, though it is interesting that Deep Thought, from its New York headquarters, was unable to find the win without Dlugy's assistance.

Match 5, Game 16
December 1, 1990
Scotch Opening

White: Garry Kasparov ***Black: Anatoly Karpov***

Annotated by GM Ron Henley

1	**e4**	**e5**
2	**Nf3**	**Nc6**
3	**d4**	**exd4**
4	**Nxd4**	**Nf6**
5	**Nxc6**	**bxc6**
6	**e5**	**Qe7**
7	**Qe2**	**Nd5**
8	**c4**	**Nb6**
9	**Nd2**	**Qe6**
10	**b3**	**a5**

A novelty, the idea of which is to secure counterplay with . . . a4. (RH)

11 Bb2

Black gets a good game after 11 a3, permitting . . . a4; e.g., 11 . . . a4 12 b4 c5 13 b5 Bb7. (RH)

11 . . . Bb4?

After 11 ... Bb4

Karpov deviates from the intended 11 . . . a4, since he saw what we had overlooked: 12 Qe3! followed by Bd3, 0-0 and Ne4, with a beautiful attacking formation for White. Portisch and I were responsible for preparing this variation. (RH)

12 a3 Bxd2+?!

Black surrenders the bishop-pair and sacrifices the c7-pawn—a terrible plan. (RH)

13 Qxd2 d5?

Spassky thought 13 . . . a4 was still playable, although White would enjoy an enduring advantage: 14 c5 Nd5 15 b4 Ba6! 16 Bxa6 Rxa6 17 0-0 0-0 18 f4 f5. (RH)

14 cxd5 cxd5
15 Rc1!

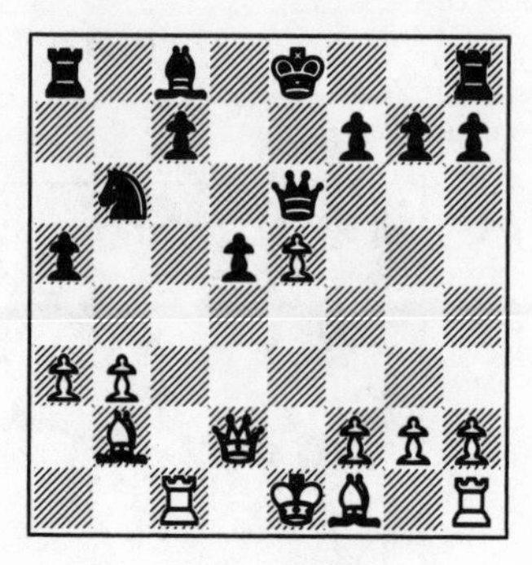

After 15 Rc1

15 . . .	0-0
16 Rxc7	Qg6
17 f3	Bf5
18 g4	Bb1

Much worse, according to Spassky, are 18 . . . Bxg4?? 19 Rg1 and 18 . . . Be6 19 Bd3.

IM Andrew Martin, in Lyon, reported the press consensus—"Karpov is getting desperate." Lein, however, was beginning to think Kasparov's own position might be vulnerable. Kasparov spent a half-hour alone at the board working out his next move. (SC)

19 Bb5!

Black is completely lost.

19 . . .	Rac8
20 Rxc8	Rxc8
21 0-0	

Karpov, alone again onstage, was beginning to look worried.

21 . . .	h5

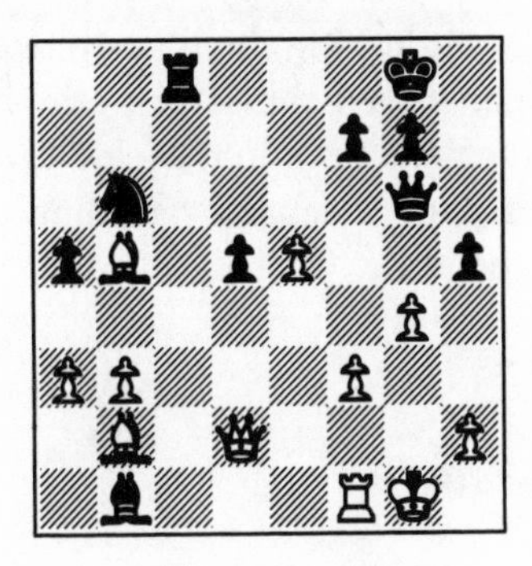

After 21 ... h5

22 h3?!

According to Karpov, the strongest continuation is 22 Qd4!, threatening 23 e6!, which wins immediately: 22 . . . hxg4 23 Qxg4 Qxg4+ 24 fxg4 Bc2 25 Bd4 Rb8 26 Rf3 Nc8 27 a4 Bd1 28 Rg3. Karpov felt that endgame was hopeless for Black, since he's a pawn down, his knight on c8 is out of play, and his a5-pawn is weak. (RH)

22 . . .	**hxg4**
23 hxg4	**Bc2**
24 Qd4	**Qe6**
25 Rf2	**Rc7**
26 Rh2	

Spassky gives 26 Qe3 a4 27 bxa4 (27 Bd4 axb3 28 Bxb6 b2) 27 . . . Nxa4 28 Bd4.

"We're in for a gruesome finish," Tisdall observed. (SC)

26 . . .	**Nd7!**

The knight heads for the kingside, hoping to stable at g6 and create practical counterchances. (RH)

27 b4

Why not 27 a4, leaving the black pawn on a5 as a target in the endgame? Here I think Kasparov had so many positional advantages he couldn't decide on a clear direction. The text helps Black's cause by trading one pair of pawns and opening the a-file. (RH)

27 . . .	**axb4**
28 axb4	**Nf8**
29 Bf1!	

A good, solid move, protecting White's king and preparing to push the b-pawn. (RH)

29 . . .	**Bb3**

The threatened push of the b-pawn forces Black to surrender the b1-h7 diagonal. (RH)

Each player had less than fifteen minutes for eleven moves.

30 Bd3!	**Bc4**
31 Bf5?!	

An unnecessary interpolation. The simple 31 Bb1 is better. (RH)

31 . . .	**Qe7**

Now the e6-square is available to the black knight. (RH)

32 Qd2	**Rc6**

No good is 32 . . . Ne6?? 33 Rh8+ Kxh8 34 Qh2+ Kg8 35 Qh7+ Kf8 36 Qh8+ mate. (RH)

33 Bd4 **Ra6**
34 Bb1

Black is winning after 34 Bc5?? Qxe5 35 Bxf8 Ra1 + 36 Kg2 Bf1 +. (RH)

34 . . . **Ra3**
35 Rh3 **Rb3**
36 Bc2 **Qxb4**
37 Qf2

Threatening Qh4.

37 . . . **Ng6**

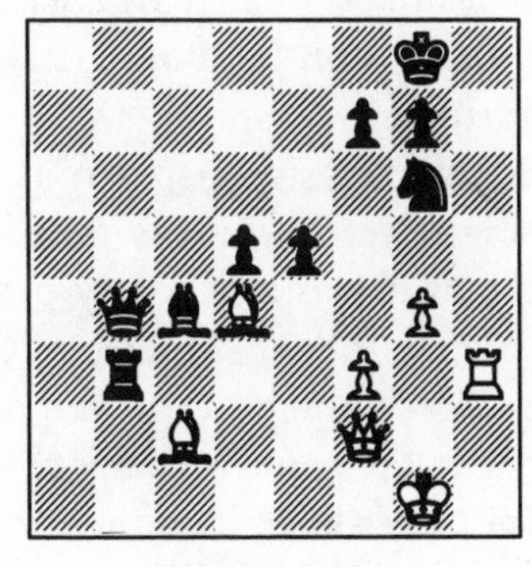

After 37 ... Ng6

38 e6?!

Though this is a serious mistake from a practical point of view, since both players were short of time, it should still be enough to win. Better is 38 Bxb3! Qxb3 39 Qb2!:

A) 39 . . . Qd3 40 e6! Qf1 + 41 Kh2 fxe6 42 Qb8 + Kf7 (42 . . . Nf8? 43 Rh8 + Kxh8 44 Qxf8 + Kh7 45 Qxg7 mate) 43 Qc7 + Ke8 44 Qxg7, and White is winning;

B) 39 . . . Qxb2 40 Bxb2, and Black can resign;

C) 39 . . . Qd1 + 40 Kf2 Qf1 + 41 Kg3 Qe1 + 42 Qf2, and White still wins. (RH)

38 . . .	**Rb1+**
39 Bxb1	

Kasparov apparently changed his mind about continuing 39 Kh2, choosing to seal in a less complicated position. With the text move, he admits he should have just played 38 Bxb3 and kept his e-pawn.

39 . . .	**Qxb1+**
40 Kh2	**fxe6**
41 Qb2!	

Kasparov's sealed move, and the best one. White's threat of 42 Qb8+ forces the exchange of queens. If White allows . . . e5 with the queens on the board, Black could mount a serious counterattack.

During overnight analysis, Kasparov's team could not find a clear win if Black set up pawns on e5 and d4 and just waited. Feeling that it was a fifty-fifty proposition between winning and drawing, they spent most of their energy on the formation with a black knight on g6 and pawns at e5 and d4 and less on the way the game actually continued. This gave Karpov a chance to get back into the game.

It's an interesting and fairly common adjournment phenomenon for one problematic and difficult variation to eat up analysis time desperately needed to examine less complex sidelines. Unfortunately for us, the steel trap armed in the first session was only weakened but not disabled.

41 . . .	**Qxb2+**

Not 41 . . . Qd3? 42 Qb8+ Kf7 (42 . . . Nf8 43 Rh8+ Kxh8 44 Qxf8+ Kh7 45 Qxg7 mate) 43 Qc7+ Ke8 44 Qxg7 e5 45 Rh7 Qe2+ 46 Kg3 Qe1+ 47 Bf2, and White wins.

When the game resumed, Kasparov, waiting at the board for Karpov, looked like he had been up all night. Karpov arrived looking fresh and cheerful. Most experts in Lyon thought Kasparov had winning chances, but slight ones. (SC)

42 Bxb2 **Nf4**
43 Rh4

After 43 Rg3?! Ne2 44 Rg2 d4, Black has good compensation due to the lack of coordination between White's pieces.

43 . . . **Nd3**
44 Bc3?!

Already Karpov is beginning to benefit from the Kasparov team's preoccupation with 43 . . . Ng6. Much better is 44 Ba3! Ne5 45 Kg3 Be2, with an enormous range of options, none of which we could prove led to a forced win or draw.

44 . . . **e5**
45 Kg3

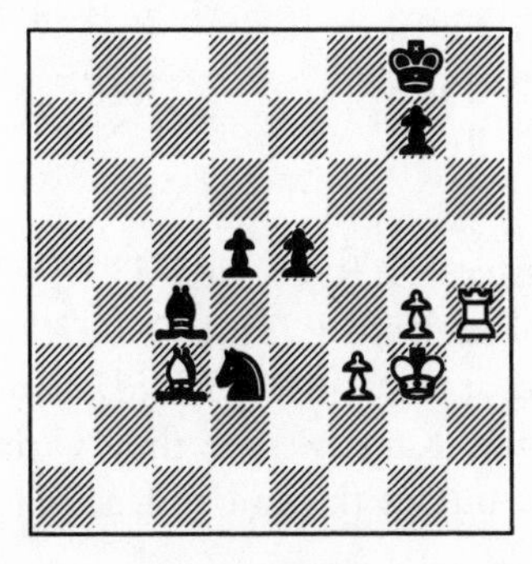

After 45 Kg3

45 . . . **d4**

After 45 . . . e4, we have another key juncture for Black. We spent a lot of time trying to determine whether the white king would ever be able to penetrate after 46 fxe4 dxe4, and concluded that he would have good winning prospects: 46 fxe4 dxe4 47 Bd4 Bf7 48 Rh1 Bc4 49 Ra1 Bf7! (the bishop must help mask the weak pawn at g7 from the white rook going to the seventh rank) 50 Ra8+ Kh7 51 Ra7 Kg8 52 Kh4 Nf4 53 Be3 Ng6+ 54 Kg5 Nh8 55 Kf4 Bg6 56 Bd4 Nf7 (now Black has a semi-fortress, but White should be able to break through with patient maneuvering; i.e. 57 Ra8+ Kh7 58 Rf8 Nh8 59 Bc3 Nf7 60 Bd2 Nd6 61 Be3 Nf7 62 Bc1 Nh8 63 Ke5 Nf7+ 64 Ke6 Nh6 65 g5 Ng4 66 Rf4, and Black's waiting game is over) 66 . . . Bh5 67 Kf5 g6+ 68 Kxe4, and White wins. (RH)

46 Bd2	**Bd5**
47 Rh5	**Kf7**

Karpov spent eighteen minutes on this move.

48 Ba5	**Ke6**
49 Rh8	**Nb2**
50 Re8+	**Kd6**
51 Bb4+	**Kc6**
52 Rc8+	

The alternatives 52 Rxe5 Nd3 53 Rg5 Nxb4 54 Rxg7 d3 55 Kf2 d2 56 Ke2 Bxf3+, and 52 Re7 Nc4 53 Rxg7 d3 54 Kf2 d2 lead to draws, since 55 Bxd2 is now forced. Unfortunately, though Karpov sees that variation now, a few moves later he misses the same idea. (RH)

52 . . .	**Kd7**

53 Rc5	Ke6
54 Rc7	

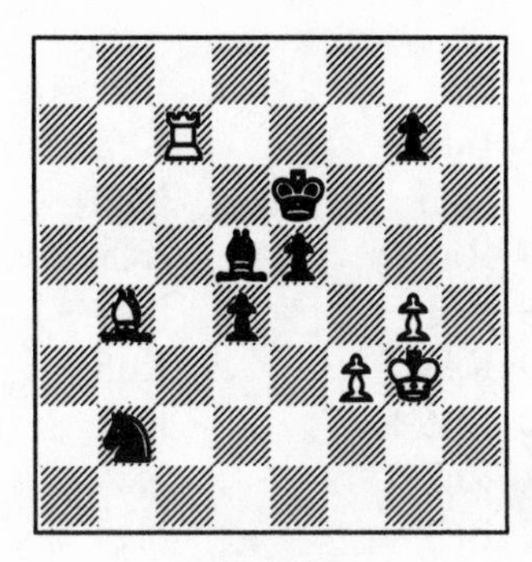

After 54 Rc7

54 ...	g6?

Necessary is 54 ... Nc4!. After putting up tremendous resistance, Karpov misses a forced draw: 55 Rxg7 (55 Kf2 d3 56 Ke1 g5!, and Black threatens just to liquidate with 57 ... d2+ 58 Bxd2 Nxd2 59 Kxd2 Bxf3, draw) 55 ... d3 56 Kf2 d2 57 Bxd2 (57 Ke2? Bxf3+, and Black wins) 57 ... Nxd2 58 Rg6+ Kf7 59 Rg5, draw. (RH)

55 Re7+	Kf6
56 Rd7	Ba2
57 Ra7	Bc4
58 Ba5	Bd3
59 f4!	exf4+
60 Kxf4	Bc2
61 Ra6+	Kf7
62 Ke5	Nd3+
63 Kxd4	Nf2
64 g5?	

Karpov pointed out after the session that White wins quickly with 64 Rc6!, scattering the black pieces around the edges of the board. (RH)

64 ...	Bf5
65 Bd2	Ke7
66 Kd5	Ne4
67 Ra7+	Ke8
68 Be3	Nc3+
69 Ke5	Kd8
70 Bb6+	Ke8
71 Rc7	Ne4
72 Be3	Ng3
73 Bf4	Nh5

Now the knight has at least found an anchor. Even so, it is still subject to being trapped by the white bishop. (RH)

74 Ra7	Kf8
75 Bh2	Ng7
76 Bg1	Nh5
77 Bc5+	Kg8
78 Kd6	Kf8
79 Bd4	Bg4
80 Be5	Bf5
81 Rh7	Kg8
82 Rc7	Kf8
83 Kc6	Kg8
84 Re7	Kf8
85 Bd6	Kg8?!

Here Karpov made a practical mistake by thinking for ten minutes on a forced move. This allowed Kasparov to make the next time control and to sacrifice forty-five minutes to seal his move. With Kasparov short of time, Karpov should have forced him to play another ten to twelve moves before adjournment. Then Kasparov would have been forced to find a win over the board to avoid a draw on the basis of 50 moves without a pawn advance or capture, commonly referred to as "the fifty-move rule."

86 Re8+	**Kf7**
87 Re7+	**Kg8**
88 Be5	**Kf8**

Kasparov appeared to be uncomfortable onstage, disappointed perhaps that Karpov had survived another session and a little concerned that he might have to settle for a draw. He sealed his next move and the game was adjourned for a second time.

The ten minutes Karpov had spent on the meaningless 85 . . . Kg8 probably decided the game in Kasparov's favor, since it allowed the champion's team to solve the position away from the board.

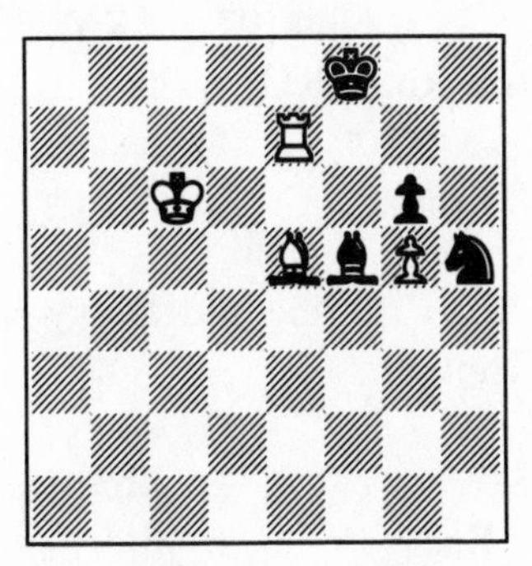

After 88 ... Kf8

89 Ra7!

This is the natural move, but the important thing is that Kasparov sacrificed forty-five minutes to seal it, leaving him eleven minutes to reach move 104 and the next time control after resumption. Meanwhile, he had two days to find a win before move 114 when a draw would result from the fifty-move rule.

Spassky gives 89 Bd6 Kg8 (89 . . . Ng7 90 Ra7 + Kg8 91 Ra8 + Kh7 92 Be5 winning) 90 Kc7 Ng7 91 Kd8 Ne6 + 92 Kd7 Kf8 93 Rxe6 + ? Kf7, when Black draws.

89 . . . Bg4

Karpov knew the position was lost when the second playing session was over. In fact, White has three methods of winning at this point. Other tries for Black are even worse: 89 . . . Kg8 90 Kc7 Kf7 91 Kd8 + Ke6 92 Re7 + Kd5 93 Bb8 Bg4 94 Ke8 Be6 95 Bh2 Bf5 96 Kf7 Bc2 97 Re6 Bf5 98 Rxg6!, and White wins (Zaitsev and Kuzmin). Or 89 . . . Be4 + ?! 90 Kd7 Kf7 91 Bh2 Bd3 92 Kd8 + Ke6 93 Ra5! Ng7 94 Re5 + Kf7 95 Re7 + Kg8 96 Be5 Nf5 97 Re6 (the weakness of the g6-pawn allows White to break down the Black defense) 97 . . . Nh4 (97 . . . Kh7 98 Re8) 98 Ke7 Bf5 99 Rb6 Kh7 100 Rb8. (RH)

90 Kd6

Kasparov selects the method Dlugy had already tested against Deep Thought.

90 . . .	**Bh3**
91 Ra3	**Bg4**
92 Re3	**Bf5**
93 Kc7	**Kf7**
94 Kd8	**Bg4**

After 94 . . . Ke6 95 Bh2+ Kd5, White can maneuver the king to h6 and trade the rook for the pawn and knight with an easy win. (Spassky)

95	**Bb2**	**Be6**
96	**Bc3**	**Bf5**
97	**Re7+**	**Kf8**
98	**Be5**	**Bd3**
99	**Ra7**	**Be4**
100	**Rc7**	**Bb1**
101	**Bd6+**	**Kg8**
102	**Ke7**	**1-0**

Karpov resigned and the two players discussed the game. The white king has achieved decisive penetration and the rest is easy: 102 . . . Ng7 103 Be5 Nf5+ 104 Kf6 Ne3 105 Rc8+ Kh7 106 Kf7 Ba2+ 107 Kf8 Nd5 108 Ra8, followed by 109 Ra7+. (RH)

Following his win in Game 16, Kasparov's supporters were quick to parade their candidate's claim to superiority, and Kasparov fever raged again in the press room. Unfortunately for them, Karpov had forgotten to read his own obituary. Aggressively answering Kasparov's 9th-move novelty with 10 Ng5!, he efficiently put the champion away before adjournment.

Although the match was tied again, 8.0–8.0, the trading of uppercuts in the middle of the ring had revived general interest. This kind of bloodletting was something even non-players could understand—there was a winner and a loser, and none of the fine distinctions between a quiet truce and a fighting draw that make a half-point so hard to explain to the average sports fan.

Match 5, Game 17
December 5, 1990
Grünfeld Defense

White: Anatoly Karpov ***Black: Garry Kasparov***

Annotated by GM Ron Henley

This game was played on my birthday, which I share with Karpov's former trainer, Semyon Furman.

1	d4	Nf6
2	c4	g6
3	Nc3	d5
4	cxd5	Nxd5
5	e4	Nxc3
6	bxc3	Bg7
7	Be3	c5
8	Qd2	0-0
9	Nf3	Bg4
10	Ng5!?	

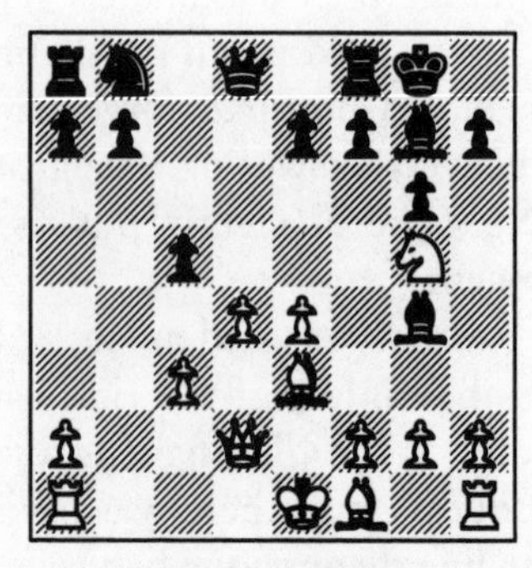

After 10 Ng5

This novelty was developed by Kuzmin and Zaitsev. Before the game, it was also suggested—coincidentally and independently—by a local chess columnist. When Karpov played it, Kasparov glanced over at Azmaiparashvili. (RH)

10 . . .	**cxd4**
11 cxd4	**Nc6**

Spassky suggested 11 . . . h6 12 h3 hxg5 13 hxg4 Nc6 14 Rd1.

12 h3	**Bd7**
13 Rb1	**Rc8!**
14 Nf3	

Bad is 14 Rxb7? Nxd4 15 Bxd4 Bxd4 16 Qxd4 Qa5 + 17 Qd2 Rc1 +. (Spassky)

14 . . .	**Na5**
15 Bd3	**Be6**
16 0-0	**Bc4**
17 Rfd1	**b5?!**

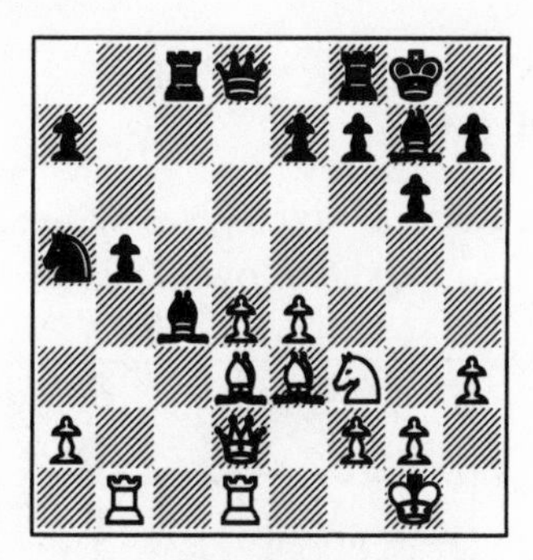

After 17 ... b5

A natural move but too loosening, according to Karpov. Preferable is 17 . . . b6 to support the knight at a5. (RH)

18 Bg5!

Karpov begins a series of fine positional moves, culminating in 27 Bc3!, that accents the defects in Black's position. (RH)

18 . . .	**a6**
19 Rbc1!	**Bxd3**
20 Rxc8	**Qxc8**
21 Qxd3	**Re8?**

Probably Black's last chance to avoid a serious disadvantage is 21 . . . Qb7. (RH)

22 Rc1	**Qb7**
23 d5	**Nc4**
24 Nd2!	**Nxd2**

Now Karpov went into a long think. Everyone in the press room was expecting 25 Qxd2 with the obvious point that 25 . . . Rc8? loses a pawn to 26 Rxc8+ Qxc8 27 Bxe7. (RH)

Both players were running short of time here—White 1:43, Black 1:57.

25 Bxd2!	**Rc8**
26 Rc6!	

Now 26 . . . Rxc6 27 dxc6 gives White a powerful passed pawn, since 27 . . . Qxc6 allows 28 Qd8+ Bf8 29 Bh6 and wins. (RH)

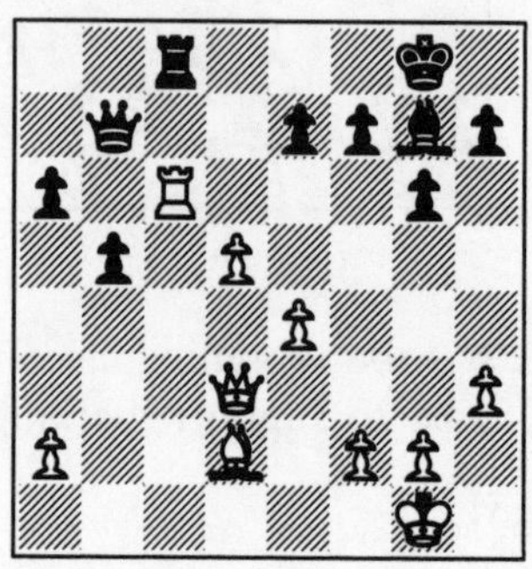

After 26 Rc6

26 . . . Be5

No better is 26 . . . Rxc6 27 dxc6 Qc7 28 Qd7 Be5:

A) 29 Bh6 Qxd7 30 cxd7 Bc7 31 e5! (a beautiful variation found by Kharitonov, in which Black runs out of moves) 31 . . . a5 (after 31 . . . Bd8 32 h4!, Black can't play 32 . . . e6 due to 33 Bg5) 32 Kf1 b4 33 Ke2 a4 34 Kd3 Bd8 35 Kc4 Ba5 36 h4 Kh8 37 Bf8;

B) 29 Bb4 (the continuation Karpov had in mind during the game) 29 . . . e6 30 Qe8+ Kg7 31 Qf8+ Kf6 32 Qh8+ Kg5 33 Bd2+ Bf4 34 h4+ Kg4 35 f3+ Kg3 36 Be1 mate. (RH)

27 Bc3!

This final stroke destroys the coordination of Black's pieces, after which Black's resistance is broken. (RH)

27 . . . Bb8

Black does no better after 27 . . . Bxc3 28 Qxc3 Rxc6 29 dxc6 Qc7 30 g3, an unpleasant queen ending in which he will have to create further weaknesses on his kingside to bring his king to bear against the passed c-pawn: 30 . . . f6 31 Qb3+ Kf8 32 Qe6, and now 33 Qd7 is a decisive threat since 32 . . . Ke8 allows 33 Qg8 mate; or 30 . . . a5 31 Qc5 b4 32 Qd5, and once again the threat of 33 Qd7 is decisive; or 30 . . . e5 31 Qc5 f6 32 Qd5+ Kf8 33 Qe6 Qd8 34 Kg2 a5 35 h4 b4 36 g4 a4 37 Qc4, and Black loses a decisive pawn.

Also winning for White is 27 . . . Rxc6 28 dxc6 Qc7 29 Bxe5 Qxe5 30 Qd8+ Kg7 31 c7 Qa1+ 32 Kh2 Qe5+ 33 g3 Qb2 34 Kg2. (RH)

28 Qd4	f6
29 Ba5!	

Karpov now overpowers the c7-square, forcing Black to abandon the c-file, since exchanging on c6 would give White an unstoppable passed c-pawn. White loses after 29 Rb6?? Rxc3. (RH)

29 ...	Bd6
30 Qc3	Re8
31 a3!	

Classic Karpov: once he has a bind he clamps down on all counterplay. (RH)

31 ...	Kg7
32 g3	Be5
33 Qc5	h5
34 Bc7	

Domination of the c-file is now complete. The black bishop has very few squares to avoid being exchanged. (RH)

34 ...	Ba1
35 Bf4	Qd7
36 Rc7	

With only a few minutes left, Karpov does not bother with 36 Rxa6, but goes for the jugular at e7. (RH)

36 ...	Qd8
37 d6	g5
38 d7	Rf8

39 Bd2	Be5
40 Rb7	1-0

Kasparov could not find a move and resigned. White threatens Qc6 followed by Be3-b6. This was Karpov's best performance of the match and the best birthday present I've ever received.

Karpov's quick comeback might have taken the wind out of many players' sails, but Kasparov responded with another haymaker in Game 18. For those of us following the match, there was something surreal about the shift from equilibrium to carnage. We had been lulled into forgetting just how uncertain a chess player's fortunes are, how little separates winning from losing. Now we were on a roller coaster, and everyone was awake for the ride.

Ironically, in this game it was Karpov who trotted out the first innovation, one which nailed the world champion to his clock (1:09 for nineteen moves to Karpov's fifteen minutes). But after 21 Qc4!, a move overlooked by Karpov's camp in their preparations, the challenger found himself in a terrible position with the clocks even. Adjournment couldn't save him: 9.5–8.5.

Match 5, Game 18
December 8, 1990
Ruy Lopez

White: Garry Kasparov ***Black: Anatoly Karpov***

Annotated by GM Leonid Shamkovich

1 e4	e5
2 Nf3	Nc6

3	Bb5	a6
4	Ba4	Nf6
5	0-0	Be7
6	Re1	b5
7	Bb3	d6
8	c3	0-0
9	h3	Nd7
10	d4	Bf6
11	a4	Bb7

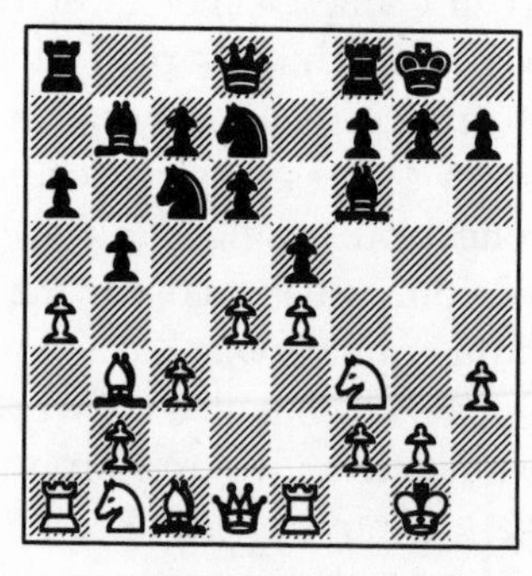

After 11 ... Bb7

Karpov had adopted this system three times before in the match, and each time Kasparov answered with a different plan. (LS)

12	Na3	exd4
13	cxd4	Nb6
14	Bf4!	

Also possible is the weaker 14 axb5 axb5 15 Bf4 b4 16 Nc2 (16 Nc4 Rxa1 17 Qxa1 Nxc4 18 Bxc4 Nxd4, with equality) 16 . . . Na5 (16 . . . Na4 17 Nxb4 Nxb2 also equalizes) 17 Nxb4 Nxb3 18 Rxa8 (18 Qxb3 Rxa1 19 Rxa1 Bxe4, with excellent chances for Black) 18 . . . Qxa8 19 Qxb3 Bxe4. (LS)

Kasparov, having spent forty-six minutes on this move, had used fifty-one minutes to Karpov's eight.

14 . . .	**bxa4**
15 Bxa4	**Nxa4**
16 Qxa4	**a5**

Karpov played this move instantly. (SC)

Black's queenside has been weakened, while White's center pawns are very strong. Karpov probably counted on pressure along the b-file. (LS)

17 Bd2

Discouraging . . . Nb4.

17 . . .	**Re8**

With thematic pressure against e4. (LS)

18 d5!

Fixing the backward pawn at c7 and taking control of the c6-square. Weaker is 18 Bc3?! Nb4. (LS)

18 . . .	**Nb4!?**

Simply bad is 18 . . . Ne7?, and White has strong pressure after 18 . . . Ne5 19 Nxe5 Bxe5 20 Nc4. (LS)

Karpov again used less than a minute for his answer, looking extremely comfortable and relaxed. Kasparov appeared nonplussed at Karpov's uncharacteristically rapid pace. (SC)

19 Bxb4 **axb4**
20 Qxb4

With chances for c-file pressure. White has agreed to fight with two knights against two bishops, but he has plenty of compensation due to the weaknesses at c7 and c6. (LS)

20 . . . **Rb8?!**
21 Qc4!

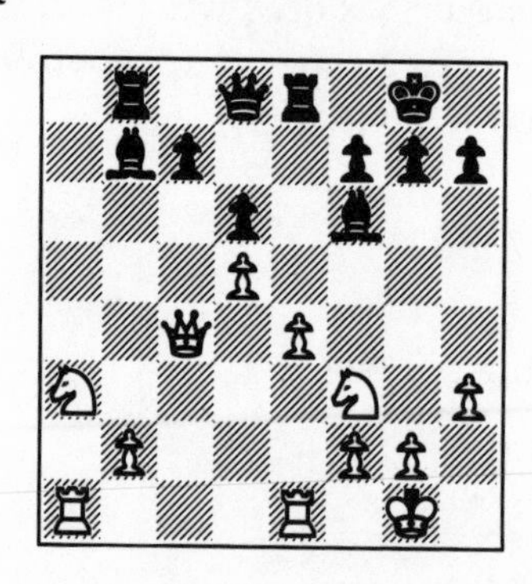

After 21 Qc4

The key move of the game, making . . . Ba6 difficult. Other moves are not as strong; e.g., 21 Qd2 c6 (21 . . . Ba6 22 Nd4) 22 Nc4 cxd5 (22 . . . Rxe4?! 23 Rxe4 cxd5 24 Rf4 dxc4 25 Rxc4 Bxf3 26 gxf3 Rxb2 27 Qd5 and White is better) 23 exd5 Rxe1+ 24 Rxe1 Ba6 25 Qc2! (24 Na5 Rxb2 25 Nc6 Rxd2 26 Nxd8 Rde2) 25 . . . Bxc4 26 Qxc4 Bxb2, with equality; or 21 Nb5 Qd7 22 Qc4 Bxb2 23 Rab1 Bxd5 24 exd5 Rxe1+ 25 Rxe1 Rxb5 26 Qxc7!. (LS)

21 . . . **Qc8**

To prepare . . . c5 or . . . c6. White is even better after other tries: 21 . . . Bxb2 22 Ra2 Bf6 (22 . . . Qf6 23 Qxc7

Rec8 24 Qd7 Qc3 25 Nb5 Qb3 26 Ra7) 23 Nb5 Qd7 24 Nfd4 Bxd4 25 Nxd4; or 21 . . . c6 22 dxc6 Rc8 23 Nd4 (or 23 cxb7 Rxc4 24 Nxc4 Qc7 25 Ra8 Rb8 26 Na5). (LS)

Karpov spent an hour and three minutes on this predictable move.

22 Nd4!

Sooner or later, Black has to play . . . c5. Unclear is 22 Nb5?!. Dorfman gives 22 Rab1 c6 as equal. (LS)

22 . . .	Ba6

Is 22 . . . Bxd4 better right away? Hardly! White wins after 23 Qxd4 c5 24 dxc6 Qxc6 25 f3, with a winner at b2. (LS)

23 Qc3	c5

After 23 . . . Qb7, very strong is 24 Nac2. (LS)

24 dxc6	Bxd4
25 Qxd4	Qxc6
26 b4	

It seems impossible that this feeble pawn will metamorphose into a queen. (LS)

26 . . .	h6
27 Re3	Re6
28 f3	Rc8
29 Rb3	Bb5
30 Rb2	Qb7
31 Nc2	Qe7
32 Qf2	

After 32 Ne3, Black plays 32 . . . Qg5, with the idea . . . Rg6. (LS)

32 . . .	**Rg6**
33 Ne3	**Qe5**
34 Rbb1	**Bd7**
35 Ra5	**Qe7**

Not 35 . . . Qc3 36 Nd5! (LS)

36 Ra7	**Qd8**
37 Nd5	

To meet 37 . . . Bxh3 with 38 Ne7+. (LS)

37 . . .	**Kh7**
38 Kh2	

White has an extra pawn and a dominating position, but Karpov is very resourceful in the kinds of bad positions that Kasparov usually abandons as hopeless. Karpov has a special talent for difficult defense. (LS)

38 . . .	**Rb8**
39 f4	**Re6**

Attacking White's only weak spot. (LS)

40 Qd4	**Qe8**

Adjourned.

"Karpov is lost, totally lost!" exclaimed IM Nigel Davies in the press room as Kasparov sealed his move.

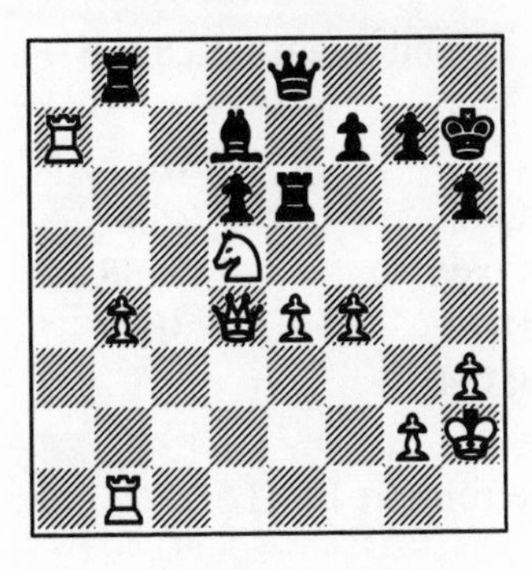

After 40 ... Qe8

41 Re1!

White also wins after 41 Qd3 Bb5 42 Qc2, but Black survives after 41 Nc7 Rxe4 42 Qd3 Qe7 43 Nd5 Bb5!. (LS)

41 ...	**Bc6**
42 Qd3!	

To prevent ... Bxd5 and threaten 43 Nc7 Bxe4 44 Rxe4. (LS)

42 ...	**Qf8**
43 Rc1!	

Forcing the exchange at d5. (LS)

43 ...	**Bxd5**
44 exd5 +	**Rg6**
45 Qf5	

Creating new threats—Rxf7 and Rcc7. (LS)

45 ...	**Kg8**
46 Rac7	

Black cannot defend against Rc8.(LS)

46 ...	Rf6
47 Qd7	Rd8
48 Qxd8	Qxd8
49 Rc8	Qf8
50 R1c4	

To restrict the rook at f6. (LS)

50 ...	Rf5
51 Rxf8 +	Kxf8
52 Rd4	

The rook is useless at f5. (LS)

52 ...	h5
53 b5	Ke7
54 b6	Kd7
55 g4!	

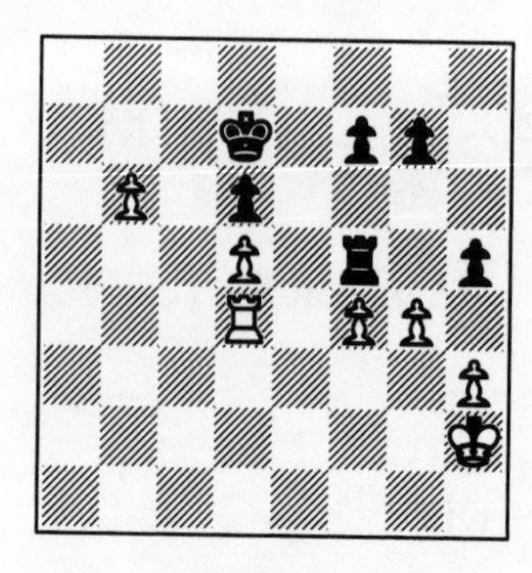

After 55 g4

Either 55 Rc4 Rxd5 or 55 b7 Kc7 gives Black a chance to escape. (LS)

55 . . .	**hxg4**
56 hxg4	**Rf6**
57 Rc4	**1-0**

Black cannot stop the b-pawn: 57 . . . Rh6+ 58 Kg2 Rh8 59 Rc7+ Kd8 60 Ra7, winning. (LS)

10

LYON, GAMES 19 THROUGH 24

Match 5, Game 19
December 12, 1990
King's Indian Defense

White: Anatoly Karpov *Black: Garry Kasparov*

Annotated by GM Ron Henley

	White	Black
1	d4	Nf6
2	c4	g6
3	Nc3	Bg7
4	e4	d6
5	Nf3	0-0
6	Be2	e5
7	Be3	c6
8	d5	Ng4
9	Bg5	f6
10	Bh4	Na6
11	Nd2	Nh6
12	a3	Nf7
13	f3	Bh6
14	Bf2	

Necessary to prevent the black bishop from taking up residence at e3. (RH)

14 . . .	f5
15 Qc2	Bd7
16 b4	c5
17 Rb1	b6
18 Nf1!	Bf4
19 g3?!	

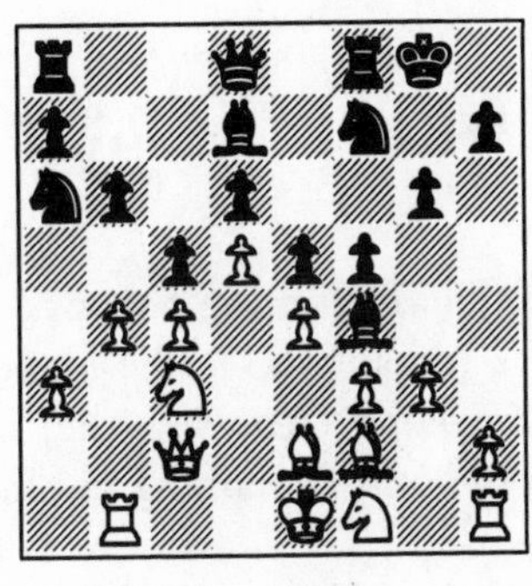

After 19 g3

After the game Karpov criticized this plan (19 g3, 20 h4, and 21 g4), since it only surrenders the f4-square to the black bishop. Better is 19 Ne3! followed by 20 0-0, when White has a slight edge since he has already secured prospects on the queenside and the black bishop at f4 can be kicked by g3 whenever White chooses. After 19 Ne3, the game might continue 19 . . . Qg5 20 Ncd1 Qf6 (20 . . . Bxe3 21 Nxe3 f4 22 h4) 21 0-0, or 21 Bd3 to pressure the f5-square. (RH)

19 . . .	Bh6
20 h4	Nc7
21 g4	fxg4
22 fxg4	Bf4!

Black has solved the problem of activating what can become the chronic bad bishop in the King's Indian. (RH)

23 Ne3	Ne8

24 Ncd1	**h6**
25 h5	**g5**
26 Rg1	

When he played 19 g3, Karpov underestimated Black's possibilities for counterplay. (RH)

26 . . .	**Nf6**
27 Rg2	**Qc8**
28 Kf1	**Nd8!**

Very flexible thinking on the part of Kasparov. More often in the King's Indian we see the maneuver . . . Na5-b7-d8-f7. Here Kasparov reverses the idea and obtains counterplay on the only remaining unblocked sector. (RH)

29 Kg1	**Nb7**

On French television after the game, Kasparov said he thought White could play 30 b5 a6 31 a4 to finish blockading the position and secure a draw. (RH)

30 Kh1	**cxb4!**
31 axb4	**a5!**

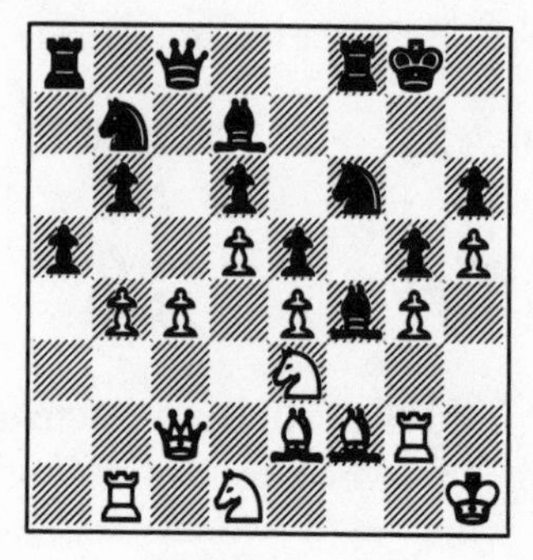

After 31 ... a5

The point of Black's plan, securing c5 as an outpost for his knight. (RH)

32 Nf5	**Bxf5**
33 exf5	**axb4**

Kasparov sacrifices the b6-pawn to consolidate his grip on the dark squares. (RH)

34 Rxb4	**Nc5**
35 Rxb6	**Nce4**

After 35 . . . Nfe4!? 36 Rc6 Qd7 followed by 37 . . . Rfb8, Black's troops should come pouring in along the queenside files. (RH)

36 Rc6	**Qb7**

Better is 36 . . . Qd7!, protecting the d6-pawn. (RH)

37 Be1

Not 37 Rb6?? Nxf2+. (RH)

37 . . .	**Ra1**
38 Bf3	**Nc5**
39 Bc3	**Rc1**
Draw	

Kasparov, realizing he had mishandled the initiative, proposed a draw which Karpov, short of time, accepted. The score: 10.0–9.0.

Adjournment Analysis

With more time on the clock, Karpov might have tried:

After 39 ... Rc1

40 Qb2! Qa8

Black threatens 41 . . . Rb8 and 42 . . . Rbb1, as well as 41 . . . Na4 and 42 . . . Nxc3, with a big edge. This was the continuation Karpov was concerned about during the game.

Black's other try is 40 . . . Qxb2, and now:

A *41 Bxb2!? Rxc4 42 Rxd6 (42 Be2 Rc2 43 Rxd6 Nce4) 42 . . . e4 43 Rxf6?! Rxf6 44 Bxf6 exf3 45 Rg1 (45 Rf2 Ne4 also favors Black) 45 . . . Ne4, with a win for Black; or 43 Be2! Bxd6 44 Bxc4 Nfd7 45 Ne3;*

B *41 Rxb2 Nd3 42 Ra2 Rb8 43 Kg2, with mutual counterchances, but White is a pawn ahead.*

41 Rxc5! dxc5
42 Bxe5 Qa4!

Weaker is 42 . . . Bxe5 43 Qxc1.

43 Bxf6

White has two other tries.

First, 43 Bxf4 Rxd1+ 44 Kh2! (44 Bxd1 Qxd1+ 45 Rg1 Qf3+ leaves Black winning) 44 . . . gxf4 45 g5! (suddenly the black king is exposed) 45 . . . hxg5 46 Rxg5+ Kh8 47 Bxd1 Qxd1 48 Qb7 Rg8, followed by:

A *49 Qe7 Ng4+ 50 Kh3 Nf2+ 51 Kg2 (51 Kh4 Qh1+) 51 . . . Rxg5+ 52 Qxg5 Qg1+ 53 Kxg1 Nh3+ 54 Kg2 Nxg5 55 d6 Nf7 56 d7 Kg7 57 Kf3 Kh6 58 Kxf4 Kxh5 59 Ke4 Kg5 60 Kd5 Kxf5 61 Kxc5 Ke6, drawn;*

B *49 Rxg8+ Nxg8 50 Qb2+ Kh7 51 Qb7+ Kh6 52 Qc6+ Kxh5 53 Qg6+ Kh4 54 Qxg8 Qe2+ 55 Kg1 (55 Qg2? f3, and Black wins) 55 . . . f3 56 Qh7+ Kg4 57 Qg6+ Kf4.*

Second, Black wins after 43 Rg1 Rc2.

43 . . .	**Rxd1+**
44 Rg1!	

Very bad is 44 Bxd1? Qxd1+ 45 Rg1 Qf3+ 46 Rg2 Qf1+ 47 Rg1 Qh3+.

44 . . .	**Rxg1+**
45 Kxg1	**Qxc4**
46 d6!	

Other tries lose: 46 Be7? Rb8 47 Qf6 Qc1+ 48 Kg2 Rb2+ 49 Kh3 Qf1+; or 46 Bh8 Rf7.

46 . . .	**Bxd6**

Weaker is 46 . . . Qd3 47 Qb7! Rxf6 48 Bd5+ Kh8 (48 . . . Kf8 49 Qe7+ mate) 49 Qc8+ Kg7 50 Qg8+ mate.

47 Qd2!

Not 47 Qb7? Qc1+ 48 Kg2 Rxf6.

47 . . .	**Qf4**

Weaker is 47 . . . Qa6?! 48 Bb2, when the threat of 49 Qc3 and the exposed black king combined with the white bishops should provide sufficient compensation for the exchange; e.g., 48 . . . Be7 49 Bd5+ Kh7 50 f6 Bxf6 (50 . . . Rxf6 51 Qc2+ Kh8 52 Qg6, with a White win) 51 Qc2+ Kh8 52 Qg6, and White is winning.

Playable is 47 . . . Bf4 48 Bd5+ (48 Qd7 Qc1+ 49 Kg2 Qd2+ 50 Qxd2 Bxd2 51 Bd5+ Kh7 52 Be7, drawn) 48 . . . Kh7 49 Bxc4 Bxd2 50 Be7 Kg7!, or 50 . . . Rc8 51 f6 Bc3 52 f7 Bg7 53 Kg2 Bf8 54 Bf6 Bg7 55 Be7, drawn.

48 Qd5+	**Kh7**
49 Qb7+	**Bc7**
50 Be7	**Rb8**
51 Qe4	**Qh2+**

Another try is 51 . . . Qxe4 52 Bxe4 Rb4 53 Bf3 (53 f6+? Rxe4 54 f7 Rxg4+ 55 Kh1 Rf4, with a Black win) 53 . . . Rb1+ 54 Kf2 c4 55 f6.

52 Kf1	**Rb2**
53 f6+	**Kh8**
54 Bxc5	**Qh3+**
55 Bg2	**Rxg2**
56 Qxg2	**Qxg2+**
57 Kxg2	**Kg8**
58 Kf3	**Kf7**
59 Bd4	**Bd8**

With a draw after all. (RH)

Game 20 resurrected Kasparov's hopes of scoring a crushing victory over Karpov. Karpov offered an improvement to theory with 18 . . . Nf6, but went into a deep think after Kasparov's reply, 19 Nh2. At the cost of a pawn, Kasparov built up an overwhelming kingside attack, eventually "downing Karpov in a pool of blood and an explosion of applause" in GM Jon Speelman's words. The score: 11–9.

Match 5, Game 20
December 15, 1990
Ruy Lopez

White: Garry Kasparov ***Black: Anatoly Karpov***

Annotated by GM Leonid Shamkovich

1	e4	e5
2	Nf3	Nc6
3	Bb5	a6
4	Ba4	Nf6
5	0-0	Be7
6	Re1	b5
7	Bb3	d6
8	c3	0-0
9	h3	Bb7

Karpov plays his favorite defense again. (LS)

10	d4	Re8
11	Nbd2	Bf8
12	a4	h6
13	Bc2	exd4

14 cxd4	**Nb4**
15 Bb1	**c5**

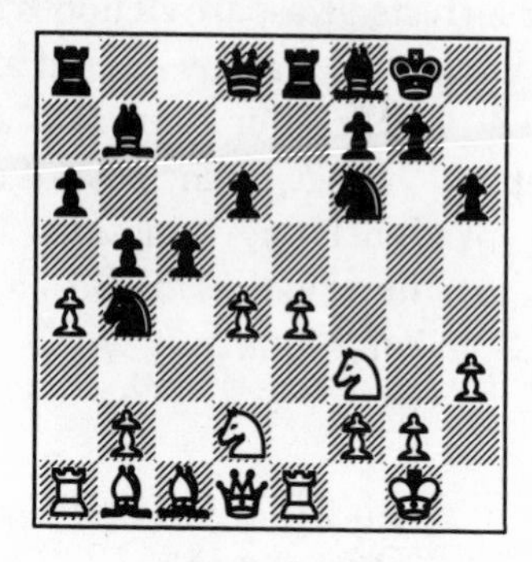

After 15 ... c5

In Game 2, White was better after 15 . . . bxa4 16 Rxa4 a5 17 Ra3 Ra6 18 Nh2 g6 19 f3. (LS)

16 d5	**Nd7**
17 Ra3	**f5**
18 Rae3	**Nf6**

Against Timman earlier in the year, 18 . . . f4 was only slightly better for White, but Karpov probably feared an innovation after 19 Rb3 Ne5 (Karpov may have decided that 19 . . . Qf6 20 Nf1 followed by Bd2-c3 is good for White) 20 Nxe5 dxe5 21 Nf3; or 19 R3e2 Ne5. (LS)

19 Nh2

Kasparov takes aim at g4, sacrificing his center for piece activity and a potential kingside attack. (LS)

19 . . .	**Kh8**

Also playable is 19 . . . fxe4, but the king is safer at h8. (LS)

20 b3	

To activate the queen bishop. (LS)

20 ...	**bxa4!?**

Also possible is 20 . . . fxe4. (LS)

21 bxa4	**c4**
22 Bb2	**fxe4**

Karpov spent another thirty-four minutes on this move. Roshal thought that Black's position "smelled." (SC)

23 Nxe4	**Nfxd5**

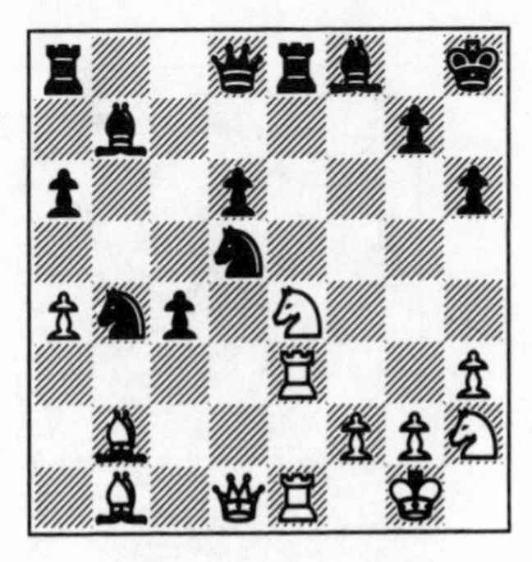

After 23 ... Nfxd5

White is even better after 23 . . . Rc8 24 Bc3 Nbxd5 25 Nxf6! Nxe3 (25 . . . Rxe3 26 Nxd5, and White is still better—the reason for . . . a5) 26 Qh5!; or 24 . . . a5, with a serious White initiative, though the position is unclear (Spassky and GM Lev Polugaevsky). (LS)

24 Rg3	

White intensifies his kingside threats at risk of a pin on Ne4.

Deep Thought gave 24 Qh5 as winning: 24 . . . Nxe3 25 Qxh6+ Kg8 26 Ng5!! mating. Black does somewhat better, however, after 24 . . . c3 25 Nxc3 (25 Qg6 c2 26 Qxh6+ Kg8 27 Rg3 Qc7, and Black may hold; or 25 Ng5 Qxg5 26 Qxg5 hxg5 27 Rxe8 cxb2 28 Rxa8 Bxa8 29 Re8 Kg8 30 Rxa8 Nc3, with winning chances for Black) 25 . . . Nxe3 26 Qg6 Nec2. (LS)

24 . . . Re6!

"A fantastic move," according to Spassky. "Maybe he can hold the position now." (SC)

25 Ng4

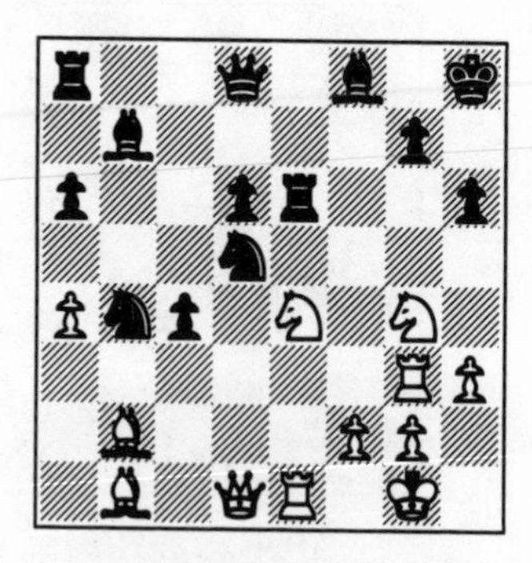

After 25 Ng4

White is preparing the sacrifice at h6. Safer and more logical is 25 Nf3 Qe8 26 Nd4 Re5, with an unclear position. (LS)

25 . . . Qe8

Apparently the best practical chance, though this move was criticized in Lyon.

Spassky's recommendation, 25 . . . Qh4?, looks very strong, defending h6 and preparing . . . Rae8, but after 26

Nc5 Rxe1+ 27 Qxe1 dxc5 28 Qe4, the black king's position is called into question: 28 . . . Nd3 (forced) 29 Rxd3 cxd3 (29 . . . Nc3 fails to 30 Qxb7!) 30 Qxd3 Kg8 (30 . . . Nf6? 31 Bxf6) 31 Ne5! (a hard move to find, preventing . . . Kf7 and threatening mate; after 31 Qh7+ Kf7 32 Ne5+, White has a strong attack but is a rook down with no decisive line) 31 . . . Nf6 32 Ba2+! (another argument for a4 in the opening!), and now 32 . . . Kh8? (33 Ng6+ Kh7 34 Nxf8+ Kh8 35 Qh7+ Nxh7 36 Ng6+—don't take the queen if you have mate!); or 32 . . . Bd5 33 Bxd5+ Nxd5 34 Qxd5+ Kh7 35 Qxa8 winning.

According to Roshal, Karpov said after the game that he saw 25 . . . Nd3 26 Bxd3 as equalizing, and everyone in Lyon accepted this evaluation, including Speelman and Kasparov. But White should retain the edge after 26 . . . cxd3 27 Rxd3 Qa5 (preparing . . . Rae8; White has a strong attack after 27 . . . Nf4 28 Rde3 Nd5 29 Ng5!) 28 Nc3. (LS)

26 Nxh6!?

Karpov, judging from the game continuation, was not expecting this shot. After the game, Kasparov said he played this move based on his feeling that the number of pieces in the attack would guarantee success. (LS)

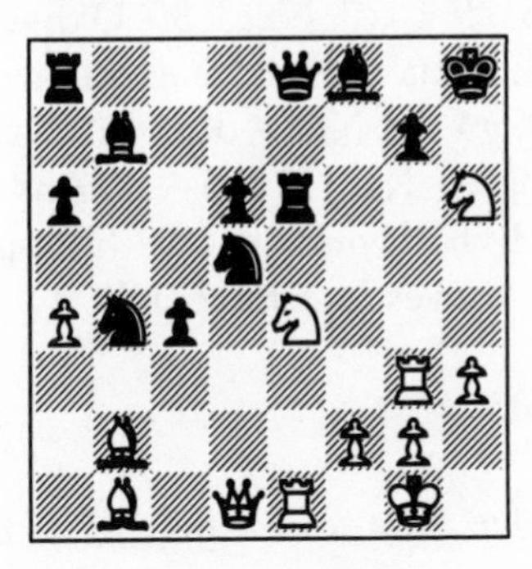

After 26 Nxh6

26 . . . c3?!

A familiar idea, but probably a mistake. 26 . . . Rxh6!? may be better, leading to some wonderful complications:

A) 27 Nxd6 is strong: 27 . . . Qxe1+! 28 Qxe1 Rxd6 29 Qe4 (threatening mate) 29 . . . Rh6 (after 29 . . . Nd3!, White is probably still better because of the lack of coordination between the black pieces) 30 Rg6 Rh7 31 Rxg7!!, mating;

B) 27 Qd2!? is a cold-blooded move requiring special attention. Here is an interesting example (Spassky and Polugaevsky): 27 . . . Re6 28 Nxd6!! Rxe1+ 29 Kh2 Ne3! (to prevent Qh6+, and threatening . . . Nf1+) 30 Rxe3 Qd7 31 Re7!! (a spectacular move, threatening Qh6+!) 31 . . . Rh1+! 32 Kg3 (not 32 Kxh1?? Qxh3+) 32 . . . Qxh3+!! 33 gxh3 Rg1+ 34 Kf4 (objectively better may be 34 Kh2 Rh1+, with a draw) 34 . . . Bxe7, and Black is all right—White's king is exposed, and Black's pieces are active;

C) 27 Ng5 Qh5 (27 . . . Qd7?! 28 Qg4) 28 Qg4:

C1) 28 . . . Bc8 29 Qxh5 Rxh5 30 Re8 Bb7 31 Nf7+ Kg8 32 Rxg7 mate;

C2) 28 . . . Nd3 (a standard method of counterplay in almost all variations) 29 Qd7 (29 Re6!?) Nc5 30 Qf5, with a complex position and a strong White initiative;

C3) 28 . . . c3 29 Bxc3 Nxc3 30 Qxb4, with a White advantage—Black cannot keep the extra piece;

C4) 28 . . . Qxg4 29 Nf7+ Kg8 30 Nxh6+ gxh6 31 Rxg4+ Kf7 32 Bg6+ Kg8 33 Bf5+ Kf7 34 Be6+ Ke8 35 Bxd5+ Kd7 36 Bxb7, winning—the bishop as superhero with five winning moves in a row! (LS)

27 Nf5

With only twelve minutes on his clock, Karpov was in desperate straits.

27 . . . cxb2
28 Qg4

White has a strong, possibly irresistible attack. Though Black has eliminated the strong bishop at b2, the knight at f5 is even stronger. (LS)

28 . . . Bc8
29 Qh4+ Rh6

No one in Lyon considered 29 . . . Kg8 30 Nh6+ Rxh6 (30 . . . Kh8 31 Nf7+ Kg8 32 Neg5! Rxe1+ 33 Kh2, and mate is inevitable) 31 Qxh6, with a decisive attack; e.g., 31 . . . Qf7 (or 31 . . . Qe5 32 Nf6+ Qxf6 33 Qh7+ Kf7 34 Bg6+ Qxg6 35 Qxg6+ Kg8 36 Re8 [threatening Qxg7 mate] 36 . . . b1Q+ 37 Qxb1, with material and positional advantages) 32 Nxd6. (LS)

30 Nxh6 gxh6
31 Kh2!

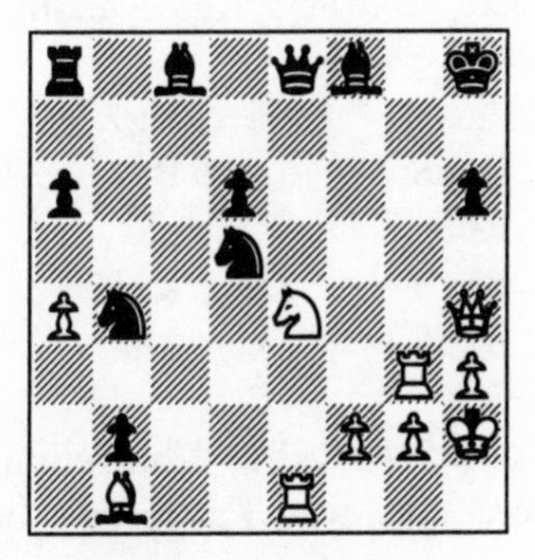

After 31 Kh2

Threatening Ng5 or Nxd6.

31 . . . Qe5

Mate follows 31 . . . Ra7 32 Nf6 Qf7 33 Re8! Nxf6 34 Qxh6+ Nh7 35 Qxh7+ Qxh7 36 Rxf8+. (LS)

32 Ng5!

A final, elegant point.

32 . . .	**Qf6**
33 Re8	

Threatening Qxh6+.

33 . . .	**Bf5**
34 Qxh6+!	**Qxh6**
35 Nf7+	**Kh7**
36 Bxf5+	**Qg6**
37 Bxg6+	

In time pressure, Kasparov played this practical move. After the game, a computer uncovered a quick mate: 37 Rxg6 Ne7 38 Rxe7 Bxe7 39 Rg5+ mate. (LS)

37 . . .	**Kg7**
38 Rxa8	**Be7**
39 Rb8	**a5**
40 Be4+	**Kxf7**
41 Bxd5+	**1-0**

With 41 . . . Nxd5 42 Rxb2, White eliminates Black's last practical chance. This was Kasparov's best game of the match. (LS)

With only four games remaining, Karpov had to come out swinging in Game 21. He returned to the provocative Sämisch Variation against Kasparov's King's Indian. In spite of an early mistake (17 Bc2), Karpov seemed to gain an edge and, in time trouble (as usual), rejected a late bid for a draw by repetition and pressed for the precious point. Kasparov held out against Karpov's desperate probing for eighty-six moves to inch closer to the title: 11.5–9.5.

Match 5, Game 21
December 19, 1990
King's Indian Defense

White: Anatoly Karpov ***Black: Garry Kasparov***

Annotated by GM Ron Henley

1 d4	Nf6
2 c4	g6
3 Nc3	Bg7
4 e4	d6
5 f3	

A return to the sharp Sämisch Variation of Game 1. Kasparov smiled—Karpov left the board.

5 . . .	0-0
6 Be3	e5

Kasparov played 6 . . . c6 in Game 1.

7 d5	Nh5
8 Qd2	f5
9 0-0-0	a6

Normal is 9 . . . Nd7.

10 Bd3

Spassky thought this was a new move, citing 10 Nge2 as a previous try.

10 . . .	**c5**
11 dxc6	**Nxc6**
12 Nd5	**Be6**
13 Bb6	**Qd7**
14 Ne2	**Rac8**
15 Kb1	**Qf7**
16 Rhe1	**Kh8**
17 Bc2?!	

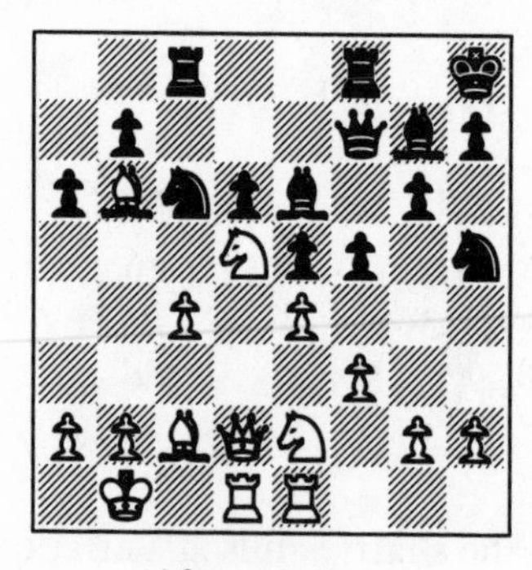

After 17 Bc2

Better is 17 Ng3! with advantage for White, as Karpov later agreed. His idea is to play 18 Bb3 to strengthen the d5-square in preparation for c5, but he changes his mind and loses two tempi. Karpov spent twenty-two minutes on this move. (RH)

17 . . .	**Nf6**
18 Bd3!	

Kasparov said this showed strong chess character on the part of Karpov, playing the strongest move in the position even if it meant showing the whole world and your opponent that the previous move was a mistake.

The same could be said for Kasparov's 25 Bg4! in Game 12. (RH)

18 . . .	**Nd7!**
19 Bg1	**Nc5**

Kasparov uses the two-tempi gift to relocate the knight from its inactive spot on h5 to a beautiful outpost on c5. Black has now achieved sufficient counterplay to equalize. (RH)

Tisdall gave Black the edge here. (SC)

20 Nb6	**Rcd8**
21 Nc3	

Alburt announced, "It is still equal. Now Kasparov has to play . . . Nb4 to prepare an exchange on d5. I don't believe Kasparov should permit White's knights to reach b6 and d5." (SC)

21 . . .	**Nd4**
22 Ncd5	**Bxd5**

Having achieved comfortable equality, Black now makes two dubious exchanges, after which White obtains prospects for an advantage. (RH)

23 Nxd5	**fxe4**
24 fxe4	**b5**
25 Rf1	**Qd7**
26 cxb5	**axb5**
27 Rxf8 +	**Rxf8**
28 h3	

Lev Alburt and I felt White might have some prospects

for a slight advantage due to his grip on the light squares and the 2–1 queenside majority. (RH)

28 . . .	**Qd8**
29 Bxd4	**exd4**
30 Qe2	**Qh4**
31 Rf1	**Re8**
32 Rf4	**Qg5**
33 a3	

Each player had nine minutes left here.

33 . . .	**h5**
34 Ka2?!	

Better is 34 h4 Qh6. Karpov had only four minutes for his last six moves. (RH)

34 . . .	**b4**
35 axb4	**Ra8 +**

Alburt now gave Black a slight advantage. (SC)

36 Kb1	**Nb3**
37 Kc2	**Na1 +**
38 Kb1?	

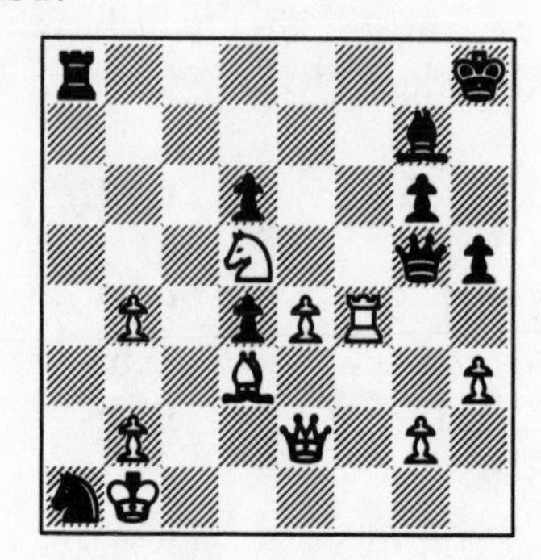

After 38 Kb1

After the game, Karpov and Kasparov analyzed for about forty-five minutes, concluding that White missed his chance for a decisive edge with 38 Kd1! Nb3 39 Qf3 Ra1 + 40 Kc2 Nc1 41 Rf8 + Kh7 (also winning for White is 41 . . . Bxf8 42 Qxf8 + Kh7 43 Nf6 +) 42 Rc8 Nxd3 43 Kxd3 Rg1 44 Rc2. (RH)

38 . . .	Nb3
39 Qf2	Qd8
40 Rf7	Qe8

Karpov, sitting alone at the board preparing to seal his move, looked troubled. After twenty-seven minutes, he put a move in the envelope and left the stage.

Desperately needing a point, we worked especially hard on the Game 21 adjournment, coming up just short of a win.

41 b5

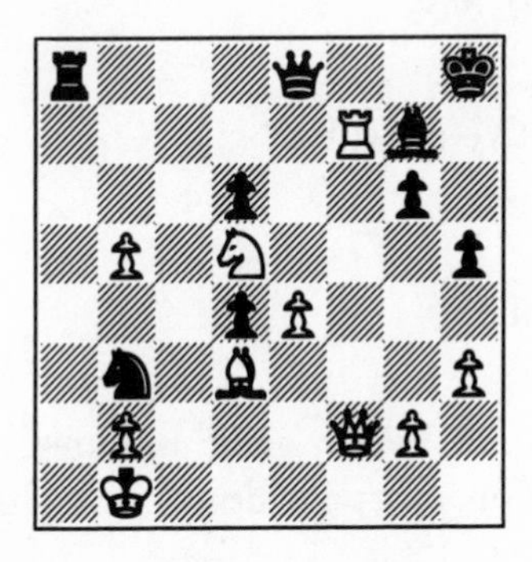

After 41 b5

"It's probably a draw now," Alburt declared. (SC)

41 . . .	Ra1 +
42 Kc2	Nc5
43 Rxg7	Kxg7

Also possible is 43 . . . Nxd3 44 Qxd4 Ne5 (44 . . . Qe5 45 Qxe5 Nxe5 46 Rc7, winning) 45 Rh7+, and White wins. (RH)

44 Qxd4+

White is winning after 44 Qf6+ Kh7 45 Qxd6 (or 45 Qxd4 Kh6 46 Bc4); but Black can turn the tables with 44 . . . Kh6 45 Ne7 Kh7 (45 . . . Ra7 46 Nc6) 46 Bc4 d3+, and Black wins. (RH)

44 . . .	**Qe5**
45 Qxe5+	**dxe5**
46 b6	**Rg1**
47 Ne3	**Re1**
48 Nc4	**Rg1**
49 Ne3	**Re1**
50 Nc4	

An alternative is 50 b4 Nd7. Karpov spent ten minutes here. (RH)

50 . . .	**Rg1**

Kasparov took twenty-eight minutes to decide on this simple repetition. Karpov, down to eight minutes for six moves, hesitated. (SC)

51 b4	**Rxg2+**
52 Kc3	**Na4+**
53 Kb3	**Nxb6**
54 Nxb6	**Rg3**

After 54 ... Rg3

55 Kc3	

In time pressure, Karpov misses 55 Kc4! Rxh3 56 Nd7 h4 57 Nxe5 Rg3 58 b5 h3 59 b6 h2 60 b7 h1Q 61 b8Q, and Black has run out of tricks.

The rest is a routine draw, although Karpov presses for another 30 moves. Queen and knight versus queen and two pawns is a dead horse. (RH)

55 . . .	Rxh3
56 b5	h4

"Now it's a draw," said Alburt. "Not a hundred percent, but ninety-five percent. It might even be an easy draw." (SC)

57 Nc4 Rxd3+ 58 Kxd3 h3 59 b6 h2 60 b7 h1Q 61 b8Q Qf1+ 62 Kc3 Qc1+ 63 Kb3 Qd1+ 64 Ka2 Qa4+ 65 Na3 Qxe4 66 Qc7+ Kh6 67 Nc4 Qd5 68 Kb2 e4 69 Qf4+ Kg7 70 Kc3 Qd3+ 71 Kb4 Qd4 72 Qh4 Kf7 73 Kb5 Qd5+ 74 Kb4 Qd4 75 Qh7+ Qg7 76 Qh1 Qd4 77 Qh4 Kg8 78 Qf4 Kg7 79 Qc1 Kf6 80 Kb5 Qd5+ 81 Kb4 Qd4 82 Kb5 Qd5+ 83 Kb6 Qd4+ 84 Kc6 Ke6 85 Ne3 Qa4+ 86 Kb6 Qb4+ Draw

This was it. Kasparov needed to control his nerves and pocket the half-point that would guarantee his title. Karpov, privately resigned to the impossibility of winning the match, had steeled himself to focus on the last four games as a "mini-match." Kasparov clinched the title with the necessary draw—the score was now Kasparov 12–Karpov 10—and both players prepared for what promised to be the biggest anticlimax of the Kasparov–Karpov series: two games played only to determine the distribution of the $3 million purse and the jeweled "Double-K" Korloff trophy studded with 1,018 black and white diamonds.

Match 5, Game 22
December 26, 1990
Ruy Lopez

White: Garry Kasparov ***Black: Anatoly Karpov***

Annotated by GM Ron Henley

1 e4

As usual, Karpov was late arriving on stage—reportedly delayed in traffic.

1	...	e5
2	Nf3	Nc6
3	Bb5	a6
4	Ba4	Nf6
5	0-0	Be7
6	Re1	b5
7	Bb3	d6
8	c3	0-0
9	h3	Bb7
10	d4	Re8

"Karpov is offering him the world championship," remarked a surprised Jon Tisdall, expecting 11 Ng5 Rf8, repeating the position. (SC)

11 Nbd2	**Bf8**
12 a4	**h6**
13 Bc2	**exd4**
14 cxd4	**Nb4**
15 Bb1	**c5**
16 d5	**Nd7**
17 Ra3	**f5**

Karpov surprised everyone in Lyon by repeating Game 20, which had been won by Kasparov in a brilliant display of fireworks. (Kristensen, SC)

18 exf5

This move got Kasparov in hot water in Game 4.

18 . . .	**Bxd5**
19 Ne4	**Bf7**

This idea was Portisch's inspiration. Later he and I spent long hours with Podgaets and Kharitonov developing it further. (RH)

Karpov left the stage, but lingered, like Polonius, just out of sight to take a last look at the board. (SC)

20 axb5

The capture 20 Nxd6? costs White a piece: 20 . . . Rxe1+ 21 Nxe1 Nb6!, and Black wins—the point of Portisch's plan. (RH)

20 . . .	d5!
21 Nc3	Rxe1 +

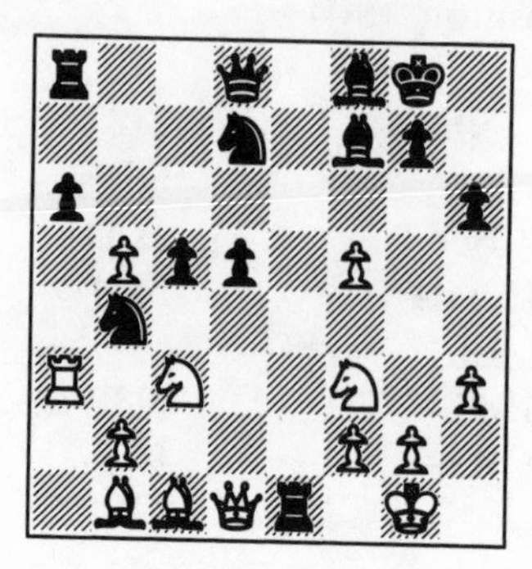

After 21 ... Rxe1+

"This is basically just what Karpov needs," observed Alburt, "a complex game in which Kasparov has committed to a kingside attack." (SC)

22 Nxe1	d4

Karpov spent forty-four minutes on this move.

23 Na2	Nxa2

Also worthwhile, according to Karpov, is 23 . . . a5. After the game, in a television interview on France's TF1, Karpov said he should have tried . . . a5 considering the match situation. (RH)

24 Bxa2	c4

Karpov sacrifices a second pawn to box in the white pieces. (RH)

25 Rxa6	Nc5

Karpov left the stage after reeling off his last three moves quickly. Kasparov did not seem pleased with his position. (SC)

26	Rxa8	Qxa8
27	Bb1	d3

Kasparov now seemed even more troubled, and Alburt remarked, "It's unclear if Kasparov will be able to save the game." GM Mikhail Gurevich, one of Kasparov's seconds, was looking for ways for White to draw by sacrificing a piece for Karpov's strong set of pawns. (Kristensen, SC)

28 Be3

Alburt: "A very interesting game from a chess player's point of view. Kasparov is in trouble, but he has many ways to try to save his position." (SC)

28 . . . Qa5

"Karpov is winning," shouted someone in the press room. Kasparov's face seemed to confirm the judgment. Spassky said White might be able to draw with 29 Nxd3. (SC)

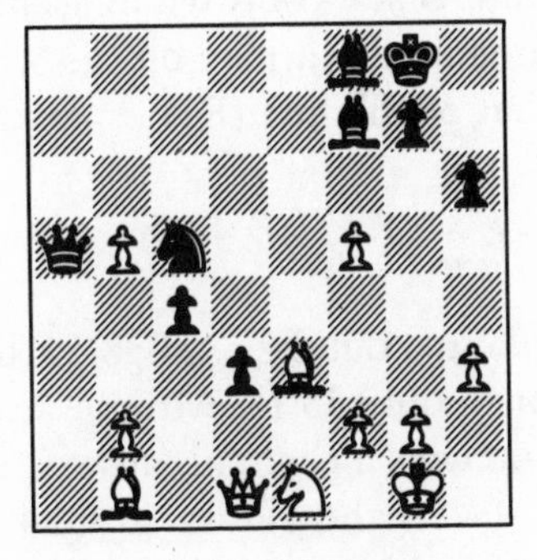

After 28 ... Qa5

29 b3!

On TF1, Karpov said the immediate 29 Nxd3 piece sacrifice is also adequate for White. (RH)

29 . . .	**Nxb3**
30 Nxd3	**cxd3**
31 Bxd3	

"Karpov is better," Alburt offered, "but Kasparov has very good chances to draw." (SC)

31 . . .	**Nc5**
32 Bf1	**Qc7**
33 Qg4!	

An excellent move, preparing 34 Bc4 to exchange light-squared bishops and threatening 34 Bxh6. (RH)

33 . . .	**Kh7**
34 Bc4!	

According to Kasparov after the game, any bishop exchange favors White. Black's only winning chance is to avoid exchanges and organize an attack on the white King. Kasparov prevents that possibility. (RH)

34 . . .	**Bxc4**

Only Roshal pointed out 34 . . . Bg8 35 Bxh6! On TF1, Kasparov mentioned only 35 f6, with an attack for White. Roshal's suggestion wins a pawn because of 35 . . . gxh6 36 Qxg8 mate, or 35 . . . Kxh6 allows 36 Qh4 mate. (RH)

35 Qxc4	**Qe5**
36 Qf7	**Bd6?!**

Safer is 36 . . . Qf6 37 Qxf6 gxf6 with a drawn ending. (RH)

37 g3	**Qe7**

After the game, Kasparov recommended 37 . . . Ne4 as more prudent. (RH)

38 Qg6+	**Kh8**
39 Bd4!?	

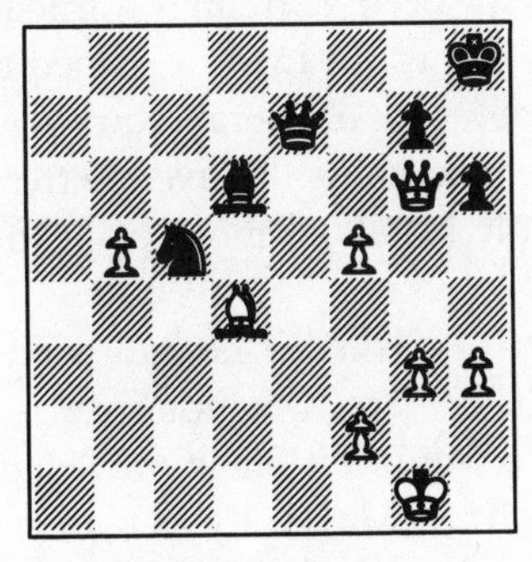

After 39 Bd4

This is stronger than 39 f6, which, however, seems to draw for White. Kasparov thought for about 10 minutes and decided to force the perpetual check and retain the title.

The strongest move is clearly 39 b6!, with a dangerous situation for Black: 39 . . . Nb7 (39 . . . Nd7 40 Qe6!? gives White chances, according to Kasparov; and Black experiences severe pressure after 39 . . . Ne4 40 Qe6!, with the threat of 41 Qxe7, 42 b7, and 43 Bf4) 40 f6! gxf6 (40 . . . Qxf6? 41 Qe8+ Kh7 42 Qe4+, and White wins) 41

Qxh6+ Kg8, with an endgame that only White has chances to win. (RH)

39 . . .	**Be5**
40 Bxc5	**Qxc5**
41 Qe8+	**Kh7**
42 Qg6+	**Kg8**
43 Qe8+	**Draw**

After clinching the world chess championship, Garry Kasparov took a few minutes to talk with reporters.

"I'm extremely happy," he said minutes after the game. "The match has been extremely difficult—much tougher than the score shows. In Lyon, I earned two points, but all of the games took a lot of energy. Karpov was well prepared, and he played great chess. I played better here than in New York. I probably benefited more from the break than Karpov did."

When a reporter asked if he had tried to win the game, Kasparov replied, "Yes. I'm not sure it was necessary to sacrifice a piece, but it left Black only slightly better. Objectively it was a draw. Maybe I was better at the end. I could have tried after he played . . . Qe7, but I didn't want to."

"I was very nervous at the beginning because I didn't know whether to play for a win or a draw. Then my life became a little easier—I got a worse position and definitely had to fight for a draw."

But there was more at stake in Games 23 and 24. Kasparov was on the verge of pulverizing Karpov's pretension to the throne. Another win would have given him the three-point margin many of his supporters predicted before the match, and a draw would have supported his claim to the "decisive" victory he had set out to achieve.

But few people in Lyon expected anything but a short draw. Everyone was ready to go home for the New Year's Eve celebrations. Karpov, tough as nails, had other ideas. He was still playing his private mini-match. Much to Kasparov's chagrin, Karpov was far from finished.

Faced with the problem of maintaining his concentration with the match already in hand against a determined opponent, Kasparov decided to join Karpov toe-to-toe in the center of the ring. The press room sleepily awaited the inevitable handshake. Although most observers thought Karpov had the better game, no one suspected that Kasparov would resign on Move 29. The score: 12–11.

Match 5, Game 23
December 29, 1990
King's Indian Defense

White: Anatoly Karpov ***Black: Garry Kasparov***

Annotated by GM Ron Henley

1	d4	Nf6
2	c4	g6
3	Nc3	Bg7
4	e4	d6
5	f3	0-0
6	Be3	e5
7	d5	Nh5
8	Qd2	Qh4 +
9	g3	Qe7

After 9 ... Qe7

This is a new move. Previously played was 9 . . . Nxg3 10 Qf2 Nxf1 11 Qxh4 Nxe3 12 Ke2 Nxc4 13 b3 Nb6 14 Rc1 Na6. (RH)

10 0-0-0	**f5**
11 exf5	**gxf5**
12 Nh3!	**Na6**
13 Rg1	**Nf6**

Another try is 13 . . . Nc5 14 g4 Nf6 15 Be2 f4 16 Bxc5 dxc5 17 Nf2. (RH)

14 Nf2	**Kh8**

Completely winning for White is 14 . . . Nc5? 15 g4 f4 16 Bxc5 dxc5 17 Nfe4. White simply plays Bd3 followed by advancing the h- and g-pawns to attack the black king-side. Meanwhile, Black would have no meaningful counterplay. (RH)

15 Be2

Karpov considered 15 f4, 15 Bg5, and 15 Bd3 worthy alternatives. He felt 15 f4 was the most complicated, but decided in favor of the text to support an eventual g4. The immediate 15 g4? permits 15 . . . f4, trapping the white bishop at e3. (RH)

15 . . .	**Bd7**
16 Bg5	**Nc5**
17 g4	

All of White's previous moves have led to this—failure to push this pawn would invalidate White's play to this point. (Karpov)

17 . . .	**e4**

After 17 . . . fxg4? 18 fxg4, White secures control of e4 and will advance the h- and g-pawns to lead a decisive onslaught against the black king.

No better is 17 . . . f4? 18 h4 Qf7 19 Bxf6 Bxf6 20 Rh1, with a thematic white advantage. (RH)

18 fxe4	**fxe4**
19 Be3!	

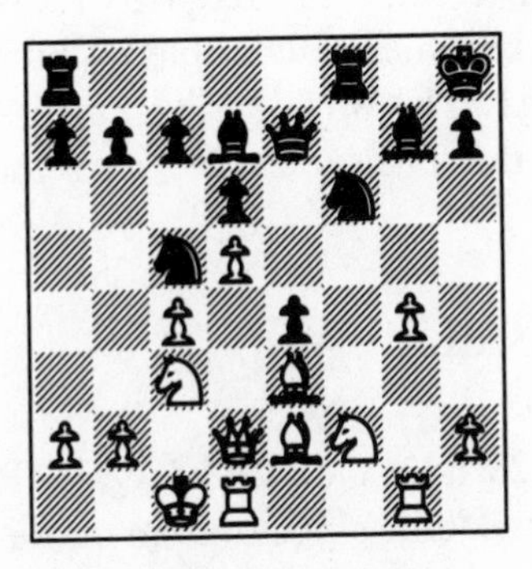

After 19 Be3

Karpov considered several plans here, but he opts for blockading the e-pawn. The text also threatens 20 g5 to kick the black knight. This threat leads to a crisis, since the knight has no good retreat square. (RH)

19 . . .	**Na4?!**

After 19 . . . Nd3+ 20 Bxd3 exd3 21 Qxd3 followed by 22 Bd4, Karpov felt that Black would have little to show for his pawn. (RH)

20 g5!

Karpov felt this was the decisive moment of the game. White has virtually a won position, but precise calculation is required—a single tempo can be decisive. (RH)

20 . . .	**Nxc3**
21 bxc3	**Ng8**
22 Ng4!	**c5!**

Karpov expected 22 . . . Bxg4 23 Rxg4!, when the black pawn at e4 becomes vulnerable. White can continue 24 Qc2 or Bf1-g2. The obvious recapture 23 Bxg4, followed by planting the bishop at e6, also looks attractive for White. (RH)

23 dxc6

Weaker is 23 h4?! Qd8 24 h5 Qa5. (RH)

"I don't like White's position anymore," said Kristensen. "Too many weaknesses and too few strong points to make up for them." (SC)

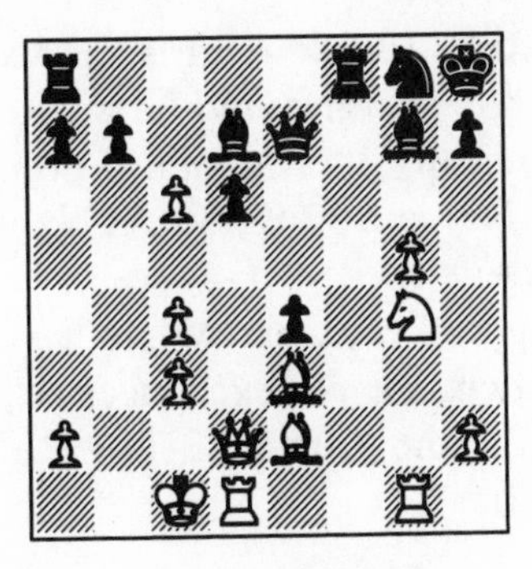

After 23 dxc6

23 . . . Bxc6?

Black's best chance, according to Karpov, is 23 . . . Bxg4 24 Rxg4 bxc6 25 Qxd6 Qb7 26 Qd7?! (Karpov intended 26 Bd4!, when White has to simply exchange queens to win; e.g., 26 . . . Rad8 27 Qb4! Qxb4 28 Bxg7 +) 26 . . . Qa6 27 Bd4 Qa3 + 28 Kd2 Ne7, giving Black good counterplay. (RH)

24 h4 d5

Karpov gives 24 . . . Ba4 25 Rdf1 as winning, followed by exchanging a pair of rooks.

Spassky and French GM Olivier Renet recommended 24 . . . Be8!?, but Karpov felt Black's compensation was insufficient after 25 Qxd6 Qxd6 26 Rxd6 Ne7 (after 26 . . . Bxc3, I suggest 27 Rd4, with the idea 28 Kc2 to force the black bishop to abandon the a1-h8 diagonal), and now:

A) 27 Nh6 Bxc3 (27 . . . Bxh6 28 gxh6! Nf5 29 Bf4! Nxd6 30 Be5 + Rf6 31 Bxf6 + mate) 28 Re6 Nf5 29 Nxf5 Rxf5 30 Rxe4, and White still has a clear extra pawn, but no forced win;

B) 27 Bd4 Nf5 28 Rf6!? Bxf6 (28 . . . Rxf6? 29 gxf6 Bf8 30 Be5 Nxh4? 31 f7 + and 28 . . . Nxd4 29 Rxf8 + Bxf8 30 cxd4 both win for White) 29 Bxf6 +, and:

B1) 29 . . . Rxf6 (Black returns the exchange to halt White's attack, but this gives White a choice of favorable endgames a pawn up) 30 Nxf6 (also decisive is 30 gxf6, with the idea 31 Ne5 and 32 f7) 30 . . . Nxh4?? 31 Rh1 Nf5 32 Rxh7+ mate;

B2) 29 . . . Kg8 30 c5, when White has a dangerous attack and two pawns for the exchange; i.e., 30 . . . Bf7 31 Nh6+ Nxh6 32 gxh6+ Bg6 33 Bc4+ Rf7 34 h5, and White wins. (RH)

25 cxd5!

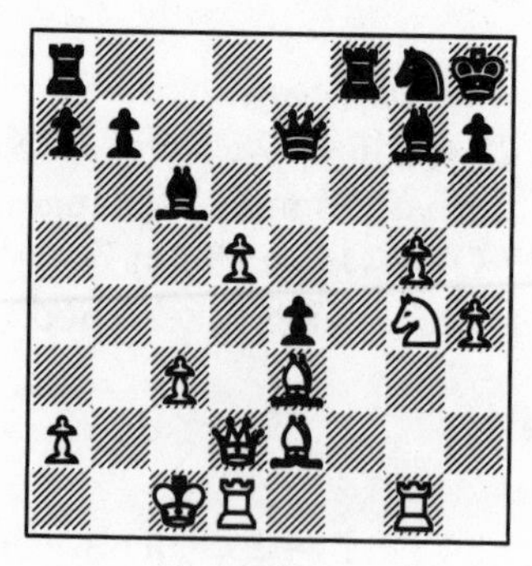

After 25 cxd5

Karpov plays the most direct move. Speculation in the press room also focused on 25 c5 b6! 26 cxb6 axb6 27 Bd4. (RH)

25 . . . Bxd5

White also wins after 25 . . . Qa3+ 26 Kb1 Bxc3 27 Bd4+. (RH)

26 Qxd5 Rac8

An interesting attempt to attack, but Karpov's reply stops Kasparov cold.

After 26 . . . Qa3+ 27 Kb1 Qxc3 28 Bd4, not only is Black a piece down, but White has achieved his strategic objective of exchanging the dark-squared bishops exposing the black king. (RH)

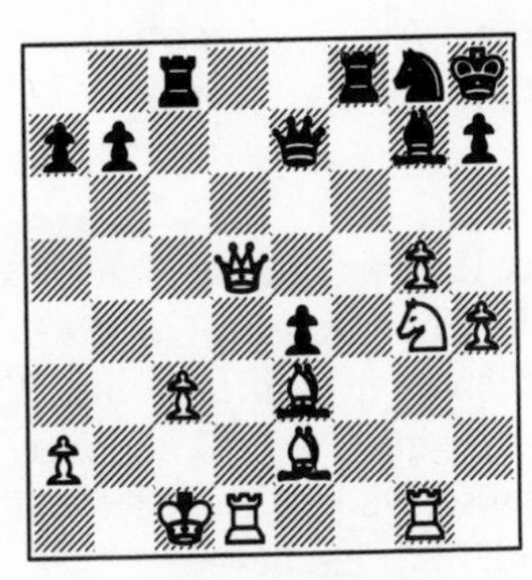

After 26 ... Rac8

27 Qd6!

Winning immediately. The black queen is cut off from attacking the white king.

Also good enough to win is 27 Bd4, but this requires greater care. Play might continue 27 . . . Rxc3+, and now:

A) 28 Bxc3 Qa3+ 29 Kb1 (29 Kd2?? Qxc3+ mate) 29 . . . Qxc3 30 Nf6 Nxf6 31 Qb3 (not 31 Qd4? Nd5!) 31 . . . Qe5;

B) 28 Kb1?? Qb4+ 29 Ka1 Rc1+! 30 Rxc1 Bxd4+, with the type of continuation Kasparov was hoping for when he embarked on his adventure with 24 . . . d5;

C) 28 Kd2!, and it is hard to find a continuation of the attack: e.g., 28 . . . Qb4 (28 . . . Rd8 29 Qxd8 Qxd8 30 Kxc3 Qc7+ 31 Kb3 Bxd4 32 Rxd4 Qb6+ 33 Kc3 Qc5+

34 Bc4 b5 35 Re1 bxc4 36 Rexe4 Qa3+ 37 Kxc4 Qxa2+ 38 Kc5 gives White good winning chances) 29 Bxg7+ Kxg7 30 Qe5+ Kf7 31 Nh6+ (or 31 Qxc3 Rd8+ 32 Kc2) 31 . . . Nxh6 32 Bh5+ Kg8 33 gxh6+, and White wins. (RH)

27 . . .	**Rxc3+**
28 Kb1	**Qf7**
29 Bd4	**1-0**

After the game, Karpov said on French television, "Kasparov last won [the championship] in 1986. We are more or less equal. I had chances in Games 21 and 22 that I failed to exploit. Bad luck for me. As the challenger, we work at a disadvantage because we are forced to disclose so many ideas in the candidates' matches."

"No, this is not my last chance. Korchnoi was forty-seven years old in Baguio, and he fought like a lion."

Asked whether, stranded on a desert island, he would prefer to play Kasparov or a computer, he answered, "I don't know what will happen in ten years, but for now I prefer to play with Garry Kasparov."

Sobered by Karpov's refusal to give up, Kasparov chose to sidestep any unexpected opening preparation by playing 1 Nf3 to close out the match. Each player used more than an hour for the first thirteen moves, jockeying for position. Karpov, forced to play for a win, pressed relentlessly, eventually falling into a losing position and accepting Kasparov's sporting draw offer.

The final score: 12.5–11.5. Kasparov thus will retain the title for another three years, but even he admits that he is likely to have to face Karpov at least one more time before this dramatic rivalry has run its course.

Match 5, Game 24
December 31, 1990
English Opening

White: Garry Kasparov *Black: Anatoly Karpov*

Annotated by GM Leonid Shamkovich

1 Nf3	

Kasparov chooses a neutral opening to avoid preparation in the final game. (LS)

1 . . .	Nf6
2 c4	e6

The same strategy used by Kasparov in Game 24 in Seville. (LS)

3 Nc3	Bb4
4 Qc2	0-0
5 a3	Bxc3
6 Qxc3	b6
7 b4	d6
8 Bb2	

"According to theory," Alburt reported in Lyon, "this is slightly better for White. Slightly." (SC)

8 . . .	Bb7
9 g3	c5
10 Bg2	Nbd7
11 0-0	Rc8

After 11 ... Rc8

The game is even. Black hopes to create counterplay on the queenside; White has chances in the center. Black can oppose the menacing battery along a1-h8 with . . . e5. (LS)

12 d3 Re8

A novelty. Spassky cites 12 . . . d5 13 b5 Qc7 14 Rfe1! d4?! 15 Qd2 Ra8 16 e3 dxe3 17 fxe3 a6 18 a4 axb5 19 axb5 h6 20 Qc3.

13 e4

Kasparov spent twenty-seven minutes on this move. He intends to meet . . . e5 with Nh4 and f4. (LS)

13 . . . a6
14 Qb3

White's queen is exposed here. Safer is 14 Qd2. (LS)

14 . . . b5

Karpov uncharacteristically plays for a direct win. Normally he would try 14 . . . Qc7. (LS)

15 Nd2	**Rb8**
16 Rfc1	**Ba8**
17 Qd1	**Qe7**

Black tries to regroup. Another try is 17 . . . Qb6. (LS)

18 cxb5

Spassky did not like this move.

18 . . .	**axb5**
19 Nb3!	

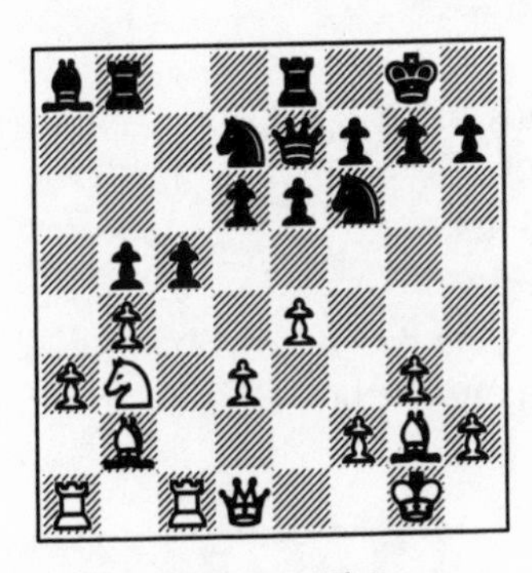

After 19 Nb3

Step by step White seizes the initiative. Black's bishop at a8 is a little passive. (LS)

19 . . .	**e5**

More logical is 19 . . . Rec8. (LS)

20 f3

A surprise to most analysts, this protects the e4-pawn to make the bishop at a8 even more passive. (LS)

20 ... h5?!

Better for Black is 20 ... Nb6!? 21 bxc5 Na4 22 cxd6 Qa7+ 23 Kf1 Nxb2. (LS)

21 bxc5 dxc5
22 a4

Interestingly enough, Kasparov plays aggressively in spite of needing only a draw to win the match. He intends to control c4. (LS)

22 ... h4

Black intends ... hxg3 and ... Nh5. (LS)

23 g4

Spassky gives 23 Ba3 b4 24 Bb2 hxg3 25 hxg3 Nh5, with serious Black counterplay. (LS)

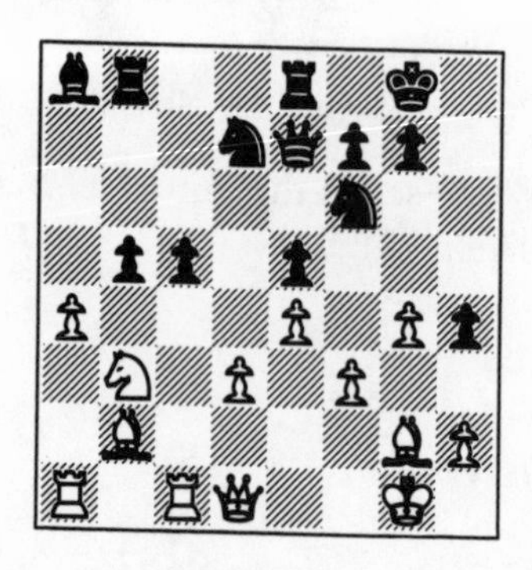

After 23 g4

23 ... c4?

Karpov felt he still had an edge after 23 . . . b4; e.g., 24 Qd2 Rbc8 25 Na5 (25 Qf2 Nh7 26 f4, and White is slightly better) 25 . . . Nf8 26 Nc4 Ng6, and Black is all right; or 24 Nd2 Nf8 25 Nc4 N6d7 (25 . . . Ng6, and Black again is OK) 26 Ne3, with a complicated position. (LS)

24 dxc4 **bxa4**
25 Ba3

Another try is 25 Rxa4 Bc6 26 Ra3 Qb4, or 26 . . . Nc5, with counterplay. (LS)

25 . . . **Qd8**
26 Nc5

Karpov said after the game that he had thought this move would be impossible, overlooking 26 . . . Qb6 27 Rab1!. (RH)

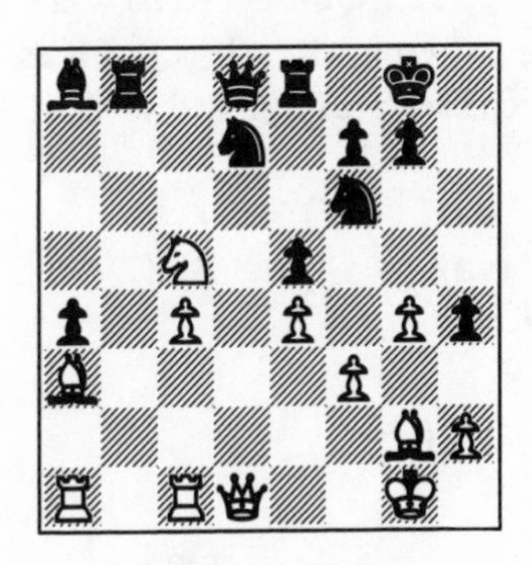

After 26 Nc5

26 . . . **Bc6?**

According to Henley, Karpov considered 26 . . . Nxc5! 27 Qxd8 Rexd8 28 Bxc5 Bc6 29 Bf2 (29 Rd1!, with equality [LS]) 29 . . . g5 30 Be3 Nh7 slightly better for Black.

Also bad is 26 . . . Qb6? 27 Rab1 Qa7 28 Qxa4. (LS)

27 Nxa4

White is clearly better. (LS)

27 . . . Nh7

Aiming for the weak g5 and f4 squares—too little, too late. (LS)

28 Nc5

Better is 28 Nc3!. (LS)

28 . . . Ng5

Another try is 28 . . . Qb6 29 Rcb1 Qa7 30 Bb4, with a draw; but White is better after 29 Qd6 Ra8 30 Rcb1 Rxa3 (30 . . . Qa7 31 Kh1 unclear) 31 Rxb6 Rxa1 + 32 Kf2 Nxc5 33 Qxc5. (LS)

29 Nxd7 Bxd7
30 Rc3

To prepare Rd3. (LS)

30 . . . Qa5

The last chance to fight. No better is 30 . . . Ne6 31 Rd3. (LS)

31 Rd3 Ba4
32 Qe1!

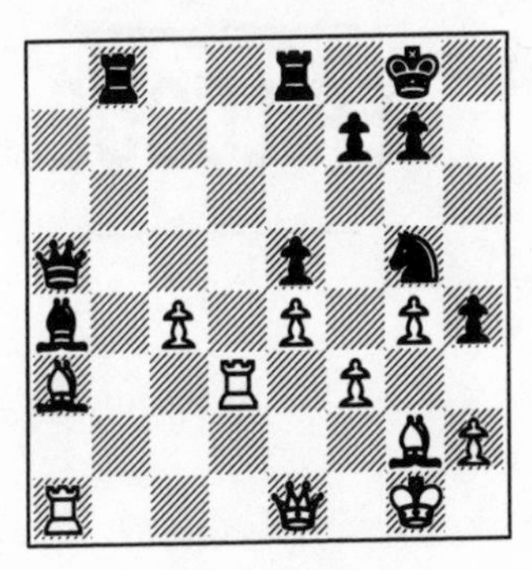

After 32 Qe1

Weaker is 32 Qd2? Qxd2 33 Rxd2 h3 34 Bh1, with a bad bishop. (LS)

32 . . . **Qa6?**

Unpleasant is 32 . . . Qb6+ 33 c5. (LS)

33 Bc1 **Ne6**
34 Rda3 **Nc5**
35 Be3 **Qd6**

Not 35 . . . Qc6 36 Qa5!. (LS)

36 Rxa4 **Draw**

White is winning easily after 36 Qa5 or 36 Qf2 Nd3 (36 . . . Nb3) 37 Qd2!, but with the match in hand, Kasparov decides discretion is the better part of valor and offers Karpov a draw in a winning position.

For their trouble, Kasparov pocketed $1.7 million, and Karpov $1.3 million. As for the jeweled Korloff Trophy with its 1,018 black and white diamonds, the young world champion donated it to the Armenian refugees driven from his home city of Baku by last January's ethnic violence.

EPILOGUE

As time goes on, the controversies that have alienated Garry Kasparov and Anatoly Karpov from each other seem less important than the talent that binds them inextricably together. Across the board, political controversy and personal animosity must eventually yield to grudging respect resulting from the intellectual and emotional give-and-take of chess.

Kasparov and Karpov may not be friends, but their growing mutual respect as players is obvious to anyone who followed this match. More and more often as the match progressed, they would sit together onstage for a few minutes going over their game. I've seen such moments of shared analysis pass for friendship between many lesser chess players over the years.

It is easy to write Karpov off for the next championship cycle: "He will be forty-two, and not likely to survive the grueling elimination matches against younger players."

But that assessment is far from the truth. Karpov is still one of the two strongest players in the world and has demonstrated his stubborn determination to win. If young superstars like GMs Boris Gelfand and Vasily Ivanchuk want to challenge Kasparov, they will still have to get past Karpov—no easy feat, as Kasparov can testify. Kasparov has proven repeatedly that he can cut through a field of "ordinary" grandmasters like a scythe, but he can't do that to Karpov. Only the world champion himself is capable of defeating Karpov, and three years from now Karpov will be as tough as ever.

As for Garry, his respect for Anatoly has made him a better player. Karpov defines the limits of Kasparov's chess universe; without him, the world champion would hardly feel subject to the laws of chess—his aura of invincibility would be absolute.

But Karpov remains an obstacle that cannot be willed into oblivion. After 144 hard-fought championship games between these forces of nature, we can expect more of the same—brilliant, inspired chess played at the edge of endurance by the world's two finest players.

Don Maddox
Manasquan, New Jersey, January 1991